NTS

THE NAVAL ACADEMY OFFICIAL MISSION

To develop midshipmen
morally, mentally and
physically and to imbue
them with the highest ideals
of duty, honor and loyalty
in order to provide graduates
who are dedicated to a
career of naval service and
have potential for future
development in mind and
character to assume the
highest responsibilities
of command, citizenship
and government.

INTRODUCTION: WHY READ A CANDIDATE BOOK?

The Naval Academy publishes a beautiful catalog. It is full of information and pictures and is must reading for any person who is thinking of becoming a candidate.

It contains a description of all the majors and minors that are offered, descriptions for all the courses that are taught and a roster of the faculty.

It explains in detail all of the academic, physical and medical requirements for admission, as well as all the admissions procedures that must be followed.

In addition, it outlines the four-year program--including summer activities and describes the job opportunities that are available for its graduates.

In short, the Naval Academy Catalog contains a wealth of valuable information for the candidate and it can be obtained in virtually any library or high school counselor's office.

Then what is purpose of this book? How does it relate to the catalog?

First, the Naval Academy Catalog is an official publication of the Academy; this book is not. This book is an independent publication, produced with the full cooperation of the Naval Academy, but without any control or official endorsement by that institution.

The Academy Catalog is like a good owner's manual for an automobile. A good owner's manual tells you everything you need to know in order to use the automobile.

But there is one thing the best owner's manual does not do. It does not tell you how to drive the car. You can read a good owner's manual from cover to cover and still never learn how to negotiate a winding mountain road during a night snowstorm.

Aside from two brief introductory chapters, which describe the Naval Academy as an institution, this book is strictly a "how to" book designed to be a companion to the candidate's owner's manual--the Naval Academy Catalog.

The main purpose of this book is to give the candidate expert advice on how to master the three major challenges that face candidates who want to attend the Naval Academy.

Who are the experts giving the advice?

Most of the experts are the students themselves--the midshipmen who are at the Academy and who have found ways to master the challenges they have encountered.

The advice also comes from a variety of other experts, including Academy Admissions Officials, key members of the staff and faculty, recent graduates, congressional staff members, and panelists who serve on the congressional boards that interview candidates.

And the three major challenges?

One of them is preparation. The Naval Academy is a rigorous institution. Before candidates even think about applying for admission, they should evaluate their motives and make certain they are mentally prepared for such an experience. This book tells them how to do that.

There are other types of preparation that are essential for candidates. The Naval Academy is a first-class academic institution and candidates must have a strong academic background to survive there. This book has four complete chapters containing advice on how to prepare for and survive the academic challenges.

In addition, there are chapters that tell how to prepare physically for the Academy and how to obtain the kinds of leadership experiences admissions officials desire for all whom they admit.

The second major challenge is competition; there are many thousands of young men and women competing each year for roughly 1100 available openings. One whole section of this book contains advice on how candidates can make themselves more competitive. It also explains what candidates can do if they lose out in the first round of the competition.

The third major challenge is survival after the candidate gets into the Academy. The midshipmen and recent graduates are the experts on that subject, and a major part of this book consists of chapters where they give advice based upon their personal experiences and observations.

All candidates need a good partner as they prepare, as they go through the admissions process and as they surmount the challenges when they get into the Naval Academy.

The ideal partner is a set of sympathetic, supportive, well-informed parents-- parents who know what to do in helping the candidate/midshipman, and what they should not do.

This book is also a "how to" book for parents who would like to become such an ideal partner. And, like the rest of the book, the advice given comes from experts. In this case, the experts on the partnership are more than 70 parents of midshipmen who were interviewed by the author. Their advice is contained in the section that concludes this book.

Now, to summarize.

If auto racers want to enter the Indianapolis 500 Memorial Day Race, they would want to know all the entrance requirements, all the rules and everything about the facilities that are available. All of this information, and more, is probably available in an official publication from the organization that administers the race. That would be an essential publication for the racers and they would not want to think about trying to enter the race without it.

Think of the Naval Academy Catalog as that kind of publication.

The potential racers also need information that cannot be provided in that official publication. They need to know all the things that must be done to prepare for the race. They need to know how to beat out much of their competition and get themselves and their cars into the race. Finally, they need to know how to survive all the dangers on the track and win the race!

Think of this book as one that will give Naval Academy candidates that kind of information.

And if you, the reader, decide to become one of those candidates, good reading and good luck!

WLS

2

THE INSTITUTION

ONE
THE ACADEMIC INSTITUTION

The United States Naval Academy opened in 1845 on the ten-acre grounds of Fort Severn. This was an old Army fort located at the mouth of the Severn River on Chesapeake Bay. It guarded the city of Annapolis, the capitol of Maryland.

The site of the present-day Naval Academy remains the same, although the grounds have been enlarged to 322 acres. Most of this land was created by a succession of landfills in the Severn River. There was little opportunity to expand in any other direction because the Academy became surrounded on the landward side by the growing city of Annapolis.

The Naval Academy began with a faculty of seven, four of them Naval Officers and the other three, civilians. At that time the students, called midshipmen or "mids," had to complete a five-year program, including two years at sea, to become naval officers.

An aerial view of the United States Naval Academy. The domed building is the chapel and the city of Annapolis starts just behind it.   *Courtesy USNA Photographic Branch.*

Now the Naval Academy is a four-year college that grants Bachelor of Science Degrees and naval officer commissions to its graduates. The students are still called "mids," and sea duty is still required before they can be commissioned as officers. However, the tours at sea are shorter and confined to two cruises during summer breaks from academic classes. Also, the faculty is still composed of both naval officers and civilians.

There is heavy emphasis upon scientific and technical education at the Naval Academy. Out of 18 possible academic majors, 14 of them are in sciences or engineering.

There is a good reason for this emphasis upon science and technology. The Navy itself is a highly complex branch of the military. Its fighting force is made up of a great variety of ships and aircraft, each with complex electronic and weapon systems. In addition it has a fleet of submarines, most with highly sophisticated nuclear power systems and many with ballistic missiles and other high-tech weapons.

The Naval Academy is fully accredited by the Middle States Association, a regional body that accredits four-year colleges. In addition, all of the Academy's specialized engineering majors are accredited by the Engineering Accreditation Commission of the Accreditation Board for Engineering and Technology.

How good are the Naval Academy's engineering programs compared to those of other colleges? One way to evaluate them is to compare how the graduates do on the Engineer and Training Examination--a test engineers take in the process of getting licensed. Of the Naval Academy graduates who take the test, 93-97 percent pass it on their first try. The success rate for graduates of other engineering colleges averages about 75 percent.

Naval Academy graduates also win more than their share of awards for graduate study. These awards include Rhodes and Marshall Scholarships as well as Guggenheim and National Science Foundation Fellowships.

Each year about eight to ten graduates go on to various medical schools, and up to 20 are eligible for that option.

In addition, up to two graduates may be selected for a special two-year graduate program in oceanography. This program is conducted at the Massachusetts Institute of Technology/ Woods Hole Oceanographic Institution and leads to a Master of Ocean Sciences degree.

What is unique about the Naval Academy's academic program and why is it so highly respected? Much of the credit is due the faculty. It is a teaching faculty. None of the professors have research obligations as they do in most other top-quality institutions. The Naval Academy professors' main job is to teach, and if they do not publish research papers in their special field of expertise, they will still keep their jobs.

Another strength of the Naval Academy faculty is its tradition for giving extra instruction, or "EI." Each professor sets aside certain hours each day that are used exclusively by the mids for EI. In addition, many faculty members encourage mids to call them at home during the evening.

Also helpful are the video-tape resources in the library. For each "core" course--a course required for all mids--there is a series of up-to-date videos covering all important topics which the mids can review at any time. This is especially helpful when a mid fails to understand something in class, or when trying to make up for a class absence.

Small class size is another strength of the Academy's academic program. The average class size is 22, small enough for each mid to become known personally by the professor.

An important advantage of small class size is that the professor will know immediately when a mid has encountered trouble in a class. Early recognition of such

A view of the United States Naval Academy over Annapolis.

Courtesy USNA Photographic Branch.

problems, combined with generous doses of EI, often saves mids who otherwise might have failed at colleges where classes of 100-300 are common.

Perhaps you are wondering why the Naval Academy, which is essentially a military institution, should place such high priority upon academic achievement. "That is not an unusual thing for a prospective student to wonder about," said the Vice-Academic Dean who was asked to comment on the Naval Academy's high standards.

"What you have to remember," he said, "is that we have to hire all of our graduates. Other four-year institutions can graduate theirs, then turn them loose and forget about them.

The professors are serious because they do not want to hear anything bad about their graduates.

Courtesy 1/C Jimmy Parker.

"Also, when our graduates leave here and take their jobs in the Navy, they have to perform well, often under adverse circumstances. If their performance was anything less than good to excellent, we would receive immediate feedback from the fleet. Obviously, we do not want to hear anything bad about our graduates so we put extra effort into seeing that we do our job right."

There is no question that the Naval Academy is a fine college, especially for those who want to specialize in science and technology. But it is more than that.

It is also a very tough military institution and no candidate should even think of going there just for the academic education. The Naval Academy's mission is to turn out high-quality officers for the naval services. How they go about doing that is the subject of the next chapter.

TWO
THE MILITARY INSTITUTION

You can attend many colleges in the United States and get an excellent academic education. But aside from some social development in a fraternity or sorority and a few off-campus adventures, that is about all you can expect to obtain.

You get a whole lot more at the Naval Academy. Besides four years of academic education and a Bachelor of Science Degree, you also get four years of leadership training. And when you graduate, you are given a commission as a naval officer and a choice from a variety of guaranteed jobs.

As a candidate, the idea of a guaranteed job after graduation can be very attractive. In addition, many of the jobs involve excitement, adventure and travel in

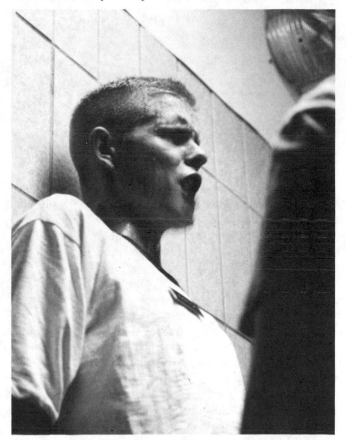

During Plebe Summer you will not be in a real steam bath but it will seem that way.

Courtesy 1/C Jimmy Parker.

The upperclassmen look at a plebe like a Corvette that has never been driven faster than 30 miles per hour. They will be determined to stretch you so you will discover your true capabilities.   *Courtesy USNA Photographic Branch.*

foreign lands. Because of this it is easy for a young person to be blinded by the glamour of the Naval Academy and think of it as a mere stepping stone to the cockpit of an F/A-18 fighter plane or the periscope of a submarine.

One purpose of this book is to clear away the glamour associated with the Naval Academy by letting you see exactly what price you must pay for that guaranteed job and a life of adventure and travel.

And the first thing you should realize is that the Naval Academy leadership training program, which is a mandatory adjunct to the four-year academic program, is roughly equivalent, in time, to a half-time job.

When you begin thinking about what it would be like going to the Naval Academy, think of attending a very demanding university like Harvard or Georgia Tech and working half time while you are doing it.

And that is just the beginning.

Next, you must realize that the leadership training is not as easy as making hamburgers at McDonald's. When you begin the first year, called "plebe" year, it is more like entering a pressure cooker than starting a job.

Actually, during the first week of July when each new class arrives in Annapolis, the temperature really is not hot enough to produce steam. It just seems that way to the new plebes because of the high humidity of the region and the pressure exerted upon them starting on their first day--Induction Day (I-Day).

Why put the plebes under such pressure?

The quote of a famous marine general can help explain why. He said:

"The first essential of a successful leader is to be able to understand and comprehend the emotions and the spirit which live in the hearts and souls of the men he commands."

That philosophy is the basis for the Plebe Indoctrination Program, which is the formal name for the first year of leadership training. The idea is that prospective naval officers should learn what is in the "hearts and souls" of those they will command by experiencing what it is like to be a follower.

In the military tradition a good follower learns to stand at attention, to salute, to accept discipline and to master the elements of close-order drill and marching. Those lessons are begun the first hours after arrival.

In addition, on I-Day the plebe receives the traditional short haircut, inoculations, a beginning clothing issue and, most important, an introduction to their upperclass trainers called "detailers."

The head detailers are the first classmen, who are the equivalent of college seniors but they are much more than that. They are the leaders of the entire brigade of

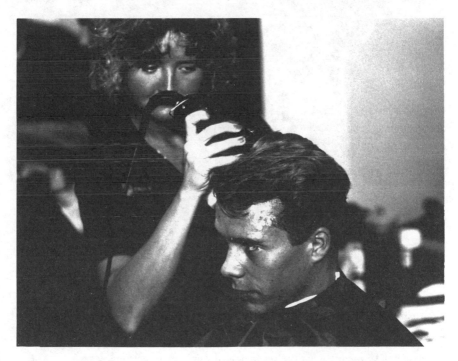

The haircut may come as a shock, but short hair is better in the heat and humidity.

Courtesy 1/C Jimmy Parker.

midshipmen (the student body), and their most important task is to supervise the Plebe Indoctrination Program. In that process, they control plebes' lives from I-Day in early July until the following May when the first academic year is completed.

The first six and one-half weeks of training, called "Plebe Summer," are considered the most difficult by many of the plebes. During this period rigid discipline is imposed and the plebes are given challenges deliberately designed to test their courage, stamina and motivation.

After Plebe Summer, during the first academic year, the entire upperclass--the sophomores, juniors and seniors, each with specific roles--continue with the indoctrination before and after classes. Also, the plebes begin their professional military training in "pro classes." These pro classes are required during all four years and must be taken in addition to a rigorous schedule of academic classes.

That is not all. In addition to plebe indoctrination and the rigors of academic and pro classes, participation in competitive sports is required.

You have to love competition if you are going to survive at the Naval Academy.

Courtesy 1/C Jimmy Parker.

10

Like sailors of old, you will have to learn how to tie knots the Navy way.

Courtesy USNA Photographic Branch.

The sports all stress the importance of developing a winning attitude--an attitude that naval officers must possess. In naval warfare there are no prizes for second place, nor are there any consolation prizes. There are only winners and losers, and losers end up down with the Titanic--at the bottom of the ocean.

The midshipmen can elect to participate in a wide variety of sports, including all the traditional team sports as well as individual sports like gymnastics, wrestling and boxing.

11

Sailing is one of the most important non-traditional sports at the Academy. During plebe summer the basic lessons of sailing and seamanship are taught. Then, during the next four years, those skills are honed and new skills are learned with the Academy fleet of sailing craft. This fleet consists of 120 craft, which makes it the largest fleet of sailing craft in the world.

The overall goal of the four years of leadership training is to produce high quality naval officers.

But what is a "naval" officer? Actually, that term applies to officers in two of the military services--the Navy and the Marine Corps. Naval officers are Navy officers if they serve in the Navy, or they are Marine Corps officers if they serve in the Marine Corps.

Each year a fixed percentage of qualified graduates may elect to go into the Marine Corps, an option that gives Naval Academy graduates a wider variety of career opportunities than graduates from the other service academies.

Those who elect to serve in the Navy may further elect to serve with the "surface" Navy, which includes ships ranging in size from small frigates to carriers. Another option, based upon qualifications, is service in the undersea branch of the Navy, the submarine service.

Roughly 20 percent (this percentage will vary each year) of the graduates elect to serve in one of the two air forces--Navy or Marine Corps. There they may become pilots or naval flight officers in fixed-wing aircraft or helicopters.

Do class grades earned at the Academy make a difference in who gets what assignment after graduation? Do those with the highest grades get the best assignments?

Class grades do make a difference but that is not the whole story. The midshipmen also are graded on more than 2000 hours of military performance during four years at the Academy. In addition, they are rated on their physical and athletic performance, and upon their performance when they are associated with military programs during summer programs.

At a civilian college, class standing is based only upon a student's academic GPA. At the Academy, class standing is based upon the midshipman's GPA and evaluations of military, physical, athletic, and professional performance.

As a general rule, most midshipmen get their first or second choice of assignment for which they are qualified. Some programs, like pilot training, require higher physical qualifications.

However, those with the highest class standings get to pick their assignments first. Thus, because there are limited quotas for certain jobs, those who rank the highest in their class are more likely to get the exact assignment they desire.

What if a midshipman discovers that he or she is not interested in being an officer in the Navy or Marine Corps? Is it possible to resign?

Midshipmen can resign after completing a specified number of weeks of Plebe Summer--the policy varies from year to year. If they resign before they start the third year, they incur no obligation whatsoever. The college credits they have earned can be transferred to a civilian college and they can continue their education.

If midshipmen resign after beginning their third year but before starting the fourth year, they are obligated to spend two years on active duty in enlisted status (not as an officer).

If midshipmen resign after beginning their fourth year, their active duty obligation goes to three years.

Is it possible to come back to the Academy after resigning and going into active service?

That has been done. Enlisted personnel who were former midshipmen have returned from the fleet. Also, there have been cases where midshipmen have been allowed to return after resigning and going into civilian life. These are exceptions, however. Those who resign normally leave for good.

One final point. If you are a potential candidate, but worried about the rigors of the military training, keep two things in mind.

First, keep in mind that the Naval Academy has one of the highest survival rates of any college in the United States. About 77 percent of all those who enter the Academy survive all four years and graduate. The national average for all colleges is under fifty percent!

Second, do not give up thinking about being a candidate until you have read what

When Plebe Summer is over, you will have learned the fundamentals of sailing.

Courtesy 1/C Jimmy Parker.

the midshipmen themselves say about surviving. Be sure to read the chapters in the survival section of this book before you decide whether or not the military training is something you can handle.

THREE
GRADUATES SPEAK: WHAT THE
ACADEMY EXPERIENCE DID FOR ME

There are three practical reasons for going to the Naval Academy. First, you will get an excellent academic education. Second, the education is free, and you get paid while you are there. Third, when you graduate, you will be guaranteed a job.

However, graduates of the Naval Academy seldom mention the three reasons just cited. Instead, they praise the Academy for the way it changed their personal lives. They all claim that the Academy experience changed them forever, and that it opened up opportunities they would never have had if they had gone to a civilian college or university.

How did the Academy change them and what kinds of opportunities were they given? That is what the author asked during interviews with nine graduates. Here is what they had to say.

Vice Admiral (Ret.) William P. Lawrence, class of 1951. Admiral Lawrence was an all-state basketball player in Tennessee, then played three varsity sports and ended up as Class President and Brigade Commander his final year at the Naval Academy. After graduation he went to flight training, became a fighter pilot, then went to test pilot school and was considered a top candidate for the initial astronaut corps, but was disqualified for a minor physical problem. Later, while commanding a squadron of F-4s on an aircraft carrier off Vietnam, he was shot down, captured, and was a POW for six years. During this time, he was an inspirational leader, and was later given citations by the two senior POW commanders which said, in part, "...among a group of heroic figures, your performance was the most heroic of all," and, "...he was consistently stalwart and resilient in the absorption of torture...he could not be intimidated..." After his release by the North Vietnamese, he attended the National War College, then obtained a master's degree from George Washington University. He went on to command a Navy aircraft wing, then continued to advance until he became Commander U.S. Third Fleet, Superintendent of the Naval Academy, and eventually Chief of Naval Personnel. Then, when he had a chance to be appointed to the top position in the Navy, his luck ran out. A latent disease, contracted while he was a POW, incapacitated him and he was forced to retire. After three years of pain and debilitation, his health slowly recovered, and he became active in civilian life. Among other things, he has served on five corporation boards, has taught leadership at the Academy in a position especially endowed in his name, has become noted for delivering inspirational speeches, and has received numerous honors and achievement awards. His youngest daughter, Wendy (also interviewed for this chapter), graduated from the Naval Academy, became a Navy pilot, and is now an astronaut.

Undaunted after six years of extreme misery and torture as a POW in North Vietnam, Bill Lawrence returned to freedom and was soon back in the cockpit of a Navy jet.

In my opinion there is no better preparation for the broad challenges of life than can be found at a service academy. You get a tremendous education, but more than that, you develop the strength of character that will allow you to make the best use of that education. In a service academy you have to stretch yourself every day, and over a four-year period this daily stretching converts young people into remarkably capable individuals. They learn to be self-starters; their daily demands are such that they cannot make it unless they become highly self-motivated. Consequently, when they graduate they are hard chargers, with a tremendous capability for achievement whether

Rear Admiral Bill Lawrence flew the A-4 Skyhawk when he was commander of an attack wing in the Pacific Fleet.

it is in the military, or the professions, or the business world. And they are not like many who graduate from civilian universities in engineering or in one of the professions--people who often have a narrow perspective and limited experience. Graduates of a service academy have had a wide range of experiences, and they have had to develop broad capabilities, which enables them to be competitive in a wide range of occupations, military or civilian.

Certainly, applying all of the above in the service of our country and for the good of society is the most important purpose of an Academy education. But I would like to explain how that experience can help an individual realize what is perhaps the most difficult achievement in life--the attainment of true happiness and fulfillment.

Young people seldom hear their parents talking about happiness and fulfillment. Instead, they hear a lot about happiness being equated with the accumulation of material things--new cars, new boats--those kinds of things. Consequently, they tend to set their goals in that direction even though that is not going to bring them happiness. They don't know that, of course, and that is why, when I speak to young people, I try to reorient their thinking. At their young stage of life I want them to understand what will bring them true happiness and fulfillment. That way they can establish goals that will get them where they really want to go.

Specifically, to achieve happiness, I believe there are four things that a person needs. First, is a close family. Second, is a circle of solid, true friends. Third, is good health. Fourth, is a personal feeling of self respect and self esteem--in other words, to be happy, people need to feel good about themselves.

Of course, the big question is: How is a young person going to achieve those four things? Well, now it is time to interject the service academy experience because, in my opinion, the four years at a service academy will allow a young person to achieve all four of them. Let me be specific.

First, the close-knit family. It was my observation as a midshipman, then later as Naval Academy Superintendent, that the academy experience does a lot to create a much tighter bond between the midshipmen and their parents, brothers, and sisters. First, families work together to provide the love and support needed by a midshipman to meet the tough demands of plebe year. Then, during the demanding upper-class years, there is further bonding because of the family pride that results when the midshipman achieves continued success. I believe also, that this heightened family awareness carries over later, when the graduates go on into their military careers, marry and produce their own families.

Second on my list for happiness is the need for a wide circle of true friends. In this regard I can state emphatically that any person who attends a service academy for four years is guaranteed to achieve that goal. The deep bonding that occurs between classmates starts with the same elements that cause the family to grow closer. The bonding forces between the midshipmen are further strengthened because no single individual can survive at the Academy without the help of others. It is simply impossible to make it through even the first summer unless the midshipmen help each other and believe they are mutually responsibility for each other's success. This mutual need for each other creates bonds that are incredibly strong. And let me emphasize that these bonds of friendship, forged during the four years at an academy, remain very strong throughout a person's whole life. Additionally, the friendships are further strengthened during later military service because of the need for close teamwork and mutual support to meet the demands of the military profession.

The third ingredient for happiness is good health, and from Day One the Academy stresses the importance of physical fitness, sports, and good nutrition. At a civilian college or university your physical welfare is not a high priority of the institution's president; you can get by without anyone caring if you stay fit or eat properly. But I can tell you from personal experience that the Superintendent of the Naval Academy is highly concerned about this dimension of your life--and this concern is not just for your physical welfare while you are at the Academy--the goal is to instill in the midshipman a lifetime desire to maintain healthy habits.

The fourth ingredient for happiness is a personal feeling of self respect and self esteem--literally, feeling good about yourself. This comes from working hard and achieving worthwhile goals. But the feeling is enhanced because at a service academy you also realize that you are going to be engaged in a very noble cause, namely serving your country and helping to preserve its freedom. Later, when serving your country, your self esteem will rise because you are in a highly respected, honorable profession.

The young people I have spoken to about the Naval Academy always like to hear about exciting things--and I don't know of anything more exciting than flying airplanes off aircraft carriers. Well, I talk about those things--about what it is like to be a Navy or Marine fighter pilot. However, I also like to tell them stories about some of the very wealthy business executives I have met who are very sad and unfulfilled persons. The

18

main reason is that they worked so hard to acquire wealth and material possessions that they neglected the four ingredients of happiness I described. They did not spend time with their families, develop close friendships or maintain good health. But most importantly, they did not gain self-esteem, because they were not proud of what they were doing. Many would swap places with me if they could, even though I am by no means wealthy.

So, yes, the Naval Academy will give you a good education and provide you a good job, and it will prepare you for many challenging opportunities. But, think of what it can also do for your long-term happiness and sense of fulfillment. Personally, I believe the latter is a more important reason for going to the Naval Academy.

Rear Admiral Don Boecker, class of 1960. Admiral Boecker grew up in Naperville, Illinois and from the time he could remember he was interested in aviation. He built model airplanes as a boy, then, with money he earned, he paid for flying lessons and learned to fly a Piper Cub. He was also very athletic and, when visited by the Naval Academy freshman football coach and told they would like him in Annapolis, young Boecker thought it must be Indianapolis, for he was from an Army family (his father was in World War I) and knew nothing about the Naval Academy. Thus encouraged, he applied, but encountered stiff opposition. But determined now, he enlisted in the Naval Reserve, then got into the Academy after going to a prep school for a year and taking an exam. At the Academy he played four years of varsity football and golf, then went to flight training after graduation. He flew F-9 Cougars and F-11 Tiger Jets, then transferred to the A-4 Skyhawk, an attack aircraft. His first deployment was on the USS Enterprise, which was put on alert for the Cuban Missile Crisis in 1963. Then, as the new A-6 Intruder came into the inventory he transferred to the first squadron and deployed to Vietnam on the carrier Independence from which he flew 69 combat missions, mostly at night over North Vietnam. On one of these missions a bomb with a bad fuze exploded as it was released and he and his bombardier/navigator ejected from their shattered airplane, evaded the enemy, and 18 hours later were rescued by a heroic helicopter crew while under heavy enemy fire. After Vietnam he went to U.S. Naval Test Pilot School, then held several command positions, including executive officer of the USS Saratoga and command of the USS Concord. After that, he held various staff jobs in Washington, then was the Director of Navy Space Systems, Commander of the Naval Air Test Center, and, at the time of this interview, was Vice Commander, Naval Air Systems Command. He is now retired.

In preparing for this interview I didn't have to think very long to make a list of the five things that the Naval Academy did for me. There were some black days when I was going there, particularly that first year, but looking back with my current perspective, they were truly golden years and it is real easy to tell you why.

First, is the discipline. It was tough at first, and I will admit that it was very hard dealing with it. But the discipline that was imposed upon me as a plebe also gave me the foundation for establishing my own self-discipline as I went through the next three years. And later, when I started flying airplanes, the rules and regulations made sense

Don Boecker (second from right) is being congratulated after his rescue from a rice paddy in Laos while Don Eaton, his bombardier/navigator (left) looks on.

to me, and allowed me to fly aggressively, but safely, because I respected the limitations and the rationale behind the regulations--and that has kept me alive while flying over 90 different models of Navy and Marine aircraft.

Second, is physical conditioning. I cannot say enough about the value of daily exercise, which I started during Plebe Summer and have continued to this day. I learned that exercise helps a person stay sharp both mentally and physically. It was a good lesson and it has helped me throughout my career.

Third, is competitiveness. The Academy requires every midshipman to participate in some kind of sport, and that is an excellent requirement. The idea of teamwork has to be instilled in young people who will become our officers because they, in turn, will have to instill that in the young men and women we have today on our ships. That is the only way we can empower and use the talents of young people; they have to learn that they can always do something better as a team rather than as individuals.

My friend and bombardier/navigator, Rear Admiral Don Eaton, USN (retired), and I have recently celebrated the 29th anniversary of our 15 July 1965 rescue from an enemy-ridden rice paddy in the remote hill country of Laos, where we were downed on a classified bombing mission. Neither of us could have lived without our military training that had given us immense self-discipline and great physical conditioning. I was 27 years old, and without the spirit of competitiveness instilled in me by the rigors of Academy life, I could not have fought through that confrontation with the enemy with self-confidence and with the spirit of teamwork Don and I used to get us through.

Rear Admiral Don Boecker after test flying an aircraft the Navy was considering as a primary trainer.

Fourth, is time management. One cannot survive at the Naval Academy with the strong academic load, professional training, and daily athletic practice without learning to manage time. It is tough, really tough, at first when there is never enough time to do everything. But this teaches one to carefully plan each day to make sure every time slot is accounted for. Also, it teaches one to avoid the kinds of things that can divert you and wreck plans. Later, when I was pressed for time and under pressure, I could fall back on this training. Now, after 34 years in many kinds of jobs, I can really appreciate what that training did for me.

The fifth thing I learned is most important, although I started with the lessons taught by my own family as I was growing up. I learned to get along with people. I learned to treat people with dignity, and like I would like to be treated. That lesson carried over in every one of my commands. There are many characteristics of a good leader, but I don't know of a single one who is really great who does not have this talent. I cannot emphasize that enough. To motivate people, you have to treat them with dignity. When I was at the Academy, there was great emphasis placed on the responsibility of an officer to be a gentleman and a moral leader. They taught us it is not enough to be bright or well-trained. They stressed that a good officer must strive to be an exemplary human being.

How would I be different if I had not gone to the Academy? I always liked math and science and I would probably have gone on to become an engineer in some company. But I would be a different person and my outlook on life would probably be totally different. In the Navy I have had the opportunity to meet many thousands of people. I have seen hundreds of countries and know about the values and culture of their people. As an engineer in some company I don't think I would be nearly as proud of being an American as I am now. My vision of the world helps me put America in perspective. My experiences in the Navy have helped me realize what a truly great country we have.

Brigadier General Charles F. Bolden, Jr., class of 1968. General Bolden grew up in Columbia, South Carolina and while he was in junior high school he was attracted to the television show, Men of Annapolis. *From then on he had only one ambition, which was to attend the Naval Academy. He began applying for an appointment when he was in the ninth grade but was told to wait until his senior year. When he reapplied, he was turned down by the local politicians, however, he wrote the new president, Lyndon Johnson (President Kennedy has just been assassinated) and soon he received a visit from a Navy chief who interviewed him. Soon thereafter he received a nomination from a Chicago congressman. At the Academy he minored in electrical science and "the two things I was definitely not planning to do were fly airplanes or become a marine." However, he had a company officer he admired very much who was a Marine Corps major, and soon, with the Major as a mentor, he was a convert to the Marine Corps. During his senior year "on a whim" he applied and was accepted for aviation training. However, the Vietnam conflict was in high gear and he was "charged up" to go fight as an infantry officer. However, a wise old, tobacco-chewing marine talked him into giving aviation a try, which he did. He went to flight training and "fell in love with flying on my first flight." From then on flying became a career and a passion. He flew over one hundred combat missions in the A-6 Intruder in Southeast Asia, completed a master's degree and several stateside assignments, then was accepted at the Navy Test Pilot School. After that, he applied for astronaut training, was accepted, and has since logged over 680 hours in space on four Space Shuttle flights--two as pilot and two as mission commander. He has also held important administrative posts at the Johnson and Kennedy Space Centers. At the time of this*

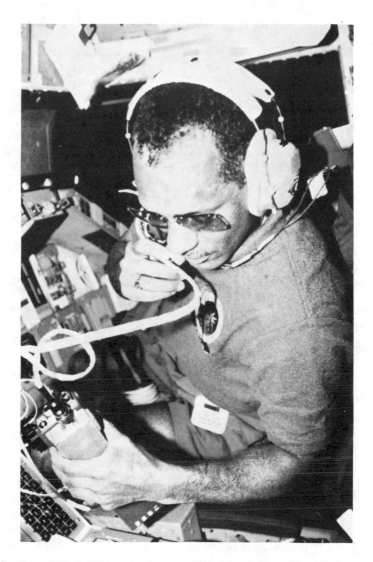

Brigadier General Charlie Bolden when he was an astronaut and in command of a space shuttle flight.   *Courtesy NASA.*

interview he was in the process of leaving NASA to become the Deputy Commandant of Midshipmen at the Naval Academy. Since then he has become Assistant Wing Commander of the 3rd Marine Aircraft Wing.

Both of my parents were teachers and they started instilling the concepts of honesty and integrity at an early age. Then when I got to the Naval Academy, I saw these things institutionalized. That is when the lights and bells really came on for me;

the moral tone of the Academy fit right into the way I was brought up and I loved the atmosphere.

The plebe year was very difficult, however, and there were many times that I wanted to go home. But I had this vision left from all the television episodes of *Men of Annapolis*--of how they were doing all these exciting things, going on ships and seeing different countries. These images gave me something to look forward to, but really, there was another factor.

All my life at home my parents had preached to me that I should never take an easy road--that I would always have to work hard for anything worthwhile. They also worked to convince me that if I was on an easy road, there was probably something wrong with it--that only the hard roads led to anything that was valuable.

So there I was, a plebe, homesick and tired of the harassment, and what was I to do? Well, that is when I learned one of the most important lessons the Academy has to teach, that is: you never give up. Instead, when faced with difficulty, you put your head down and charge. I learned that you may take some dings and some hits when you do this, but you get where you want to go.

So I hung in there and refused to let anything intimidate me. It was tough but it was a good lesson--one that has carried over throughout my whole career.

Another big thing I gained from the Academy was an appreciation for the heritage of freedom in this country. We studied the Constitution and discussed the concepts of liberty and freedom and what they mean. These concepts stuck with me, and when I got out and traveled, they meant even more.

And what if I had not gone to the Naval Academy? I got out of high school at the height of the civil rights movement, and when the Vietnam antiwar movement was starting. I could easily have gone down either one of those forks in the road. I almost surely would not have ended up in engineering. I would never have been exposed to aviation. I would not have been a test pilot or an astronaut. My guess is that I would be quite a different person.

Rear Admiral Mike Mullen, Class of 1968. Rear Admiral Mullen was raised in North Hollywood, California, with both parents working in the movie industry. He was a recruited basketball player out of high school, and elected the Naval Academy "because I knew I needed the discipline." The day he arrived the temperature was 95 degrees with 90 percent humidity and he thought he had landed in hell. Besides the physical hazing, which was prevalent then, he also suffered academic shock and by Christmas that first year he was on the borderline of failure with a .8 grade point average. In addition, one of the first classmen (who Admiral Mullen still calls a "jerk") made it his personal crusade to drive Mullen out of the Academy. But Mullen persisted and went on to graduate, selecting surface warfare as a career. His first assignment was the antisubmarine warfare officer and navigator on a destroyer which deployed in Vietnamese waters during the war. After that, he went to another destroyer as weapons officer and operations officer, then, while still a lieutenant, went on to command his first ship, a gasoline tanker. He returned to the Naval Academy for a three-year tour (two as a company officer), then went to sea as chief

Rear Admiral Mike Mullen when he took command of Cruiser/Destroyer Battle Group Two.
Courtesy USN.

engineer on a cruiser. Following that, he became the executive officer of another cruiser, took a tour at Naval Post Graduate School and obtained a master's degree in operations research, then went to sea again as the commanding officer of a guided missile destroyer. Then, after two stateside jobs and a three-month stint at Harvard for young business executives, he took command of the USS Yorktown, an aegis cruiser. After that, he served in the Pentagon, then was assigned as Commander, Cruiser/Destroyer Battle Group Two.

I will start out with a little story that will help explain the main effect the Academy had on me. I was a young lieutenant, 26 years old, when I took command of the USS Noxubee, a small gasoline tanker with a crew of about 100 men. In that tour we had to return to the United States from a deployment in the Mediterranean. As we got into the Atlantic, this huge storm front extended from Nova Scotia to South America and, all alone in the Atlantic, we hit 40-foot seas and we were stuck in that storm for 96 hours--four days, around the clock. We were in the infamous Bermuda Triangle at the time--the young boots from Iowa and Nebraska and Idaho--kids on their first cruise who had never dreamed of anything like we were experiencing--started coming to me with these books about the mysterious sinkings in that Triangle. But throughout those 96 hours, when I probably got a total of four hours sleep, and when the ship was rising, then slamming down so hard that it seemed like it would break, and when the waves were 15 feet above my eye level from my position in the bridge, and when one wrong move would have caused the ship to capsize and kill us all, it never entered my mind that we might not survive. I was totally strong and confident the whole time, and my point in saying all this is because the Naval Academy gave me a massive package that let me do all that with supreme confidence.

I remember walking on the USS Collett, a destroyer, for my first assignment. I wasn't sure the Navy was for me, or that I would even like being on a ship. But, from the minute I walked on that deck, a feeling came over me and I knew that I was in the right place. That, too, is what the Naval Academy did for me.

How did the Academy do that? It was a very simple, but very hard lesson. From that first day, when the temperature was 95 degrees and the humidity was 90 percent, I had to learn discipline and perseverance. I had to learn to overcome adversity. And, later, when this jerk decided he was going to run me out of the Academy, whatever raw leadership ability I had, came out. I said to myself that I was not going to let someone like that beat me--that I am going to persevere and turn what he thinks is going to be a big loss into a big win. And I did. I survived, and that jerk really did me a favor because the experience gave me confidence. Of course, throughout the other three years, I went on to learn more about leadership, and when I hit the deck of that first destroyer, I was ready. I was confident. I was ready for the excitement and the challenges that I knew we would face on a day-by-day basis.

So the Naval Academy took the raw material I had for leadership and gave me the knowledge, the strength, and the confidence to become a good leader--one who is never better than when things are at their absolute worst.

There are some other things the Academy did for me that I should also mention. I learned the importance of teamwork, and learned to place team goals ahead of personal goals. It taught me humility, which is a very important trait for a leader to have. Also, I thrived in an environment based upon honesty and integrity. I didn't see much of that in my high school; cheating was common and an everyday occurrence. I welcomed the atmosphere at the Academy where one learned to trust your classmates.

Speaking of classmates, I should mention the strong bonds of friendship that are established at the Academy. When I went back for a high school reunion after twenty years, I felt like a stranger to most of my classmates. We had little in common. But when I went to my 20-year Academy reunion, we picked up on conversations with each other just as though we had seen each other just yesterday. The feeling was totally different, and having so many close friends is a bonus the Academy gives its graduates.

Finally, I should mention something personal. I have always had a social conscience and I like the idea of serving others. Consequently, it was a bit of a shock for me when I went to Harvard with all these hot runners--young men and women

26

executives on the fast track. Don't get me wrong; they were good guys and gals--very bright and capable. But their narrowness of experience and goals just flabbergasted me. But that is the business world--we studied a whole bunch of companies and there were only two or three that I would even consider if I were looking for a job. Service to society is more important to me, and more satisfying. In fact, when the day comes for me to leave the Navy, I want to give service to somebody. I'm sure that the Academy, along with my career experiences, helped develop that attitude.

Captain Jim Garban, Class of 1973. Captain Garban grew up in a suburb of San Francisco and was a star fullback, rushing close to 1000 yards his senior year. He caught the attention of a local Blue and Gold Officer[1] who suggested that Garban had the leadership potential to become a good naval officer. From this seed grew a desire to attend the Naval Academy, but, because of his mediocre academic performance in high school, he accepted the offer of a year at the Naval Academy Prep School (NAPS) after he applied to the Academy. However, after a year at NAPS, he still tested low on the SAT verbal assessment and agreed to attend a junior college in Texas. After a second year of prep school, he was found qualified and was admitted to the Academy where he played varsity football as a 5-10, 195 pound inside linebacker. When he was elected captain of the team his senior year, his coach said, "Pound for pound, Jim Garban was the physically-toughest football player I've ever been associated with." After graduation Garban became a surface warfare officer, serving on a cruiser, the USS Sterett, for three years. Then he served a tour at the Naval Academy teaching leadership, navigation and ship handling, and as the defensive coordinator for the 150-pound football team. He then transferred to the Navy Supply Corps, completing various tours including two afloat supply officer assignments as well as shore duty that included a tour on the staff of the Secretary of the Navy. In 1985 he was diagnosed with cancer and was put on two years of limited duty. Luckily, his therapy gave him a 100 percent recovery. At the time of this interview he was the executive officer of the Fleet and Industrial Supply Center in San Diego, California, happily remarried, and enjoying his parenting responsibilities for five girls.

In high school I was just an unfocused, C+ kind of student, full of mischief, and with no plans for college. I lived for the day with no thoughts of the future. However, when the whistle blew and the coach yelled, that's when I reached my greatest intensity. But there was no self-motivation. I lacked confidence and I have doubts about what might have happened to me had not Tom Teshara, a Naval Academy Blue and Gold Officer, seen some potential in me that I had not realized. He thought I had potential as a leader and encouraged me to consider the Academy. I applied, and at NAPS, where they sent me for academic preparation, I continued with some of my

---

[1]A Naval Academy regional representative. The important role of the Blue and Gold Officers as advisors to candidates will be discussed in later chapters.

Captain Jim Garban (left) relaxing at home with Tom Teshara, the Blue and Gold Officer who originally got him interested in the Naval Academy.

high school-type pranks and very nearly got expelled. But at the second prep school I buckled down and got serious, then when I was accepted into the Academy, the two years of additional maturity really helped me in that rigorous environment. Also, the prep schools gave me two more years of football experience, which helped me compete for a varsity position.

At the Academy I was totally challenged in all aspects of my life and that experience changed me. Before, I needed the coach to blow the whistle or shoot the gun before I performed at my highest level. I needed somebody standing over me in order to perform at 150 percent. At the Academy I learned how to push the envelope on my own. The Academy taught me to be a self-directing coach. It taught me to blow my own whistle whenever I needed maximum performance. It also taught me to apply my very best effort at each and every facet of my life.

The Academy also enabled me to gain confidence in myself--real confidence that I was to have for the first time in my life. It was the intense environment and the hard work that did it. My Academy lesson was simple: hard work and determination can get you through anything.

However, with the confidence you get something else. You get what I call a "tool kit" for mastering all the challenges you will face for the rest of your life. In my own case, I was going through a divorce when I was diagnosed with cancer. This was a time when I was facing my "dragons" and needed to reach deeply for inner strength. I credit the Academy experience for giving me the confidence and strength to successfully battle both challenges. I simply applied the tools from the kit that the Academy gave me.

Another valuable Academy lesson was learning the power of teamwork. In all of the experiences there, whether athletic, academic or social, you learn how performance is enhanced by building on the strength of the team. There are so many opportunities at the Academy to learn this lesson well, and it was easy to transfer what I learned working with classmates to my shipmates when I went to the fleet. Now my role as a senior military leader has allowed me tremendous opportunities for coaching teams to the highest levels of excellence.

Finally, I have to mention the value of the close friendships I made while I was there. Twenty-three years after graduation, I still find that the friends with whom I shared the Academy experience--no matter what they are today--are still the people I can really count on. My mentors made a promise to me before I went to the Academy. They said that the friendships you will make there will not tarnish with the years. They were 100 percent correct. The friends from those years are friends for life.

Commander Walter Scott Gray IV, Class of 1979. Commander Gray grew up in a Navy family. His father was a Navy pilot and young Scott was involved with airplanes as long as he can remember. He watched his father perform in air shows, and he got to meet the members of the Blue Angels, the Navy's elite aerobatic team. However, after his first year at the Naval Academy, he found out that his eyes were no longer 20-20 and that he was ineligible for flight training. His next choice was nuclear submarines, and after his training preparing for that branch, he served tours on two different attack submarines, first as an engineering officer and weapons officer, then a navigator and operations officer. His third tour was on a Trident submarine as an engineer, and after that, he served as an Admiral's aide and then as a White House Fellow. Following a tour of duty as Executive Officer of the USS Houston he was given command of the USS Maryland. He was also elected to the Board of Trustees of the Naval Academy.

What did the Academy do for me? The first thing that comes to mind is the instant credibility we have. Wherever I go and whomever I meet, in the business world or the political world, when people find out I am a graduate of the Naval

Academy, they get a special glint in their eye. There is an automatic trust there, a level of respect that is not there before they know I am an Academy graduate.

Another thing the Academy did was teach me at a young age the correct outlook on responsibility. You learn responsibility between 18 and 21, which is an ideal time in a person's life. You don't wander through life and then, with a wife and kids, discover that you have to be a responsible person. So many young people, when they graduate from high school, find that they have to take on a scary world. They discover that nobody is going to hand you anything. That can be frightening. At the Academy we were protected from the outside world during those critical years when we were learning responsibility. We were given the tools in a very controlled environment while we were being monitored and taught by responsible people.

Since graduation I have never once been concerned about being employed.

Commander Scott Gray standing beside the submarine, USS Maryland, which he is commanding.

Maybe my pay as an ensign was not great, but that improved. And, once a graduate has paid back the service obligation, that's a nice ticket punch--you can put on your resume that you graduated from the Naval Academy and served in the Navy, and you can't go wrong. Young people need to understand that it is tough out there in the world these days. I know college kids who are staying in school because there are no jobs available. Just two nights ago, for example, I had dinner with a 23-year old microbiologist, a real smart young man who was laid off right after he went to work. He has been driving around the country for months looking for a job and has no prospects. That is frightening, especially after the years of hard work that went into his education.

You also learn things at the Academy that will make you a better employee, whether it is in the Navy or in the business world. For example, you have to learn time management and prioritization. Because of this training, I can work several projects at once. I can channel incoming data, process and prioritize in such a way that I can get all of them done. This is very hard to learn and, of course, people can learn that out on a job when under the gun. But it is nice to learn while in college so you have those skills on your first job.

I also learned the importance of attitude and how attitude can work for you. You learn that you can never have a defeatist attitude, and that all problems have solutions. When I left the Academy, I knew how to research problems and I knew how to solve them. Also, they build in a kind of stubbornness--to the point where you can't let yourself quit until you have solved a problem.

There is something else they teach you and I don't quite know what name to put on it. But, in the military we can get ourselves into some difficult predicaments. Quite frankly, things can go to hell real fast and what is happening can be life threatening. Now picture yourself as a leader when all this is going on. The troops under you, who are starting to worry, look to you. And, unless you are totally confident, they are going to get nervous and perhaps not even do the job they are supposed to do. What I am saying is that learning leadership is learning how to control yourself so that those around you cannot see the stress that you are feeling. Let me give an example of how that is taught.

When I was a plebe, I was getting slam dunked by this first classman. I mean he was on me big time. But I had been told by my father that you must never let one of them see any chink in your armor--that you had to play the game so that they can never see you stressed. And that is what I did. However, there were some who didn't learn that lesson as plebes. Later, however, they saw it from another side. When we were first classmen, the plebes were told, "Now if there is a problem that you think you can't handle, go to this particular first classman and he will help you." Well, when they would come to me and say, "Mr. So and So is really down on me and I can't handle him," I would tell them, "Hey, you go off and deal with it yourself. You have to be strong; you have to play the game." That was hard advice because some of them would break down and cry. But I tried to get them to see the point; when they are out in the fleet, or a Marine in combat, they cannot let their stress show. Of course, I was lucky to have a father who told me all about this. Over and over he stressed that it was just a game--that thousands of people have gone through it, then wound up later on the same team, working together as close friends. He also used the "no pain, no gain" routine, trying to get me to see that the only way I was going to learn to maintain poise under stress was to experience the stress in a controlled environment.

Back in 1985, when I completed my service commitment, I thought of getting out. I took leave and did some job applying--and had some really great offers. But I stayed in because none of the jobs seemed exciting--there would have been just the same thing day after day and not a lot of responsibility. I mean, think of my own experience, which was fairly typical. Here I was, a young lieutenant, 25 years old and on my first assignment on a submarine, with 40 people working for me, and as weapons officer I was in charge of all the nuclear weapons, all torpedoes, a mega-million dollar fire control system, the sonar system, as well as the Tomahawk and Harpoon missiles. This was incredible responsibility, and it built after that on each new assignment. Now here I was, thinking of getting out of the Navy and taking a boring job with little responsibility. Obviously, I decided to stay in, and I will confess; if I do nothing else in my professional career but command a nuclear sub, then wave the flag for duty, honor, and country, I will consider my life's work a complete success. Sure, someday I would like to run for an office and maybe even become a U.S. Senator, but that would be just gravy. None of that would equal being the commander of a nuclear submarine.

Lieutenant Commander Wendy Lawrence, class of 1981. "Flying was in my blood," said Lt. Cmdr. Lawrence when she was interviewed. "My grandfather, who was in the Class of 1930, flew in several campaigns in the Pacific during World War II, and my father, Class of 1951, was a test pilot and fighter pilot in the Vietnam War. My dream was to become an astronaut--an impossible dream when I started at the Academy the summer of 1977, but a reality 15 years later. Now I am an astronaut." So said Lt. Cmdr. Lawrence as she trained for her first mission in the space shuttle Endeavor. However, prior to becoming an astronaut, she went to the fleet as an H-46 "Sea Knight" helicopter pilot--one of the first of three women to make a long deployment supporting a carrier battle group. After that tour, she was sent to the Massachusetts Institute of Technology to obtain a Master's Degree in Ocean Engineering, then back to flight operations, flying an H-2 helicopter doing oceanographic research. After that, she went to the Naval Academy to teach physics and coach one of the women's crew teams. After that, she was accepted for astronaut training.

The best thing about the Academy is what it teaches you about yourself. The environment there encourages you to be the best that you can be, and it gives you the opportunities to do that. You really learn about yourself through failure, and during your plebe year the system makes sure that you experience failure. Then, after you have failed, you are faced with a choice. Do you pick yourself up and move on, or do you stay flat on your back, defeated? From this, if you persevere, you become dedicated and determined, and, because of the demands of the system, you become committed to excellence.

Plebe year is tough. Every day there is a new challenge. You are always tired because you never get enough sleep. The stress and the pressure are always there and the easiest thing is to give up, especially after you think you have tried as hard as you can. But the great strength of the Academy is the support that comes from your classmates, the faculty and the officers who are stationed there. So, with this support, you find the strength and continue, and, after that, you begin to feel good about

Lieutenant Commander Wendy Lawrence gives a thumbs-up for her first space shuttle mission.
Courtesy NASA

yourself. You then look inside yourself and you see a new person, a better person; you have learned that there is more inside yourself that you ever imagined.

Another thing I carried away from the Academy was an attitude toward failure. I am not afraid of challenges. I am not thinking about failure. The attitude I developed was to always do your best, then you never have to hang your head if you fail.

It is also important to point out some of the enjoyable things about the Academy experience. For me, the close personal relationships I developed are the most memorable. There is a very strong bond that you develop between your classmates. Later, you realize that this bond is going to last throughout your lifetime. In addition, if you are on an athletic team, the rowing team for example, you perform physically demanding work every day, in the rain and in the cold, and the adversity you share causes you to develop a very, very strong bond with your teammates.

But the Academy is not for everybody. I stress this when I speak to high school students. You are not in control of your life when you are there. It is not like a civilian school where you can go into town when you wish, and where the choice of studying is your own. You have a schedule laid out for you, you are told which uniform you have to wear, and you have to perform when you don't feel like it.

But that is the way it is when you are in the fleet. You are not in control. You go where they send you. And, if you are on flight operations 24 hours a day and don't feel like flying, that's too bad. You have a job to do and you have to do it.

Personally, I never found the regimentation a problem. I like organization and structure; I am comfortable in that kind of system. Also, now I can realize the importance of the training at the Academy. At the time, it seemed stupid to memorize menus and other information when there wasn't enough time to do it. We had to do that under deliberate pressure from the upperclassmen. But then, when I was out over the North Atlantic with 20 passengers in a helicopter, knowing that going down in that cold water would end our lives in minutes, I knew that a split-second reaction using a memorized emergency checklist could make the difference between living and dying. That's the way it is in the military; your decisions and your reactions don't just lose money as in the business world; when things go wrong in the military, people's lives are on the line and whether they live or die can depend upon your ability to perform.

There is a rationale behind the stress and pressure you experience at the Academy. So, it is an individual decision whether or not you want to become an individual who can handle that. But let me say this: the good part of it is that you develop confidence in yourself after those kinds of experiences. And self confidence is a key component to success in any field.

Of course, I have to add one more thing. For me there is a lot of satisfaction knowing that I am serving my country, especially after it has given so much to me. I don't make a big thing out of it, but that makes me feel good about myself and makes me believe that what I am doing goes beyond my personal sense of accomplishment.

Mr. Greg Zingler, Class of 1983. Mr. Zingler was in high school when his older brother was one of the top football players at the Academy. He, too, wanted to go there, but was not qualified academically. He applied to the Naval Academy Foundation and received a scholarship to a prep school in Texas, after which he raised his college board test score 300 points. He was then admitted to the Academy, was a company sub-commander and played lightweight football. Upon graduation he became a supply officer and, during a Mediterranean deployment, was awarded the Navy Commendation Medal. He then returned to the Naval Academy where he enjoyed a variety of positions. Upon completion of his active duty service, he was hired to manage Alumni Hall, the 30-million dollar complex that is a home for professional as well as cultural and athletic activities.

First of all, the Naval Academy helped me become a mature person because of the responsibilities that were given to me. There were numerous challenges, 24-hours a day, and I had the choice to react to them in a positive or a negative way. I went the positive route, as did most of my classmates, and, now, looking back, it wasn't the physics or the drill or what I learned out of the textbooks that helped me. It was knowing, as an upperclassman I was in charge of the lives of other young men and

Greg Zingler with wife, Kathy, and his three children.

women. I was challenged, and when I performed well in this leadership position, I developed a positive feeling about myself.

For me, the great thing about the Academy, was that I had good role models in front of me every day. I was blessed; my parents were great role models when I was growing up. And here at the Academy, I could emulate leaders the same way as my parents.

Another good thing is the camaraderie that develops here among teammates and classmates. At our ten-year reunion, with 830 classmates and their family members attending, it was like greeting friends you had seen just yesterday.

When I speak to high school students, I emphasize all the service academies are going to develop them physically, morally and academically. Also, I stress after they graduate, they are going to have much more responsibility than if they had gone to a civilian college. In the Navy, for example, they can immediately be given a responsibility critical for the safety and welfare of 30+ subordinates and millions of dollars worth of equipment--a responsibility that they *might* have at 35 years of age in the civilian sector.

After graduation, I was able to get out on a ship and see different countries and the way many people have to live. I just wish it were possible for many more of our young people to take a cruise to some of those places so they would realize what this country has to offer. Then they could appreciate why service to their country, in or out of uniform, is such a worthwhile profession.

Lieutenant Junior Grade Morgen Paul, Class of 1994. Lieutenant Paul was one of ten graduates from a small high school in Alaska. She went directly to the Academy, which was a shock coming from a four-teacher high school. She struggled at the beginning, particularly in academics, but soon caught up with her classmates and went on to major in physics. As a first classman she was a regimental commander, with the supervisory responsibility for 2100 midshipmen--half of the Midshipman Brigade. After graduation she went to the Navy Surface Warfare School, then to the USS Nimitz, an aircraft carrier. She was interviewed on the Nimitz as it was returning from a six-month deployment to the Persian Gulf. At the time of the interview she was in charge of the 90 enlisted personnel who ran the combat operations center on the ship. Since then, she has attended Aegis weapons training and will report to the USS Port Royal, a Ticonderoga-class cruiser. She will be the fire control officer.

"On I-Day they broke us up into two groups before the swearing in ceremony. That is when I realized that the 500 in the group waiting with me was more people than my entire town. I felt overwhelmed and sure I was going to get lost in the shuffle. I just knew there was no way this hick from the sticks was going to make it. I felt that everybody around me had advantages I didn't have. So I was very intimidated at first, especially after Plebe Summer in my academic classes where every single person in each class was just as bright and just as quick. I knew when I went there that the academics were going to be tough, but I didn't realize how much tougher they would be.

My problem was that I had no time management skills. I was used to getting every assignment done, so I might spend all four hours of my study time doing a history assignment, then not have any time for my calculus or chemistry homework. My grades were horrible the first semester--by my standards, at least. For a long time, even though I was terribly homesick, I was afraid to call home because I was ashamed of myself and I was afraid I would cry.

But I never ever thought of quitting. No way could I have lived with myself if I had. What helped me was my track experience. I am not a graceful runner. I don't have natural running skills. I can't run sprints nor can I run long distances. So I ran the half mile--a distance too long for the sprinters and too short for the distance runners, but races you can run if you have heart. I would win those races because I wouldn't quit and let anybody beat me. From that experience I found that if something was just hard and didn't take natural talent, I could hang in there with almost anybody. In other words, if all a task requires is guts, I can do it.

36

Lieutenant Junior Grade Morgen Paul with one of her technical support personnel in the combat operations center of the USS Nimitz. *Courtesy PAO USS Nimitz.*

That's the attitude I had when I went into the Academy and it is the attitude that got me through. There was just no way I was going to quit; if they wanted me out, they would have to kick me out. That thought, especially, got me through the first semester. Then things began to click. I saw that people weren't necessarily so much smarter than me and my confidence factor rose. Also I learned to manage my time, and by the end of the second semester I ended up on the Superintendent's List. I went to jump school at Fort Benning the following summer, and, after that, was picked to be second in command of the sophomores in my company. Things went straight up from there.

As a female I never had a single incident where I was harassed or felt any kind of prejudice. My roommate and I had the same attitude: you don't have to be careful around us; you don't have to treat us with kid gloves; treat us like everyone else.

I have heard stories that some parents don't want to send a daughter to a service academy because it takes away their femininity. I don't understand that. I have never felt any less feminine. Sure, I had to wear a plebe uniform for a year. But I still love being able to dress like a girl. I love pink and I love to wear flowers. I don't think the four years in the Academy changed my femininity at all.

But it did change me in one important way. It gave me great confidence in myself. When I came aboard the Nimitz, I had absolute confidence that I could do whatever was required. I knew I would have to learn things, but whatever was thrown at me would be nothing like that first year at the Academy. Back then, for each day, I had ten hours of homework plus class time for a 22-credit hour course schedule, four hours of sports practice, and a couple of hours for studying professional knowledge, yet I had to sleep and eat--this added up to like 48 hours a day and I had to figure out how to do everything in half that time. In addition, I had to learn how to convince my upper class to support me instead of being against me--I had to figure out how to respond to get them on my side. I didn't have the ability or the confidence to do any of that coming out of high school, and I sure wouldn't have learned much more in a regular college.

I also learned how to be successful socially--everybody has to learn that because you will fail if you don't have the support of the people around you. From day one you learn that there are only five basic responses to your superiors: "No, sir; Yes, sir; Aye aye, sir; No excuse, sir; and I'll find out, sir." Therefore, when given a job, you cannot respond with: "I can't figure out how to do that, sir." You learn that a response like that is what comes from an independent person and you cannot be such a person at the Naval Academy. In a hundred different ways you are forced to go beyond yourself and seek help from those around you--those with knowledge or talents that you don't have. You don't learn how to do that in other colleges, and I doubt if I would have ever learned that on my own.

Now, I am in charge of 90 lives and it isn't just getting those 90 people to do their jobs. I also have to deal with their pay, their morale, their leave, their advancement--I am their legal counselor, their financial counselor, their home counselor--and I have to support them when they are in trouble. That's what being a good manager is all about, but I can't go to the officer above me and say, "I'm sorry, I can't do this job." That's not an option. But my job now is not that much different from when I was a battalion commander during Plebe Summer. The plebes depended upon me for their food, their sleep, and for all of their other problems. Then, when I was regimental commander, I sat on numerous Honor Boards and had to make hard decisions that deeply affected the lives of the midshipmen accused of honor violations. I would not have had those managerial types of experiences in a regular college.

Because of the Academy, I am also a tougher person. I had setbacks as a plebe and I had never failed at anything in my life. Many of us came in thinking we were God's gift to the Academy. Then it was wham, bam, you're not God's gift to anyone; you have to prove to the upperclassmen that you're a worthy person just to sit at the table and dine with them. I failed in a lot of little things, and I was humbled. I also had an overwhelming feeling that I might fail everything. I remember going home for Christmas. I was so relieved to be home, it was like I had lost my mind. I ran around like a crazy person, irresponsible and silly. And I dreaded horribly going back. I had reached my mental limit. But, as I said before, I could not have lived with myself if I had quit. The key was going back with the right attitude and, sure enough, things got a whole lot better. And I was a tougher person. Then things got even better the next year and I continued to grow and become even stronger.

What if I hadn't gone to the Academy? I wouldn't be the quality of person I am now. Also, there is one other thing: I would be seriously in debt. What is it, $20,000 a year to attend a top college or university? Instead of being obligated for that huge amount of money, I got paid for going to college and, unlike my friends who went to regular colleges and can't even find jobs, I had a guaranteed job when I got out. Now, I have good pay, I love what I do, I am getting leadership experience that is unbelievable, and I am seeing the world. Sometimes I get asked: Would you do it again? My answer: "Good Lord, yes, I would do it again." And I tell others: "If you can possibly get there, go!" And when they say to me, "The military life is not for me," that's fine. But, I reply, "Don't complain when you graduate from college and have trouble getting a job."

There are great opportunities at the Academy and in the Navy *if you want them,* and if you're willing to say, "I can hack it; sign me up!"

HOW TO PREPARE

FOUR
MENTAL PREPARATION COMES FIRST

"If you had a brother and sister in high school, what would you tell them to do to prepare mentally for the Naval Academy?"

That question was asked of a group of midshipmen gathered around a table discussing various aspects of preparation. One second classman responded immediately.

"I wouldn't tell a little brother anything until I knew WHY he wants to come here," he said.

The others agreed immediately and they began to tell why. "It's easy to get caught up in the glamour of this place," said one. "I'll bet I had 50 calls after the newspaper article came out telling that I had been accepted here. You get to thinking, wow, I'm really somebody special."

"And then you get here," said another, "and you're all puffed up thinking you're just going to whiz through four years, get into a jet and be a Top Gun."

Then what? For the next several minutes the mids competed to see who could tell their stories first--stories about themselves and stories of mids who did not make it. Their stories cannot be repeated here. But the lessons can, and perhaps they can help with your own mental preparation.

On I-Day you go from being somebody to being nobody. The consolation is that some of America's best and brightest are right there with you.   *Courtesy 1/C Jimmy Parker*

Every day during your plebe year you will be under relentless pressure to prove yourself worthy of being a midshipman. *Courtesy 1/C Jimmy Parker.*

The shock is hardest on the "Top Guns"--those with puffed up egos because of their prowess in high school as top students, football captains and prom kings. When they get to the Academy, they suddenly discover that they are not "Top Guns" any more. They start looking around at their fellow plebes and they see more than a thousand others who were equally as good in their high schools, *or better*!

So right away the ego of most mids gets a hard blow. Then the detailers take over. They begin to pile it on. Criticism...on top of plebe knowledge to memorize...on top of duties to perform...on top of more criticism...on top of seamanship to learn...on top of physical challenges and obstacle courses...on top of more criticism...

The pressure builds and the stress on the plebes rises. But the detailers keep pouring it on, relentlessly.

Why do they do this?

They want to pile it on until all plebes reach what they *think* are their limits. They want the plebes who think they are operating at 100 percent to realize that they are only at the 60 percent level.

Thus, all will fail to operate at the level demanded of them. However, the failures are not catastrophic. It is not failure that damages the mind or body. It is failure in small things, like not memorizing some requirement perfectly or failing to pass a room

No matter how much you clean, your room will never be clean enough.

Courtesy USNA Photographic Branch.

inspection after a uniform race.[1] But such failures, minor though they be, result in important lessons learned.

It is through failure that the detailers learn about the plebes and the plebes learn about themselves. When a plebe is on the verge of failure, straining to avoid that fate, what kind of a person will emerge? Will the plebe get angry? Will the plebe break down and cry? Will the plebe just give up? Until these kinds of undesirable behavior surface, they cannot be modified and strengthened.

Much more important to the detailers, however--because few have learned to fail gracefully--is what the plebes do after they have failed.

Does the plebe admit failure and think about what can be learned from the experience? That is a healthy response. Does the plebe say, "I have done my best and

---

[1]A graduate who reviewed this chapter described a uniform race--a common exercise used to produce frustration and failure. "A uniform race is where you are in one uniform and are sent scrambling to your room to change into another and report back in just a few minutes. It teaches uniforms but guarantees failure. On one particular occasion we were laughing after our second or third change, but ready to cry by the eighth or ninth. By then, all our carefully put-away clothes were scattered around the room and we had just a few minutes to put them all away. Of course, we failed--as intended."

failed; now give me another challenge and see if I can do that." That, too, is a good response.

There are some who have such egos that it is difficult to admit failure. Some are chronic excuse makers; they blame the failure on anyone or anything but themselves. Others give up before they fail, or they want to quit after they fail.

How would you survive such pressure? Without such experiences it is hard for a young person to answer such a question.

But do not worry about that. According to midshipmen who have survived those experiences, you, too, can survive if you are properly prepared mentally. Here is what they say you must do.

First, you must program your mind to believe that if you are selected by the Naval Academy, *you can survive there and that the Academy wants you to survive.*

Think about that statement, and as you do, realize that it may be difficult for your mind to accept it. This is partly because of the false reputation that has been perpetuated about the Naval Academy. It is common to hear that the philosophy at the Academy is to weed out the faint-hearted and the quitters by making it so rough they cannot survive.

That is not true. They do make it rough for the reason already explained--because they want to teach the plebes how to function under pressure and stress--and to expand their perception of their own limits. They want to build a new foundation of inner strength in the plebe.

They do not want you to quit and leave. They want you to stay and fight. That is the *system* at the Naval Academy. If you can believe in that system when you are

You should at least complete the first year to prove to yourself you can do it, and to get a year of college credit. The bonus is the opportunity to help one of your classmates climb the Herndon Monument, the ritual that finalizes the plebe year.   *Courtesy 1/C Jimmy Parker.*

going through the rough times, say the mids, you will grow stronger. And, according to the mids, you will enjoy the pride of being a better person and be grateful to the system that made that possible.

How else should you prepare your mind? You should program it to be like that of the wrestler. When down on his back and about to be pinned, the wrestler must never let himself give up. His mind must say, over and over, "I will not give up; I will not quit; I will fight back with everything in me to keep from being beaten."

Do not be the kind of candidate who thinks, "Hey, I'm going to go and give it my best shot but if I don't make it, I can always come home."

Drive such thoughts out of your mind. It is almost guaranteed that if you go to the Academy with an escape route in your mind, you will end up taking it before the first year is over.

And then what? You go back home and you face all the people who have helped you and what do you say? "I've failed?" That is really not the truth, although you and many others will have a tendency to think that. You did not fail. You simply made a mistake and did not prepare your mind correctly.

What you should do is to program your mind so that *nothing* will make you quit until you have finished your first year. That way, if you decide to quit, you will have one year of college credits you can transfer. Also, neither you nor anybody else can think of you as a failure.

Why? Because you completed what is by far the most difficult year at the Academy. You survived the worst that anybody, in any institution, could throw at you. If you make it through the first year, you can leave the Academy with your head high, saying to anybody, "I tried it. I took everything they threw at me and I handled it successfully. I gave it a fair trial, but the Naval Academy is not for me. I decided that I wanted more options in my life."

The preceding is not a statement of failure. It is the statement of a winner. The person who makes it through the first year is a winner--a successful person. The person who can survive that first year can feel good inside, and that feeling will always be there.

Be that kind of a person. Do not be the kind of person who goes for awhile and quits, then spends a lifetime with guilt feelings. Life is difficult enough without taking on that kind of mental burden.

Believe in the system and have your mind programmed not to give up during the first year. Those are two steps toward proper mental preparation for the Naval Academy. But there is more.

"Make sure you are coming here for the right reasons," was a statement repeated over and over by the midshipmen. Are you coming just for the education? If so, forget it, say the mids. You can get a good education at many colleges.

Are you coming because you want a *free* education? That, too, is a mistaken belief.

First of all, the education is not free in the sense that you get it for nothing. You must work much harder for it than you would at a civilian college, and you owe the

U.S. Government five years of service[2] when you graduate. The government gives you four years of expense-paid education and you pay the government back by giving them at least five years service--with pay, of course.

Also, there are easier ways to get an expense-paid college education. If you are good enough to get into the Naval Academy, there is a good chance that you can win a scholarship at a civilian college.

But you want to get an expense-paid education and become a naval officer, too? If that is true, you still do not have to go to the Naval Academy. There are about 1000 openings each year (the number will vary with the needs of the service) for Naval Reserve Officer Training Corps (NROTC) scholarships at civilian colleges. If you are eligible for the Naval Academy, you will also be eligible for an NROTC scholarship.

Upon graduation from an NROTC program, you can become a naval officer and be eligible for any job available to the Academy graduate. In addition, you will have more personal freedom during your four years of college and more freedom to select from a wide variety of academic programs.

Do you want to come to the Naval Academy because your parents or grandparents want that for you? If that is your sole reason for applying, you are strongly advised to forget about the Naval Academy.

You might "get through the cracks" of an admissions system designed to detect that motive and screen out such candidates. But if you do make it into the Academy, you will almost surely get fed up with the grind and decide to quit. That is not just the author's opinion. That is the unanimous opinion of midshipmen, Academy officials and faculty who commented on the matter.

Then what is a good reason for wanting to go to the Naval Academy? There is not just one--there are three good reasons, which, together, make the Naval Academy worth all the effort of preparing for it, getting in, and then surviving for four years.

First, you should want to become a naval officer of some kind and want to serve your country in that capacity for at least five years or, better, for a twenty or thirty-year career.

Second, you should want to experience great personal growth, and in the process develop an inner strength that will condition you, not only to survive difficult challenges, but to look forward to such challenges.

Third, you should want to attend a very high quality college, with small classes taught by a faculty 100% committed to the process of teaching.

If you truly want all three of those things, *and* if you program your mind never to give up and to believe in the Academy system, your head is okay. Now all you have to do is to make sure you are prepared academically and physically.

---

[2]The required amount of active duty time may have changed by the time you get to the Academy

FIVE
WHY MANY PLEBES SUFFER
ACADEMIC SHOCK

It was the author's second visit to the Naval Academy. It was mid-May and the plebes who came in shifts to tell about their first-year experiences were just hours away from becoming upperclassmen. And they were in a joyous mood. As each group gathered around the conference table and pondered the list of topics that they would be asked to discuss, they bantered and joked with each other. For this was a rare day in their lives. It was a day of leisure, a day free of upperclass harassment, a day when they would eagerly tell a stranger how they had managed to survive while some of their classmates were falling by the wayside.

Among the topics to be discussed was the subject of academic preparation. "How well did your high school prepare you for this place?" was the lead-off question that was asked.

That question elicited smiles all around--in every group. Then came the comments, cautiously at first, then as a flood as the plebes competed to tell their personal experiences.

The following is a sampling of their opening comments taken from those notes:

"I graduated from high school with a 3.89 GPA and afterward I got straight A's during one year at a junior college. Then, when I came here, I struggled to get C's. I became very depressed, and now, with a 2.0-something at the end of this year..."

"I was a very good student in high school, got straight A's...my idea of studying was popcorn and TV...I just listened in class and crammed before the tests. When I got here, I was in trouble immediately...I went into my final exam in chemistry scared to death with a 1.7 average..."

"The academic competition here hit me hard...It was the first time I was ever challenged...I didn't think I was a brain but I thought I was good. I got A's with no effort in high school. But I started falling apart as soon as I got here. I had to admit I wasn't going to be the best or even close to the best. That was hard. I felt I wasn't living up to the goals I had set for myself. I had to not let failure on a test get me down..."

"I never studied in high school and was the valedictorian. When I got here, I began struggling and thought I wasn't going to make it..."

"I graduated from high school with a 4.07 GPA because the AP courses I took were weighted more than regular classes. Academics here was a big surprise...I used to get by with my way of studying but here I soon found myself in trouble. I was very scared and had to stay in Saturdays and try to hang on by changing everything..."

"I graduated near the top of my high school class and had top SAT scores. Here, my cume [cumulative] GPA at the end of the first semester was 1.41 and I had received the first F of my life. I went before the Academic Board and was inches from

In the small classes at the Naval Academy you cannot meld into the background like you can in many high school classes. With small numbers to deal with, the professors can hold you accountable every day. *Courtesy 1/C Jimmy Parker.*

being kicked out...The fear of God was in me with all those officers sitting around the table. The problem was that I was studying the way I did in high school..."

"I was valedictorian of my high school and had the option of several scholarships The academic shock here was so great I almost quit. I didn't realize what I was getting into...It was a shock to fail tests...I just couldn't accept going to class unprepared..."

On and on they went--with similar comments, then with advice on how candidates should prepare for the academic challenges of the Academy--advice that is included in a later chapter.

This chapter has other purposes. One of them is to get your attention. Chances are good that if you are reading this, you, too, are a good student. Perhaps you know what it is like to take home "A's" on your report card. Perhaps you have taken one of the College Board tests and have high scores. Perhaps, too, your parents, teachers and counselors have commended you for your fine academic record and you are looking forward to similar success in college. Do the comments of the midshipmen telling of their academic shock at the Academy cause you to question your own academic ability? Are you wondering if you, too, might be in the same predicament should you go to the Naval Academy? If so, this chapter has already fulfilled one of its purposes.

Another purpose of this chapter is to help you understand *why* good high school students suffer academic shock when they go to the Naval Academy. As you will see, the problem is usually not caused by any lack of natural learning ability--in fact, in the words of almost everyone interviewed for this book, including midshipmen, admissions counselors and professors, "If they let you in, you have the natural ability to make it through." So do not despair if you feel that you have good natural learning ability. The problems of most good high school students are related to attitude and experience, both of which can be changed and improved.

But first, before you can change anything, you have to understand the problems. Here are the main ones:

THE LETTER-HUNTING ATTITUDE. Try asking some of your friends who are good students what they want to get out of some class they are taking. Will they begin talking about how they want to learn more about simultaneous equations, anaerobic respiration, the Second Battle of Manassas or the Miller's Tale from Chaucer?

Or will they start talking about letters of the alphabet? Not "M's", "T's" and "Z's", of course. They will only want to talk about the first letters of the alphabet--the "A's" and, perhaps, if the course is very difficult, the "B's".

Why letters? Because most students have been conditioned throughout their entire school career that it is the letter, not the knowledge, that is the important achievement in any class.

The result is that most good students do whatever they have to do to get the first or second letters. And when they get them, they have something that brings great prestige and, more important, will last forever. Fifty years after the letter is awarded, it will still be on a permanent transcript for all who are interested to see. The first and

If you studied high school math just to get good letters, you are in for a shock at the Academy. You will be expected to use high school math in your freshman chemistry class.
Courtesy 1/C Jimmy Parker.

second letters of the alphabet are permanent merit badges for good academic achievement.

But what of the knowledge? How long does the student remember how to apply simultaneous equations to problems with two variables? How long will they be able to relate any of Chaucer's tales to types of human contemporary behavior? Will they even remember how to determine the density of a substance if they know the volume and its mass?

What do you think? Would you agree that many, if not most good students, retain the knowledge from their classes only until they are tested on it for the last time?

That, of course, is one of the reasons why plebes at the Naval Academy suffer academic shock. In calculus class the professors expect that the students will be able to simplify algebraic fractions and work with sines and cosines. In chemistry, the professors expect that students will be able to compute the volume of a sphere if they know its radius. In English class it is assumed that the plebes will know why different pronouns are used with transitive and intransitive verbs.

In summary, the typical student attitude that letters are most important and that knowledge is just something to "cram and dump"--to remember just long enough to get through the last test--is a bad attitude. It should be changed if you expect to do well at the Naval Academy.

And if you will change your attitude, you can expect a nice bonus. If you change your attitude so that your main goal is to master the material in your classes, you will get the knowledge *and* good letters. In addition, when you master knowledge, you will have it to build upon during the years ahead. That, too, pays off with another bonus. For you will then have a much better chance of earning good letters in the future.

THE COPYING PROBLEM. What do you do when a teacher assigns you to write answers to questions at the end of a chapter?

Do you read the assignment two or three times, then sit down and write out the answers in your own words?

Of course you do not answer the questions that way--that is, if you are the typical student.

The typical student might skim the reading assignment once. Then, after looking at the first question, the student will turn back through the pages (If it is question number one, the answer is sure to be somewhere near the beginning of the chapter.) until something is found that relates to the question. The student will look at the question again, then at the text, then...

Begin copying!

If possible, the student will try to get by with copying just one sentence. If the student is a first-letter-of-the-alphabet-hunter, he or she will probably copy an extra sentence or two just to be safe.

Is that technique familiar? Or is it something that you used to do or something only your friends have done?

Then what about this assignment from your English teacher. "Next Friday I want you to turn in a report on one of the authors in Unit Twelve."

Where do the students go to do that assignment?

To the library, of course.

And what do they do there? They may only go to an encyclopedia and copy whatever is written about the author they have selected.

But the more conscientious students may also find a couple of reference books and copy part of the report from them.

More sophisticated students may do much better. They may take quotes from several sources, identify them with footnotes and references, then string the quotes together with occasional, original prose.

And in all cases the report is copied. The only difference is in the selection of references and whether or not the student has been honest about acknowledging the copying.

Why is copying a problem? First of all, doing a writing assignment that way is strictly a "no-brainer." No mental exercise is needed to mindlessly copy something from a book.

Much worse is that the copier never learns to organize information and thoughts and get them down on paper in clear, logical prose. In short, the copier never learns to write.

And that is a terrible handicap to carry into any college, especially those that demand original compositions from the very beginning of the freshman year. Of course, the Naval Academy is one of those.

THE MEMORIZERS. Another common problem of many good students is the almost robotic way they go about learning their assignments. Typically, they are happy just to memorize fact after fact, and they are equally happy when they can parrot back 90 percent or more of those facts on a test.

But they are usually not pleased when their teacher forces them to go beyond the memorization of facts. When teachers ask them to apply what they have learned to unfamiliar problems, panic sets in and the students often flounder helplessly.

Here are examples of this problem that were given to the author by two Academy chemistry professors who teach the plebes.

Said the first professor: "I can tell them the formula for computing density, which is: mass divided by volume.

"If I give them numbers for the mass and volume, they can plug them into the formula and most will come up with the correct answer. However, if I give them the density and the mass and ask them to compute the volume, there will be some who will struggle with it.

"It is worse when they have solved the above problem and I tell them that the substance we are working with is the shape of a sphere and that I now want to know its radius.

"Believe me, I might as well have asked them the size of the universe. Of course a few--maybe one out of five--will remember the formula they all learned in high school, volume equals 4/3 time pi times the radius cubed, and from that they will think of using the formula to compute the radius. The problem with most of them is that they learned with blinders on and they can't take them off to look at a problem from a broad point of view.

Said the other chemistry professor: "An example of this mind set is what happens when I ask them to estimate the answers to problems before they begin their calculations. Here is what happens.

"Suppose the problem requires them to multiply 85.983 times .4972. If I said, 'quickly, before you go to the calculator and multiply that out, give me an estimate of the answer,' many would hesitate or look worried.

"Those types are so caught up into the blind robotics of arithmetic that they fail to think about the basic problem itself, which is simply to take about half of 86 and that the approximate answer would be 43."

It is not always the fault of students that they memorize a lot of facts but have difficulty applying them in novel situations. Some teachers place far too much emphasis upon the learning of facts and give students too little practice with problems that require the facts to be applied. More about this problem and what you can do about it will be discussed in the next two chapters.

THE SPOON-FED CRIPPLES. Probably the most important reason why plebes suffer academic shock is because of the way they were taught in junior and senior high school. An example will help explain.

Imagine that you are observing a typical high school class and it is near the end of the period. Just before the bell rings, the teacher gives the class its homework assignment. "Read pages 40-49 in the textbook," says the teacher.

Now it is the next day at the beginning of the period and, again, we are observing the class. What does the teacher do?

Usually the teacher starts talking about the material that was in the assigned pages. The teacher would probably call this a "discussion," however, in most cases, it is a one-sided discussion with the teacher doing most of the talking.

And what are the students doing? Some are listening and a few may be taking notes.

And how about the teacher? How is he doing?

His explanation of the lesson is very good. He uses good examples and his chalkboard diagrams are excellent. If he were to be graded on the quality of his presentation, he would deserve an "A" grade.

Now imagine that we have let one week pass and we are back in the same classroom again. It is the day before a test--a test that includes the material that was explained during the previous visit. Again we see that the teacher spends the whole period talking. All of the important topics in the unit are explained again. Every possible question that might be asked is answered in some way. At the end of the period we could probably take the test and get a good grade even though we only observed one class. We are equally confident that any student who has paid attention in the class should be able to get a good grade on the test.

In other words, we would give the teacher another "A" grade for the thoroughness of his review.

Now let us ask ourselves some questions about this teacher. From what we have observed, does the teacher appear to have a good knowledge of his subject?

Yes, that was obvious from his explanations.

Is the teacher hard-working and dedicated to doing his very best for the students?

Yes, he is hard-working and appears to be very dedicated.

Does he seem to have a genuine interest in seeing that each of his students do well in his class?

Absolutely. One can tell just from the way he looks at his students that he cares about each of them. In fact, one gets the impression that he would gladly stay after school to reexplain anything for a student if that seemed necessary.

Now the final question. Is he a good teacher?

No, he is a poor teacher.

Why? Perhaps an example from another kind of class will put his poor performance into perspective.

We will go to the community swimming pool. It is June and we are observing swimming classes. Beginning swimmers are splashing around in the shallow water in two groups, each with a teacher.

One of the teachers has her children putting their faces in the water and trying to front-float. And as we watch, we cannot help feeling a twinge of pity for the children. After coming up out of the water they cough and spit and rub their reddened eyes. But the teacher has them repeat the exercise time after time, with lots of encouragement and sympathy, of course.

And do the children in that group learn to swim that day? No. Nor the next day, nor the next week, nor, in most cases, the next month. It is just the same old thing for those children every day: water in the eyes, water in the nose, water swallowed and coughed up, and very little progress.

Now let us focus on the other swimming teacher. Every day he starts out having his children put their face in the water and attempt to front-float. They are eager and they all try it. But they come up sputtering, coughing and rubbing their eyes. Now this teacher is a very caring person and after a few minutes, when each child has tried once and failed to front-float, the teacher gives each one of them a paddle board to lie on. Then he lets them paddle to him and when they do, he whoops with joy and the kids love it. And that is what he does for twenty-five minutes of the thirty-minute lesson.

We continue to watch this teacher for several days and the same thing happens each day. The kids try to front-float for a few minutes, then they spend the rest of the lesson enjoying themselves on the paddle boards.

Now let us evaluate the teachers.

Is the first teacher a good swimming teacher?

We cannot say for sure because we did not observe any single child actually swimming. But from what we know about that teaching process, we could say that she is probably a good swimming teacher. If she keeps working at it, most or all of the children will eventually learn to swim.

And the other teacher? Is he a good swimming teacher?

That answer is easy. No, he is a poor teacher. Why? Because if he continues with the technique he is using, his students will be on paddle boards forever. Children would never learn to swim with this kind of teacher.

Now let us return to the high school teacher whom we observed.

He is a poor teacher because he never lets students learn on their own. He might ask them a question or two at the beginning of the period, but chances are, only a few would know the answers. Then he gives them the equivalent of a paddle board. He spoonfeeds them for the rest of the period, and he repeats the process day after day. Eventually the whole school year passes and he has told them absolutely everything that they need to know, but should have learned on their own.

And what is wrong with that?

Students who are taught that way end up like the children on the paddle boards who never learn to swim. They end up as educational cripples who must depend upon someone telling them everything they must learn.

Students who are spoonfed day after day never learn to read and analyze material from a printed page.

Nor do they learn accountability. Day after day they can get by without studying their homework because they know it is going to be explained for them the next day. Some do not even have to pay attention in class. They can listen to the review before the tests and, if extra effort is necessary, they can always open the book and cram that same night.

And what do the students learn? Using the cram and dump technique, they learn enough knowledge to take tests and to achieve the letter that they desire to have on their permanent record.

Of course, those who aspire to go to the Naval Academy have to earn a lot of good letters. Also, they have to retain enough of the knowledge that was spoonfed to them to do well on the College Board tests.

Then they become plebes. They take English and calculus and chemistry and enough other subjects to make their load at least 30 percent heavier than that of normal college students. And they are pressured every day to memorize all the plebe knowledge piled on them by the upperclassman. And they have mandatory athletics and plebe duties.

And are they spoonfed in their classes? Some of the time. By some professors. But many days they will be held accountable for their assignments just minutes after they walk into their classes.

And what gargantuan assignments! (Compared to what they had in high school.) In chemistry: "Start with the section, "Quantitative Analysis by Precipitation on page 118. Then study the sections on Gravimetric Analysis, Acid-Base Reactions, Volumetric Analysis, and Acid-Base Titrations over to page 129. Also do problems five through fourteen at the end of the chapter. Expect a quiz at the beginning of the period tomorrow; then be ready to explain your problems on the board."

In English: "Write a 500-word paper telling what 20th century person Othello most closely resembles and why."

In calculus: "Do the eight problems at the end of Section 24, page 109. Be ready to go to the board and explain your solutions to the rest of the class."

And how well are spoonfed cripples going to do?

Can they wave their transcript with good letters at their professors and get by? Can they go off and do those assignments by memorizing? Can they do their assignments by copying something out of a text or an encyclopedia?

No. They must call upon a variety of skills to complete all their assignments, few or none of which were learned from their spoonfeeding teachers.

So they flounder. And occasionally fail.

That is the bad news.

But there is good news. At the beginning of this chapter you read the words of midshipmen who were good students in high school and who suffered academic shock at the Naval Academy. But *all* those comments you read were from plebes who *survived* the first year!

Remember that. All those who said they were shocked by the academic rigors of the Academy were also able to learn how to study and were able to maintain the minimum 2.0 GPA that is necessary to remain in the Academy.

So there is more to the story. You will get some of it in the next two chapters, one of which consists of advice from Academy professors on how you can best prepare for the Naval Academy.

Later, in a chapter in the survival section of the book, the same midshipmen who complained about academic shock give advice on how to avoid some of the problems they encountered. It is good advice. To benefit from it you just have to be open-minded enough to accept it.

SIX
THE PROFESSORS SPEAK:
WHAT YOU CAN DO TO
PREPARE FOR THE ACADEMY

The plebes say they have trouble with all their first-year classes. But they suffer the most in three of them: English, calculus and chemistry, which are required, full-year courses.

After listening to the plebes and their troubles, the author interviewed professors from the English, mathematics and chemistry departments. They were asked to give their opinions on why the plebes had trouble in their classes. They were also asked for advice on what candidates can do to better prepare themselves for their courses. Here is what they had to say.

COMMENTS FROM THE ENGLISH DEPARTMENT

The English professors broke the typical plebe problems down into three categories. The first and most significant problem comes under the heading of poor writing ability.

Professor Michael Halbig, Associate Dean of Faculty: "Kids who have been very bright in high school and, therefore, not pressed too hard by the high school system will get a big shock here..."

Said one professor who also is a naval officer: "Plebes come in here and have no idea how important it is for a naval officer to be a good writer. That is partly because they do not understand how the naval services really work. For example, they think everybody does everything in response to an order--that everything is just cut and dried--that a senior officer gives an order and it is passed down, adapted, then blindly obeyed. They are shocked when they realize how much give and take there is at each level of command.

"Most commanders seek input from the officers below them when they make their decisions. And when a junior officer comes up with an alternate approach or a different idea during an oral presentation, often he is told to 'put it in writing.'

"So it is very important to the career officer to have good writing skills. One never knows when a written proposal will be sent up through the chain of command. It is really out of one's hands then--it is too late to amplify a point; it must stand on its own. "Also, it is possible for a brand new junior officer to write something that a senior officer such as your captain thinks is a good idea. In that case the senior officer may use much of the junior officer's prose when he passes on the idea to the officers above him. That is a heady experience for a young officer the first time it happens. Needless to say, it also is good for the young officer's career."

Another professor made some of the same points while justifying the English Department's emphasis upon developing good writers. But he added, "I tell these kids that you have to become a good editor as well as a writer. As a junior officer you will have to write things for your superior--sometimes because he is lazy or because he is not confident of his own writing ability. Then you are in potential jeopardy because if you write something for him and he finds fault with it, this might cast a cloud over your other abilities and cause you to be misjudged. If you are careless enough to submit something with errors that he can discern, then you are leaving yourself wide open to criticism. We don't want someone taking those kinds of cheap shots at you; we want to teach you to write in such a way that you can avoid them. We want you to develop enough writing and editing ability so no writing assignment will make trouble for you."

If you go to the Naval Academy, you will learn immediately that writing is a serious business. For example, during Plebe Summer you will have to take a writing proficiency test. For this test you will be given a topic--or perhaps a choice from several topics--and you will be given an hour and fifteen minutes to write an essay on that subject. That essay will then be graded by members of the English Department and your score will be used to place you in one of three levels of English.

What can a candidate do to become a better writer?

Said one professor: "If there is a creative writing course in your high school, take it. If one is not available, check into the availability of a night course in the local community adult education program.

"Those who do not have such opportunities can do other things. What is important is to do a lot of writing. Write letters--lots of them. Write your friends. Write your relatives."

Said another: "Writing is like an athletic skill; the more you practice, the easier it becomes. But kids don't get a lot of practice in many high schools, so if they want to improve their writing, they will have to do things on their own.

"In that regard I think one of the best things they can do is to keep a daily journal. It doesn't have to be a soul-searching diary. It can be a factual account of one's activities with emphasis upon descriptive writing."

The director of the Academy's Writing Center had a number of comments about plebes and the kinds of deficiencies she has seen over the years. She said:

"One of the most common deficiencies is a lack of library research skills. Many of the plebes are used to going into a library, pulling a book or two off the shelf, then doing a report.

"They can save themselves a lot of time if they will learn how to use a library before they get here. I suggest that they go to a big library and get a tour...find all the nooks and crannies. I also recommend that they pick a topic and research it thoroughly--without doing a paper. Just pick topics that are interesting and see how much can be found. "Many plebes have no idea how to research periodicals and it is a skill that they will have to use here. My advice is to get good at this kind of research before you get here.

"Another problem I see is that plebes waste a lot of time when they are reading and gathering material for a paper. They should think as they read, and they should jot down their thoughts and ideas as they go along. This speeds up the organization process and helps them sort out ideas that can be implemented when they begin to outline their paper. It would help them if they would practice this in high school.

"Another problem with many plebes is that once they write something, they think they are finished. They are naive about the writing process and look upon it solely in terms of composing, not of composing and revising. We have to change that attitude so they will write, then rewrite and continue rewriting until the work is polished.

"And this leads me to another recommendation. But first some background. Every midshipman has a personal computer and a word-processing program. All written work must be done by word processing, including all the writing that is done for the English Department.

"This creates a problem for some of these kids, not because they don't know how to use computers--most have lots of experience with flight simulators and video games--but they have not learned good keyboard skills. In other words, they haven't learned to type.

"This is a problem because during plebe year they are under tremendous pressure from all their classes and from the upperclassmen. Then, when they have to do a written homework assignment, they waste precious hours hunting and pecking around the keyboard trying to get the paper written on the word processor. That is one reason why they resist rewriting their papers--it takes too much time pecking around on the keyboard.

"I strongly recommend that candidates learn to type and, if possible, get some word processing experience. After that, they should keep using and improving their skill by writing letters. They should not let it get rusty. If they come here and don't know how to type, it is like being in grade school. Learning to do it here will suck up hours of time that should be spent on other things.

The lack of reading experience was the second problem discussed by the English professors.

Said one: "A lot of the kids have not read much when they get here. And from my experience, after many years of teaching plebes, those who have the most trouble in our English classes are those who have read the least. Reading is a subliminal way to learn grammar and syntax. Unfortunately these kids, having been raised with television, have heard good English spoken, but they have not read much of it. Therefore, they can't reproduce it like they would if they were used to seeing the printed words."

Professor Michael Parker, Head of the English Department: "I think the main thing we would like to see in midshipmen is not so much having read specific individual works, but having the habit of reading--of wanting to read and doing so whenever they get a chance."

Said another: "To prepare for this place I would advise any candidate to do a lot of reading. Ideally they should read some of the classics--any English teacher could give them a list of 8-10 titles that would give them good reading experiences. *The Illiad* and *The Odyssey* would be on my list, and a plebe who doesn't know who Plato is or anything else about Greek literature is going to find himself behind the eight ball. Shakespeare would be on the list; I would recommend any of his plays. I would also recommend a number of classic novelists, such as Dickens, Shaw, Conrad, Hemingway, and Fitzgerald."

"But if they won't do that," continued the professor, "there are other things they can do to help themselves. For example, I personally would recommend that they subscribe to a good, large-city newspaper during their senior year. Then they should

59

get in the habit of reading it every day. Especially important is the editorial page, which is often a gold mine of good writing. Also, by reading the editorial writers every day, they will be knowledgeable of all the major issues of the times.

"I also recommend that they get into the habit of going to the library during their spare time. There they should look over the periodicals and find one or two that can be read for enjoyment. This is a pleasant way to relax, yet it provides additional reading experience. Some periodicals--*Rolling Stone* is an example--would appeal to many high school students while at the same time giving them a chance to read a number of good writers.

"To summarize, I think the main thing we would like to see in midshipmen is not so much having read specific individual works but having the habit of reading. We want to see midshipmen who want to read and who do so whenever they get a chance."

Another professor added: "I agree that candidates should do a lot of reading. And I really wish that they would read the Bible. It's the owners manual of Western civilization. All our Western Literature is based upon it, directly or indirectly. If students don't know what is in the Bible, they will have lost half the meaning of much of our literature."

Still another said: "My advice to the candidate is to read more than you have ever read in your life and don't be too concerned with what. I think it is unrealistic to expect high school kids to read the classics--although it would be good for them. I would tell them to read anything in which they are interested, or anything that gives them pleasure. That way they at least will have some motivation to keep reading."

The third problem mentioned was the plebes' problems with grammar.

Said one professor: "Many of the plebes come here without much knowledge of grammar. That is a problem here because most of our teachers believe that a knowledge of grammar is important; that is the way they were educated. Of course, it is important when discussing writing. It facilitates the communication process. Students who understand grammar are easier to teach."

Said another professor: "The students who have the most trouble are those who do not know basic grammar. When they have written a bad sentence, for example, I might say, 'Let's break this sentence down and see which pronoun, who or whom, should be used. First, where is the noun?' Typically, that is where the trouble begins. We cannot even get into a discussion of the nominative or subjective cases because the kid cannot identify the noun. It's as bad as trying to diagnose car trouble when you get under the hood and don't know where the carburetor is or what it does."

What should a candidate do to correct such a deficiency?

"Get a handbook of grammar--there are many good ones out there," said a professor. We use the Simon and Schuster handbook[1] and it is very good. But get any handbook and go through it systematically. Do the exercises and when you stumble

---

[1] *The Simon and Schuster Handbook for Writers*, Lynn Q. Troyka, Prentice Hall, Third Edition.

on something, ask yourself why you are having problems. Then get at the root of the problem or get an English teacher to help you.

"It wouldn't take most students long to review the basics of grammar and it would really help them to have this knowledge fresh on their minds when they arrive. Many have had good training but it was in the eighth or ninth grade. That is too long a lapse for many of them."

Another recommendation is for candidates to familiarize themselves with a spell checker and a grammar checker. These are software programs used in conjunction with computer word processors. The midshipmen all have computers with this software[2] and they are expected to use it when they begin their first year English classes. For example, it is rare to see a paper with a misspelled word because the students learn that they must do a spell check.

COMMENTS FROM THE MATHEMATICS DEPARTMENT

All midshipmen must take two years of mathematics. During plebe year they take two semesters of calculus. The second year they take a third semester of calculus and one semester of differential equations.

Each plebe is given a math placement test during Plebe Summer. This allows the math department to place the plebe in one of three different calculus courses, all covering the same material but at different rates. The regular calculus meets three days a week, the slower classes meet four days a week and the slowest classes meet five days a week.

Each year a few plebes are found to be mathematically deficient and must pass a special non-credit class in algebra and trigonometry before embarking on the two-year sequence of calculus and differential equations.

Why do many plebes have trouble with their math classes?

"I think most of them have trouble," said one professor, "because they can't do the algebra. I see it all the time--when they start working with algebraic fractions, for example. They get into trouble adding fractions, inverting fractions, dividing fractions...they tend to write down what they think is right and they just push on and don't stop--they waste a lot of time that way. And they do dumb things--they will add one over A, plus one over B, and put down one over A plus B. Those are the kinds of mistakes that just tear them apart."

"I agree," said another professor. Many are deficient in algebraic skills all across the board. That is so frustrating because we don't teach algebra here--not in our calculus classes. It is very frustrating when they can't manipulate fractions or

---

[2] Currently the midshipmen are using Word Perfect 6.0 which includes a spell checker, thesaurus, and "Grammatic," which checks "grammar, mechanics, and style." An older, but excellent grammar checker that candidates might find in their community is "Right Writer."

quadratic formulas, can't do simplifications and factoring or do not understand the properties of exponents. Those are just a few of the deficiencies that I see."

Why are students with good math backgrounds deficient in algebra?

Said one professor: "I think it is because of the attitude they had when they were taking the course in high school--that the algebra was something to be learned long enough for a test--and not something that must be retained and built upon in later courses. Even when they are taught well, I think eleventh graders--typically that is the last year they take algebra--do not realize that they will need to use what they have learned. It's an attitude. They don't realize that they have to keep their learning intact."

Said another professor: "I think the problem is more in the way they learned the algebra. Many learn by rote memorization. They want to know how to manipulate the letters and numbers without doing too much thinking--without understanding how or why they can do the manipulating. Then, when they get here, they expect to use the same approach and it doesn't work. They have to apply their algebra and think their way through a problem. That is a new experience for many of them; a tough experience. That is why many have trouble with calculus."

The math professors were asked what candidates could do to come better prepared.

One professor repeated the obvious: "Learn your algebra. Get good at it. Work especially hard applying algebra in word problems--that is the real test of whether one really understands it or not."

Professor Jim D'Archangelo of the Mathematics Department: "I see a change in the plebes coming in. Their algebra and geometry skills are degraded from what we saw in the past. Maybe it is because kids are taking algebra earlier than they used to. Maybe it is a maturity factor. Maybe they weren't ready for algebra at the time they took it. But, they definitely need a strong algebra background when they come in here."

Said another professor: "Don't forget trigonometry either. Know and understand how to work with sines and cosines. I see kids hit trig and it becomes a real hurdle for them. When they have to work with sines and cosines, it becomes a psychological barrier and they think they can't get through it."

The professors also gave advice that was heard from many midshipmen--advice that will be expanded upon in a later chapter.

The advice: *do not allow yourself to get behind.*

Said one professor: "I see it all the time. A plebe gets under pressure, often from the upperclassmen, then sloughs a homework assignment. Then he gets snowed in class but thinks he can dig himself out that evening. But then something else happens--more pressure, perhaps, then the inevitable happens. He gets behind.

"Don't let that happen. Every professor hands out a sheet during the first day of class. That sheet explains when the professor is available for EI [extra instruction]. Every plebe should use that EI time immediately when something is not understood. The problem is that the plebes are not used to classes where so many concepts are interrelated and built on each other. Therefore, they don't realize what kind of a jam they are getting themselves into when they get behind."

A professor from another department summed up the same advice with an expression that dates back to the days of the sailing ships. "A stern chase is a long chase," he said. "It is very difficult to catch up when you once get behind. So the best advice is not to allow yourself to get behind in the first place."

COMMENTS FROM THE CHEMISTRY DEPARTMENT

The midshipmen call the first-year chemistry course the "plebe killer." The professors who teach that course were asked if it deserved that reputation and, if so, why?

"There is no question that chemistry is a difficult course for most plebes," said one of the professors. But it isn't because we set out to flunk all the plebes. It is because of a combination of problems, some related to the nature of the subject, but many related to other factors. Let me try to explain.

"First of all, chemistry is a class that demands a lot of daily attention. We go through 10 to 15 pages a day and that is a lot of material that must be absorbed. And unlike history and some other subjects, one cannot just wait until the night before a test and cram for several hours. That won't work and it takes the plebes time to realize that. Of course, by that time they are in trouble.

"Just keeping up on a daily basis is a problem because of all the other pressure that is on the plebes. If they were in a normal institution, they could spend more hours each day on their studies. But they can't do that here. Their time is limited and they are not efficient in the way they allocate it. Of course, most of them were never pushed in high school, so it takes them a while to adapt after they get here."

"Chemistry itself is not the problem at all," said another professor. "The primary problem is the lack of ability to apply algebra to word problems. They are used to memorizing facts and regurgitating them. When they have to analyze a problem, then set it up using an algebraic equation, they find themselves lost.

"Another weakness is their reading ability. The reading vocabulary of the average chemistry textbook--the number of terms and concepts introduced in a short time--is one of the highest of any college subject. And, while many problems are done in math, the concepts on which they are based must be comprehended from the written word.

"Partly because of their problems with reading comprehension, but also because of their lack of discipline in doing their work on a daily basis--all of which is aggravated by the pressures of the plebe indoctrination system--the typical plebe is going to fall behind. What they have to realize is that studying chemistry is like studying a foreign language; there is so much terminology that must be absorbed and utilized and if it is not mastered on a daily basis, they cannot function or communicate."

Another professor said: "I think these kids are preconditioned during Plebe Summer. In that program they have to memorize, memorize, memorize, day after day. Of course, they are smart and they figure out tricks that help them--they get good at memorizing after a while. But then they come to our chemistry classes and want to do the same thing. It seems like they are always looking for the magic trick that will allow them to solve chemistry problems, and, of course, there is no such thing. Except for a couple of chapters, rote memorization will not work with chemistry. They have to use reasoning...."

Then what should candidates do to prepare themselves for the chemistry classes at the Naval Academy? That question was asked of all the professors who were interviewed. Here is how they replied.

Said one: "I don't care too much if they have even had high school chemistry. We start from scratch and they can learn it here. What I do care about is their knowledge of algebra, their ability to read quickly with comprehension and their ability to do word problems. So I would tell them to master algebra to the point where they can apply it.

"Also I would tell them, if they do take chemistry, to concentrate on all the word problems--do them even if they are not assigned. Of course, I can't imagine high school kids doing that."

Said another: "I disagree with my colleague who says that high school chemistry is not important. It is, and I would hate to think of a kid coming into my class without some background, without some basic knowledge of the subject.

"What I am against is AP [Advanced Placement] chemistry. So many elect that and do not take physics--which is a real mistake. Of course, if they can take both, more power to them. However, it would still be a mistake to take AP chemistry for the purpose of testing out of our chemistry here. They would miss too much. If they take AP chemistry, they should not do it at the expense of either physics or calculus.

"Also, if I was giving advice to a young high school student, a freshman, for example, I would say take all the math that you can and do not look for the easy ways out. Take all the tough classes and never take a study hall. Push yourself and try to develop study habits that demand that you give a certain amount of attention to your classes every day, not just before tests. Most important, you must demand more of yourself than the high school does."

Professor Mark Elert of the Chemistry Department: "I encounter a large number of students who come to me and say, 'Sir, I read the assignment--I read it two or three times but I still failed the quiz.' It is because they read the assignment but didn't learn to solve the problems. Most got by with their intelligence in high school and didn't have to learn how to solve problems. My advice: learn to solve problems; that's the best preparation."

Said another: "I recommend that they change their attitude about their high school math. They think of it as a subject to itself, unrelated to chemistry or physics. They should think of it as something to be mastered so it can be used in other subjects.

"Also, there are specific kinds of math knowledge that I see lacking in our chemistry students that could be mastered in high school. Our kids have trouble working with basic trigonometry functions so learn those and feel comfortable using them. It would also help to understand natural logarithms, which they can do if they take calculus. Natural logarithms are introduced here in our calculus classes, of course, but it is done too late for when they are needed in chemistry. They are used when we get into kinetics and first-order rate laws.

"In addition, they should master simple algebra concepts. They should know how to apply the binomial theorem to problems. They should be comfortable working with base-ten logarithms. Also, they should really work at understanding graphing. The typical kid comes in here thinking of a graph as being like a pie chart--something like a graph that is used in business. Even though they have had it in their algebra courses, they do not think of a graph as x-y plots. They don't grasp the concept of plotting a function with a variable even though they have probably done it many times in their high school algebra."

One final bit of advice came from the father of one of the chemistry professors who is an award-winning high school chemistry teacher. He said: "Students always have trouble with word problems. My advice is to tackle that deficiency head on.

When you take high school chemistry, do the word problems on your own, before you go to class. Do them even if they are hard and require a lot of work. Take pride in going to class and watching how your fellow students have to be spoonfed--who have to have the method for solving the problems explained to them by the teacher. Of course, you won't be able to solve all the problems without some help. But develop an independent attitude--an attitude where you will get great satisfaction out of needing the teacher as little as possible. A kid with this kind of independent attitude will survive anyplace.

"Oh, and one more thing. When you are in the chemistry lab, do your own work and get your own results. When you write up a lab, never copy anyone else's results. I know that is sometimes done and I don't condone it, but if it is routine in your own chemistry lab, at least you should take pride in being the person whose work is copied."

SEVEN
PREPARING ACADEMICALLY:
SUMMING IT UP

By now you should be convinced that the Naval Academy will offer a tough academic challenge to most who would go there.

But now what?

Do you want to improve your chances of surviving that academic challenge?

Do you want to prepare yourself in ways that will make the academic challenge of the Academy less traumatic and more satisfying or, perhaps, even enjoyable?

Would you like to excel academically at the Naval Academy?

Proper preparation is one key to achieving any of the above goals. Here is what you can do.

TAKE THE RIGHT COURSES.

It is tempting for high school students to want to sample from the buffet of electives that is available in many high schools. But if you are really serious about going to the Naval Academy, restrain your appetite for those electives. Go for the basic courses, the solid courses and, yes, the *hard* courses taught by the *hard* teachers.

An example is the mathematics courses. Many students elect to drop out of the math curriculum after they complete a sophomore course in geometry. Do not be one of those dropouts. Take math courses during all four years in high school. Take advanced algebra, trigonometry, analytic geometry and, if possible, a full year of calculus.

And as you take those advanced math courses, heed the advice that you read in the last chapter--the advice from Academy math and chemistry professors. Do not learn algebra just to pass the next test. Master the algebraic concepts--factoring, simplification, manipulation of fractions, the binomial theorem, quadratic equations, graphing, etc., and when you have completed the final test, do not erase the tape. Think of the algebra you have learned as a set of tools that you will use over and over, not only in future math classes, but in your future science classes as well. You want all that you have learned in algebra to remain in your hard drive.

Constantly evaluate yourself as you are taking the advanced math classes. And the question to ask is: How am I doing with the word problems?

You read the comments of the professors. Word problems drive plebes crazy. Why? Probably because in high school, students were spoonfed on techniques for solving them, tricks actually--tricks that get the problems solved but do not give students the opportunity to reason on their own. Nor does the spoonfeeding allow students to suffer failure and thus learn that they do not understand the concepts on which the problems are based.

So what can you do about the word problems? Do what the award-winning high school chemistry teacher suggested in the last chapter. Do word problems at every opportunity, even if they are not assigned. And if they are assigned, take pride in doing them on your own before going to class. Ignore tricks and shortcuts that a teacher might use to get struggling members of your class through the word problems. And every time you have to depend on your teacher to spoonfeed you with a solution, be aware of your status as a learner. You are still teacher dependent. Also, you probably do not completely understand the math concepts that must be applied to the problems.

In the high school science curriculum, biology is usually the last course that is required. But do not stop there. Go on and take chemistry and be sure to take physics. And, if Advanced Placement courses are offered in chemistry or physics, take them, too, if possible. However, do not take them with the thought of testing out of either course at the Academy. Take them so you will have a better background and can excel in the courses at the Academy.

Most good high schools require four years of English and that is a good requirement for students aspiring to attend any college. However, you may have an option for electives to satisfy that requirement. If you do, here are some suggestions.

Give first priority to any English course where creative writing or the writing of reports is emphasized. You need the writing experience. And you need to practice researching, organizing and writing reports.

Give second priority to a course in speech or debate. Why? It will build your confidence. It will help you develop poise. It will teach you to control and project your voice. Most important, it will teach you to think on your feet and while you are under pressure. In short, it will help you develop the kinds of skills that are needed to survive the plebe indoctrination system at the Naval Academy.

Your third priority should be a review of grammar and punctuation. However, there is only a slim chance that you can take a course in your English department that will give you that kind of review. Of course, if there is, take it. But, if there is not, do as the English professors recommended in the last chapter. Purchase a handbook of grammar and do the review on your own. Also, familiarize yourself with grammar checking software so you are comfortable using it when writing with a word processor.

What else should you take?

You should take at least two years of a foreign language. And if you take more than that, you might be proficient enough to validate, or be exempted from a year of language at the Academy.

And by all means, *learn to type*. Do not go to the Naval Academy and be one of those who has to sit for hours pecking away on your computer with two fingers--while all your other homework and plebe responsibilities are languishing.

Most high schools offer a personal typing or keyboarding class. If you have no other choice, take that course. But also look for options. You might be able to take such a class during the summer at a local community college or adult education program. If you have lots of self-discipline, you might also obtain a typing book and advice from a sympathetic teacher in your high school business department, then practice and learn on your own at home. But whatever the method, plan on having good keyboard skills when you arrive at the Academy.

Also, learn to use a word processing program--it does not matter which one; they all have a lot in common. The time you spend learning to edit, search, move blocks, and manipulate print commands will more than pay off when you are buried under long assignments and the crunching time schedule you will experience as a plebe.

LEARN TO RESEARCH

If you were assigned to do a research paper titled, "What Chain of Events Led to the Berlin Airlift?," what would you do?

You would go to a library, of course. But then what would you do, especially if your instructor requires at least six citations and the library is a large one like you would use at the Naval Academy?

Chances are good that you would be less than proficient at such a research task. Most high school students never have to do that kind of research.

But you *will* learn to do that kind of research if you go to the Naval Academy. So the question is: Do you want to wait until you get there and waste precious hours learning those skills while you are a plebe and under terrific pressure?

It is recommended that you learn how to do research in a good library before you go to the Academy. The easiest way to do this is to take a day or two of your summer vacation and visit your nearest college. If you call ahead of time and they know you are coming, some member of the library staff will give you a tour. In the words of the Academy Writing Center Director, use such a tour to discover all of the "nooks and crannies" in a good library. Learn what different types of media are available and how to search each type.

Most libraries are either computerized or are in the process of becoming so. If possible, get a library staff member to teach you how to use the computer system. You will have to use one when you get to the Academy.

That is the first step.

The second step is to conduct a number of searches on your own, perhaps with intermittent help from a staff member. Pick fun topics--topics that you might find interesting. For example, you might research for a paper called "When the Beatles Came to America" or "How Girls' Basketball Used to be Played" or "The Public's Reaction to the First Corvette."

Such research will be tedious at first and you may waste some time spinning your wheels. But keep at it, asking for advice when you need it and, if the library staff is cooperative, for an evaluation of your efforts when you think your research is complete.

Your goal is, first, to learn research strategies, then the mechanics of searching. There is no way to do either without practice. And just remember, if all of this sounds like a lot of work, just imagine what it will be like learning these techniques when you are stewing in the plebe pressure cooker.

LEARN TO STUDY EFFICIENTLY.

"How were your study habits in high school?" That question was asked during many of the interviews with Academy midshipmen.

And the answers? First there were grins and chuckles. Then came the answers.

"Study? In high school? Are you kidding?"

"Study habits? What study habits?"

"What a joke. I thought I was studying when I had a book open and the music cranked up."

"Study? I didn't need to except before tests. I got by just listening in class."

"I thought I studied a lot but I know now that I wasted a lot of time."

Those comments were typical. They were given jocularly, but as the conversation moved around the conference table, the mids grew more serious. And they started telling of the problems they had as plebes because they did not know how to study.

Their main problem can be summed up with one word: *time*. They discovered that the clock was always against them; they never had enough time. They never had enough time to sleep. They never had enough time to eat. They never had enough time to memorize their "pro stuff" (required plebe knowledge). They never had enough time to clean their rooms and prepare for inspections. Most important of all, because success or failure depended upon it, they never had enough time to study.

You, too, will say the same thing if you end up at the Naval Academy. You will never have as much time as you need to study. Nothing you can do now will change that. However, there is one thing you can do that will help with the problem. You can learn to study efficiently and thereby give yourself more study time than you would have otherwise.

For example, try the following routine. When you sit down to study, look over the first assignment that you must complete. Then make an estimate of how long it should take you to do it. When you decide upon a time estimate, set an alarm clock so it will go off at that time. Then do your best to complete the assignment on time.

After that, take a break. Call a friend. Watch some television. Reward yourself with a snack or a coke. Enjoy the leisure of the break.

Then go back to work. Look over the next assignment, estimate how long it should take, set the alarm and repeat the process. And do not forget the breaks and the rewards afterwards. They are important. You will feel more like working hard if you know they are coming.

Follow this procedure for several weeks. During this time evaluate yourself objectively. Am I being realistic in my estimates of the time needed for the assignments? How is the work paying off in my classes? Am I learning more? Am I earning better letters? Am I still wasting time? Could I cut the time down and do the assignments even faster?

All of the above questions are important but the last one is the one to examine carefully. At the Academy you will often have six hours work and only three hours in which to do it. You will always have to prioritize--that is, you will have to let some work go and "take the hit" while you are doing other assignments that have a higher priority. So it will be crucial to use what study time you have with the highest efficiency.

That is why you should be hard on yourself when you are preparing for this regimen. When you estimate the time needed for one of your assignments, do not be afraid to shave ten minutes off your estimate when you set the alarm. You might be surprised how much faster you can work when that clock is ticking in front of you.

And that is the point. At the Academy you will hear the clock ticking every minute you are awake. It is relentless. It will never leave you alone. It will control your life. So get used to it.

Better yet, learn how to beat it. Learn to work faster so you can still squeeze things into your schedule that are pleasurable--things that are fun. The mids learn to do that eventually. They learn how to work and to have fun, too.

TRY TO BECOME INDEPENDENT OF YOUR TEACHERS.

Stop and consider for a moment what your teachers actually do in your classes. Most of their work falls into three categories.

First, they give an assignment.

Second, they "teach" the material that was assigned. That is, they either explain to you what you should have learned, or they do the same thing indirectly by letting students discuss and recite so the rest of the class will understand what was assigned.

Third, they hold you accountable for some of the things that were taught. Usually they account by administering a written test.

And what happens to you? You become careless about doing your assignments. You know the teacher is always going to spoonfeed you before the accounting takes place. So, year after year, you become teacher-dependent. You become the classic spoonfed cripple--the cripple, who, when you wish to learn something, thinks you must sit in a chair and have it explained by a teacher. In the worst cases, you become a total educational cripple; you can't read something as simple as an employment form without being spoonfeed without having the form explained.

If you have a lot of good letters on your transcript and good College Board scores, you obviously escaped some of the crippling process. But, in view of the rigor of classwork at the Academy, and considering the kind of severe competition you will experience from your talented classmates, the extent of your crippling, relatively speaking, could be significant. In short, because of the way you have been taught, you are likely to encounter trouble in your classes at the Naval Academy.

So what can you do?

First, you must always assume that step two and three in the typical teacher's routine will be reversed. You must assume that your teachers will demand an accounting *before* they explain what it is you are supposed to have learned.

Many of your professors at the Academy will do that. They will give an assignment and expect you to write or recite on the material before they spoonfeed you. (They call it lecturing, which is usually nothing but a formal explanation of the material that you were supposed to have learned.)

But forget for the moment that your professors at the Academy may do that. You are still in high school where most teachers do not do an accounting before they explain the assignment. So you can still slide by, day after day, accepting what the spoon brings.

Does it make you angry to read that? Do you resent being called a spoonfed cripple? More important, do you resent being one?

If so, there is hope for you. Because anger, disgust and wounded pride are powerful emotional incentives that can drive you to break this dependency.

But what must you do?

First, you must convince yourself of one thing. You must convince yourself that the only way you can become free of such dependency is to work hard on your assignments.

You must say to yourself, "I must read the material in this assignment twice, three times or four times--or whatever is necessary so I can go into tomorrow's class and know everything that the teacher is going to explain. Everything. Absolutely everything. With no exceptions."

Second, you must have the desire to be critical of yourself. When the teacher explains something that you do not fully understand from the assignment, chalk up one for the spoon. Your mind must accept the fact that the spoon has won and you have lost.

Third, you must make up your mind that some of the time you ARE going to lose and the spoon is going to win. After years of dependency, you cannot expect to free yourself after just one evening of determined homework. It will take weeks, or months of hard work to dig yourself out of such dependency.

It sounds like a lot of work, doesn't it? Well, it is. But it will not be as bad as you think.

Why? Because there is an immense amount of satisfaction that results from being free of the teacher's spoon. And that satisfaction comes quickly. The first day you go to class knowing everything the teacher will spoonfeed the others, you will feel good. You will feel good knowing that you are free of depending upon that teacher. You will feel good knowing that you may accomplish the same thing in more difficult classes--classes that are more likely to keep you teacher-dependent.

More important, you will feel good about yourself. It is a type of freedom that you have won. And freedom, when you have not had it, is a delicious reward.

DO NOT CATCH SENIORITIS.

You have just started the second semester of your senior year. You look around for your friends and many of them are missing. They are winding down their high school careers. They earned extra credits during their first three years and now they are paying for their cars by working at McDonald's or Burger King. Or they have elected an extra study hall. Or they are down in the gym shooting baskets. Or they are taking a course called "Cooking for Boys" in the home economics department. They are everyplace but in the hard classes where you are heading.

Would you like to join them? Would you, too, like to start winding down? After all, you will soon have twelve years of schooling under your belt--thirteen, if you went to kindergarten.

That is a long time, isn't it? You deserve the chance to slack off, do you not? After all those years of work, you have earned the right to coast downhill for awhile. Right?

If coasting downhill is what you want, go for it.

But just be aware of the steep hill that is just ahead of you if you intend to go to the Naval Academy. If you want to coast downhill during the last semester of your senior year, be ready for the hard work that will result when you have to start up the next hill. It is a steep one.

It is said that those who begin coasting during the last part of their senior year are afflicted with senioritis. It is not a disease but it is very contagious; you can catch it easily.

It is recommended that you avoid senioritis. Instead of coasting, use the last part of your senior year to peddle harder than ever. Keep increasing your momentum instead of losing it. Take a full load of classes. Take hard courses taught by hard teachers. Keep your brain in shape. Stay in the habit of studying.

That does not mean that you have to be grim about it. If you have learned to study efficiently, you will still have time for fun. You can still do things with your friends. You can still go to parties.

It is a matter of attitude. Those with senioritis have a tendency to feel badly about all the effort they have expended during the past years. They look at school as something to escape from. They think of it as a tape recording that they can soon erase and replace with something more pleasurable.

It is that attitude that you are being asked to avoid. If you aspire to succeed at the Naval Academy, you cannot erase the tape. Nor should you want to do so. To achieve success at the Naval Academy you will use everything that you have learned. And, because of the types of advanced courses you may be taking during your senior year, what you learn during the last semester of high school may be more important than everything else!

However, you should realize that senioritis is seldom a fatal affliction. Many others have caught it and survived. They just had to peddle harder going up the next hill.

What you have to decide is whether you want to keep your momentum and perhaps beat the others up the next hill, or whether you want to struggle along with the rest of the pack. It is your decision.

EIGHT
PHYSICAL PREPARATION

Do not go to the Naval Academy unless you like physical challenges. The Academy is a physical place and wimps are scorned by all.   *Courtesy USNA Photographic Branch.*

Do you like physical activity? Do you like it well enough to look forward to it?

Answer "yes" or "no" to those questions and then you may want to rethink whether the Naval Academy is for you or not.

If your answer is "no," and physical activity is something you dread, or something you do only when it is required, you should probably forget about going to the Naval Academy.

Why?

The Naval Academy is a physical place. Every day the midshipmen are engaged in some activity that is physically competitive. Half-hearted participation is scorned by all. "Wimps" are not wanted on anybody's team.

Wimps are not wanted in the naval services either. The Navy expects its officers to remain trim and fit throughout their careers. In fact, an overweight or out-of-condition officer will be dismissed--after suitable warning, of course.

The Marine Corps is even more strict about physical conditioning. Marine Corps officers take pride in their combat readiness and their ability to keep up with the youngest and best-conditioned recruits.

Most important, according to a physical education professor at the Academy, is a favorable attitude about physical activity. "If the attitude is there," says the professor, "everything else will fall in place. The midshipmen will do well here with the physical challenges. And, when they go to the fleet, they will stay in shape because they want to--not because they have to and feel threatened if they do not."

"On the other hand," continues the professor, "if the individual reading your book does not enjoy physical activity, I will make a flat statement to that person: do not come to the Naval Academy. If you do, you will not enjoy it here. You will always be forcing yourself to keep up and that is too heavy a burden to carry for very long."

A first classman put it another way. "Just as soon as they get here I can tell by their faces if they're dragging. You know then that you can eat them for breakfast--you know they're going to have problems."

Let us assume that you answered "yes" to the question at the beginning of the chapter. You do like physical activity and you look forward to it. What then?

You should convince yourself that it is important to prepare yourself physically for the Academy. This should include endurance training as well as activities that develop strength.

Running is the best type of endurance training. The midshipmen who were interviewed for this book stressed that preparation should include the running of distances longer than just a mile or two. A general consensus of one group was that you should be able to run three 7:30 miles with no strain.

A recent female graduate did not put a time on it but recommends running four miles a day and to be in good enough shape so that those are "easy" miles.

A female midshipman also had this comment: "As a girl it is a little harder because you are running at a pace with guys who are six feet tall that have legs a foot longer than you and you are not going to keep up. I didn't keep up at first. I have a short little stride and that was my biggest problem. When I couldn't keep up, the detailers pulled me out and started yelling at me--that is the quickest way to draw their attention. They will yell at you for that and then you start to feel depressed and think you are never going to make it. Because you are depressed, then you go and try to learn rates and all the other stuff and you think, I can't do it. It is the mind frame you are in. It carries over into everything else. I really got down. The first week or so I thought I was never going to get through it. I didn't think the summer would ever end. I didn't think I would ever be able to keep up on the runs. But, the more you keep going, the more you improve. You just have to keep a positive attitude and keep going and you will make it. Definitely, if you are a short person, practice lengthening your stride when you are running and preparing to come here. It would have helped me a lot if I had done that."

A male midshipman who was listening to the previous comments added: "I think you have to be aware when you come in here that the mental preparation is as important as the physical. I ran cross-country in the fall and track in the spring just to prepare for Plebe Summer. I was okay the first four or five weeks, but then I peaked and just got really worn out. Your body gets so taxed that you are no longer making the muscles any stronger; you are just breaking them down and getting weaker. There

Make up your mind before you go that you will get yourself in shape. Plebe Summer is difficult enough without the extra struggle with the physical routines.

Courtesy USNA Photographic Branch.

were some days when it was really bad. Prepare yourself mentally; no matter what you do it is going to be difficult. Take things a day at a time. Keep saying, 'I can do this.'"

One of the PE professors recommended that running should be combined with other strengthening exercises. He said: "You can start doing push-ups and sit-ups in combination with your distance running. Stop after every one-half mile or mile and do six or seven push-ups and 15, 20 or 25 sit-ups. As you become more fit, do more of both."

The midshipmen cautioned those who play football or basketball to take their physical preparation seriously. According to them, the "jock types" sometimes have the most trouble because they think they are in shape when they are not. If you are one of these and you are in doubt, it is very simple to test your endurance. Go for a run, time yourself, and see when you start getting tired.

Weight machines are the most helpful in developing strength. This is especially true for developing upper-body strength, which is where midshipmen are most likely to be deficient according to members of the physical education department.

Pull-ups, sit-ups and the standing long jump are activities that the Academy uses for measuring applied strength for males. Of these three exercises, pull-ups are most difficult. They must be performed with the palms facing away on the chinning bar. Male fourth classmen have to do three pull-ups to receive a passing grade of "D." First classmen have to do six to pass.

Like the males, women are given applied strength tests using sit-ups and the standing long jump. Pull-ups, though, are not required since most women lack the

If you are out of shape, be prepared for the upperclassmen to give you extra attention.
Courtesy USNA Photographic Branch.

upperbody strength needed to perform them. Female mids are encouraged to eventually do one pull-up to earn an "A"; however, they can pass this part of the test by performing the flexed arm hang for 20 seconds. The special techniques that will help them develop upper-body strength are discussed in Chapter 23.

Swimming is an important activity at the Academy. You do not have to be a good swimmer when you arrive but it helps. Those who are good swimmers may be able to validate (be excused from) the course and use that time for other purposes.

The poor swimmers have to keep working at it, and each year the demands are increased. Before completing the first-class year, all mids have to be able to swim one mile in 40 minutes in full clothing!

What if you are not in good physical condition when you come to the Academy? Can you survive?

Mixed replies were given to those questions at the Academy. According to one PE professor, "If they can walk when they get here, they can survive."

Another PE professor said, "Don't scare prospective candidates by making them think they have to be in top physical condition when they get here. The important thing is for them to be in good enough shape so they don't get blisters or muscle strains. If that happens, they can get behind and find themselves in trouble."

The midshipmen were more persuasive with their comments. One said, "I went overboard getting in shape before I came and during the first few days it was almost a letdown because I expected it to be more difficult. But then I looked around and saw those who were not in good condition. They were dragging and all the other pressures of Plebe Summer were getting to them while I was almost enjoying it. It was then I realized how glad I was that I had trained before I came. Definitely those who were not in shape suffered a lot more than I did."

Another midshipman restated the warning the physical education department gave about injuries: "The worst thing that can happen is for someone to get injured, like pull a muscle. Then you cannot participate; you get behind and you get left out. Come with your muscles in shape--make that a good strong recommendation."

There is another reason for preparing physically that has nothing to do with surviving the physical challenges. A female first classman put it this way, "One of the best ways of attracting the attention of the first classmen during plebe summer is to be out of shape. It seems like those who are out of shape are always picked on more than the others. Also, those who are a little overweight seem to draw more than their share of attention. On the other hand, if a plebe looks sharp and is in good shape, I think the first classmen have a tendency to think, 'Well, that one looks squared away; we can leave him alone for awhile.' So my advice is to come here in top shape just so you won't catch as much flak from the upper classmen."

A third classman listening to the above comment added, "She's right, but I think what's important is to show energy, energy, energy--that's what the upper classmen respect. Show energy and you'll get their respect. Drag it and they'll stay on you and ride you. Lots of times I didn't know my rates (required fourth-class knowledge) but I shouted the answers with energy and they left me alone."

Another third classman added, "That's really true, and those I felt sorry for were the overweight ones. Face it; if you're a slob, you're going to get picked on. I wouldn't want to come in here overweight. They make you lose the weight--we got weighed every week during Plebe Summer and they weigh you each semester during the year. But what a hassle trying to lose weight with all the other pressure that you have the first year. That's just something else to worry about and you have more than enough already."

So what is the best advice?

Both the PE professors and the mids are probably correct. It is probably true that you can go to the Naval Academy and if you can walk, you can survive. Probably nothing is so difficult that a healthy young person with average strength cannot ultimately do it after participating in the Academy physical conditioning program.

However, there is no doubt that the midshipmen are correct on two points.

First, if you are in excellent shape when you arrive, Plebe Summer will be easier.

Second, if you can demonstrate excellent physical fitness, you are probably going to be harassed less than those who are out of shape. This probably applies even more for females than for males.

So the bottom line is this: Be in excellent shape when you arrive at the Naval Academy because it will make your first year easier and give you one less thing to worry about.

NINE
OTHER PREPARATION

You cannot get into the Naval Academy just by being a good student--even with outstanding College Board scores. You have to offer more than that.

You must demonstrate that you have had experiences outside the classroom. You must prove that you have developed skills other than strict academic skills.

What kinds of experiences are necessary?

In high school they are the kinds that can be obtained in many different kinds of extracurricular activities (ECA). Examples include team sports, clubs, student government, newspaper and yearbook staffs, dramatics, band, drill team, chorus and debate.

They also may include ECA outside of school such as Explorer and Eagle Scouts, church and community volunteer service, Civil Air Patrol and fraternal organizations.

Why are ECA so important for those who want to go to the Naval Academy?

Because participation in ECA demonstrates that the person has qualities that are valuable at the Naval Academy and in naval service. For example, a student who has played football or run on a cross-country team has experienced hardships and has had to learn self-sacrifice and self-discipline. Also, such a student has learned the value of teamwork and has developed a competitive attitude.

Participation in ECA also demonstrates that candidates are not selfish with their time--that they have a desire to contribute as well as take from their community. The desire to serve others is an essential part of a naval officer's makeup. Those who are self-centered and selfish with their time are better suited for other work.

The ability to get along with people is an essential trait for a naval officer. Participation in ECA does not guarantee that a student has that ability, but it is a favorable indicator.

When a candidate can demonstrate ECA leadership experience, that is an even better indicator of one's ability to get along with people. To those who evaluate candidates, it is far better to have been the elected president of one club than just a member of three. Likewise, it is better to have been a team captain, a newspaper editor or student council president than to have been just a member of those groups.

A student who has held leadership positions has learned something else that is considered valuable by those who evaluate candidates. That something else is called time management.

At the Academy there is never enough time to do all the things that are supposed to be done. In order to survive, the midshipman has to compromise and prioritize. Some things have to be left undone and others have to be done in their order of importance. That is called time management.

High school students who take hard academic classes and who hold ECA leadership positions have had to learn some of those time management skills. Thus, a candidate who is both a scholar and a leader is considered to be better prepared for the rigors of the Academy than one who has not been pressured for time.

In addition to ECA, work experiences also are considered important by some persons who evaluate candidates. For example, several panelists who serve on congressional screening committees have flatly stated that they prefer candidates who have had real-world work experiences.

Why are work experiences considered so important?

You must realize that for most panelists their main goal is to evaluate the motivation and potential dedication of the candidates who come before them. Some panelists believe

A midshipman photographed his well-worn copy of *Reef Points* for the author.

Courtesy 1/C Jimmy Parker.

that students who have worked at summer jobs or at part-time jobs while attending school are more likely to have the kind of motivation and dedication that is needed to survive at the Academy.

Others see work experiences as just one more opportunity for the candidate to learn to manage time.

Certainly, while being interviewed by a panel, if you are asked what you have done during your last two summer vacations, the interrogator is not likely to be impressed if you answer, "I spent my last two summers having fun."

Some other types of preparation for the Academy are not essential for getting admitted. However, there are things a candidate can do prior to enrollment that will make life at the Academy much easier.

An example relates to various kinds of naval knowledge. As soon as plebe summer begins, the new plebe is required to master seamanship terms, naval engineering terms, standard ship commands and a host of other facts. All of these are contained in a little book called *Reef Points*, which is issued to each plebe. If possible, find an upper-class midshipman or Academy graduate and borrow a copy of *Reef Points*. You can make it easier on yourself by memorizing, or at least familiarizing yourself with much of the material in that book.

Plebes are also expected to read the daily newspaper and keep up with current events. It is recommended that you start this habit several months before going to the

Anything you can learn about sailing will be helpful.

Courtesy USNA Photographic Branch.

Academy. It is a good habit and it will help you to have the background and perspective for what you will read about later.

All midshipmen learn the theory and techniques of sailing. If you can get a head start and learn the theory, you will have more time just to enjoy the sport.

A recommendation passed on by some midshipmen is to learn how to shine shoes. When learning that skill at the Academy, it may take as much as an hour to get your shoes shined to the satisfaction of the upperclassmen who will inspect you. It is better, say the mids, to solicit the help of a former military person and have this person teach you to shine shoes to military standards. Do this before you go and while you have plenty of time. Then, when in the time crunch of Plebe Summer, the chore can be reduced to a few skillful minutes of work.

Another recommendation--one that is given enthusiastically by everyone who knows anything about the Academy--is to make a personal visit and see for yourself what the Academy experience is all about. There are two good ways to go about this.

The best way is to obtain admission to the Naval Academy Summer Science Seminar. This is a six-day program that is offered three times during the month of June. It is an invitation-only program where 320 high school students (per session) who have just completed their junior year come to the Academy for a variety of experiences. They first arrive on a Saturday where, under the supervision of upper classmen selected just for this assignment, they are assigned quarters in Bancroft Hall

It is strongly recommended that you visit the Academy and spend time with the midshipmen. That is the only way you are going to learn what it is like there.

Courtesy 1/C Jimmy Parker.

and then organized into squads. Each morning at six o'clock they are called out for light exercise, and, during the weekdays--Monday, Tuesday, Wednesday and Thursday--they participate in eight out of 20 academic workshops, which correspond to the 20 different majors that are available at the Academy. These are two and one-half hour workshops so the students can attend two per day. In addition, the participants engage in a variety of sports--the idea being that they should appreciate the physical demands of the institution because sports participation is mandatory of all midshipmen. Finally, the midshipmen who supervise the program also introduce the participants to some of the military indoctrination that they would experience if they became midshipmen. There is not a lot of yelling in the face, but the participants move to their classrooms as a squad unit and they have drill practice and competition. On the last evening, those who volunteer, are offered more realistic experiences where the midshipmen actually give about an hour of actual plebe-type indoctrination training. (About 96 percent of all participants volunteer for the training and 90+ percent rate that experience as the highlight of their six days.) The whole goal of the program is to introduce potential candidates to what the Naval Academy experience is all about--and that includes making them aware that it is routine for midshipmen to perform at peak levels during 18-hour days.

How does one get invited to one of these seminars? First, if you have taken the P-SAT and done well, there is a good chance that you will be on the Academy mailing list and will receive information on how to apply. But, if you really want to attend one of the seminars, do not wait around to hear from the Academy. Go after it on your own by contacting the Blue and Gold Officer in your region. All instructions for doing this are described in the next chapter.

If you do get an invitation, you will be expected to provide your own transportation to the Academy in Annapolis, Maryland, or to Baltimore-Washington International Airport (BWI) where a free shuttle will pick you up and transport you to the Academy. You will also be expected to pay a $175 fee, which covers all expenses while you are at the Academy. And what if you feel you are a good candidate for the seminar but that the cost of transportation and the seminar fee is far beyond what you and your parents can afford? Limited financial help might be available to you, but you must let the official who sent your invitation know your situation.

The second good option is to take advantage of the offer made to all known candidates, which is mailed in August or early September. This is for a weekend visit sometime between October and late April. The Academy sponsors ten of these weekend visits for 100 candidates, and if you wish to be one of the 1000 selected for such a visit, closely check your mail or contact your Blue and Gold Officer. The weekend visits start on Friday morning and, after an orientation meeting, each candidate is paired with a third or fourth-class (freshman or sophomore) midshipman and "shadows" that midshipman until Saturday noon. During this time the candidate gets to go to classes, observe plebes in the indoctrination program, participate in sports, and, because the Friday night schedule is the lightest of the week, time is available for informal discussions with midshipmen other than the candidate's escort. Again, the candidates have to arrange and finance their own transportation. However, for this weekend visitation program, candidates must also pay the fee for the Super Shuttle that picks them up at BWI and transports them to an Annapolis Hotel--one that offers special rates for the weekend visits. In addition there is a $14.00 fee that covers the weekend meals.

HOW TO GET IN

TEN
GETTING IN: THE PROCEDURE

It is not easy to get into the Naval Academy. Every year there are more than 10,000 applications for 1180 openings.[1] That is the bad news.

The good news is, the admissions process is long and involved, with paperwork, deadlines, letters of recommendation to solicit, interviews, a physical performance test and a medical examination.

Why is this good news?

Because many young men and women who apply do so half-heartedly. These types, most of whom are not highly motivated, make mistakes in the admissions process that either hurt their chances of getting in or cause them to be eliminated from the competition. That is good news if you are a serious applicant. The complex nature of the admissions process eliminates part of your competition.

How does a serious applicant proceed? The first step, *even if you are only in the ninth or tenth grade,* is to call the Naval Academy at number 410-293-4361.

A receptionist from the Admissions Office will answer. Tell that person that you think you are interested in going to the Naval Academy. The receptionist will not be surprised by your call; that office handles thousands of calls each year!

To APPLY you must be
* At least 17 and not yet 22 years old on July 1 of the year of admission.
* Unmarried, not pregnant, and have no legal obligation to support a child, children, or other individual.
* A U.S. citizen (expect for the limited quota of foreign midshipmen especially authorized by Congress).
* Of good moral character.

To be ADMITTED you must also
* Be found scholastically qualified by the admissions board
* Be medically qualified.
* Pass the Naval Academy Physical Fitness Aptitude Examination
* Receive an official nomination

The receptionist will probably ask you a few questions to determine your status as a potential applicant. If you are not yet a junior in high school, the receptionist will probably handle your request for information. If you are a high school junior or senior,

---

[1]This is the current number. The actual number admitted can vary from year to year.

The Admissions Board carefully studies each qualified applicant.

you will be transferred to an admissions counselor. This is a naval officer trained to interview you.

You are encouraged to ask any questions you desire. But regardless of who fields your call, there is one question you should not fail to ask. That question is: How do I contact my local Blue and Gold Officer?

There are about 1750 Naval Academy Blue and Gold Officers in the U.S. Each one serves under an Area Coordinator who is generally responsible for one state, or a region within a state.

The counselor you are speaking with on the telephone will most likely give you the name, address and phone number of the Area Coordinator. In addition, if you are in or beyond the second semester of your high school junior year, you will be sent a Precandidate Questionnaire.

At this time, unless counseled differently by the person you spoke with on the phone, *temporarily* forget about the Precandidate Questionnaire.

Your most important next task is to contact the Area Coordinator for the telephone number of the Blue and Gold Officer who is closest to you. Then phone that officer.

The Blue and Gold Officers are the best allies of candidates applying to the Academy. They are experts on the admissions procedures and their main desire is to advise candidates on all aspects of that process. In addition, if you apply, your Blue and Gold Officer will have to write an evaluation of you--an evaluation that will probably influence your chances of getting an appointment.

Spirited discussion often erupts around the Admissions Board table when individual candidates are being considered.

What do you say to the Blue and Gold Officer? Describe yourself, including your age and grade in school, and explain that you would like a meeting. Explain that you may be interested in attending the Naval Academy and that you would like to learn more about it.

If you are still in junior high school, the officer may just want to talk with you on the telephone. But that is okay. A year later you can request another meeting. Then you can remind the officer that you called earlier, and in this way show you are not just calling on a whim--that you are genuinely interested.

Before your first meeting with the Blue and Gold Officer, borrow a Naval Academy Catalog from your school counselor or librarian.

Read the Catalog thoroughly, and any brochures that the Academy might have sent you. Then, during your first meeting with the Blue and Gold Officer, ask specific questions about the Academy based upon what you have read. If you do this, you will be making a good impression.

Why? Because most potential candidates want the Blue and Gold Officer to spoonfeed them with information they could have learned on their own. By demonstrating that you have already obtained knowledge of the Academy by your own research, you have indicated that you are motivated and capable of personal initiative.

Your Blue and Gold Officer can also help you locate others who can give you information about the Academy. This might include visits with midshipmen who come home for Christmas or summer leave. It may also include interviews with active-duty or retired naval officers who can tell you what it is like being a career officer.

If you are a second-semester junior or senior, you will have received a Precandidate Questionnaire from the Academy. This will be the first of many forms you must complete in the admissions process.

Never begin filling out any form until you have read *both* the instructions and the questions thoroughly. Make absolutely sure you know exactly what you are to do before you start writing, and if you have any doubts, ask for another opinion.

If possible, make a photocopy of the forms and fill out the copies first. That way you have a record that you can keep, and you can be more certain that the original form will be filled out correctly.

It is important for you to follow instructions with the Precandidate Questionnaire because it is read into a computer by an optical scanner. Since the Academy uses this information to make a preliminary assessment of your qualifications, you do not want to make a mistake and let a computer determine that you are poorly qualified.

With the receipt of the Precandidate Questionnaire the Admissions Office will open a pre-admission file in your name. That file will be used for any other information that the Academy receives about you.

The Precandidate Questionnaire asks for scores on the Preliminary Scholastic Aptitude Test (PSAT), Scholastic Aptitude Test (SAT), or American College Testing Program (ACT) test. Here is what you should know about those tests.

After all discussion is complete, the individual members of the Admissions Board vote with a two-colored block; green is a vote for appointing the candidate; red is a negative vote. The three blocks shown in this photo have the green end up.

The Director of Admissions (standing) supervises the Admissions Board proceedings. In this photo, the Academy head physician (right) is still trying to decide how he is going to vote.

Ultimately, you will have to turn in scores on the SAT or ACT. (They must be taken no later than February of the year you want to be admitted.) Just remember this about those tests. You can take them as many times as you wish and you will be credited with the highest score you make on them. The Naval Academy used to average the scores. They no longer do that and they advise candidates to take the tests more than once because experience usually pays off; most do better the second time they take them.

There are books available on the SAT and ACT--books that contain sample tests and advice on how to answer the various types of questions. Ask at your local bookstore for the latest books of this kind, or check with your high school counselor.

Another possibility, if you think you might not score well on the tests, is to take a special class that will help you prepare for the kinds of questions that are asked. These are available in most metropolitan areas and the ideal time to take one of them is the summer between your sophomore and junior years.

Admissions officials do not like to discuss minimum SAT and ACT scores required for admission because there are no set rules and there are always special cases.

However, they want all prospective candidates to know generally what kind of competition they will encounter. In recent classes the average SAT scores have been running about 550 on the verbal and 630-650 on the math--about 1200 on the total score. Also, unless your scores are at least 450 verbal and about 550 math, you are not likely to be considered unless you are a candidate for a prep school, which is a subject for a later chapter.

Now for the most critical part of the application: the personal statement.

You must write a short essay explaining why you want to go to the Naval Academy. According to admissions officials and Blue and Gold Officers, candidates can really hurt their chances of getting in with this personal statement. On the other hand, if you write a good personal statement, it can really help you. Here is some of their advice.

Do not try to make yourself into something you are not. Academy officials always smile when they speak of personal statements like that. "You can spot a con job a mile away," laughed one official. "They can't fool us. We've read too many of these things. We can tell somebody who is being natural and somebody who is pretending to be somebody he isn't. My advice: be natural. Be yourself. Tell it honestly. Tell it the way it is. Don't think you have to puff yourself up. We've got your record to look at. What's bad is when you tell us that you really believe in community service, yet have nothing like that listed among your extracurricular activities. We also get these beautifully written essays that you know were written by a parent. You can just see it; this wasn't written by a kid; this was written by an adult."

Think of the personal essay as one of the most important compositions you will write in your whole life. Therefore, you should take lots of time thinking about the essay before you start writing. Ask yourself: Why do I want to go to the Naval Academy? Get your reasons clearly outlined in your mind, then prepare to give supporting information for those reasons. If you say, "It has been a dream of mine to attend the Naval Academy since I was in the seventh grade," then you should be able to list ways you have already tried to fulfill that dream. For example, "When I was in the ninth grade, I bugged my parents so much that they finally took me to Annapolis to see the placc."

Or, "Since the seventh grade I have read twelve war books to see if I could picture myself killing people in a war. The books I read are: (list of titles)."

Or, "When I was in the tenth grade my Blue and Gold Officer told me about the Naval Academy parent club picnic where the new appointees were honored before they left for the Academy. I have gone to three of those picnics and have heard visiting midshipmen giving advice to the appointees. Nothing they said scared me. I like challenges. And I have never quit anything I've started. The talk at those picnics just increased my desire to go to the Academy."

Do not try to use fancy language to express yourself. Write the way you would speak to an older friend or to a midshipman.

Now for some comments that turn off members of the admission board. You had better not say that you want to go to the Naval Academy because your parents are poor and you need a free education. They will jump all over that statement because, if you're good enough to get into the Naval Academy, they know you are probably good enough to get scholarships at civilian institutions. So why do you want to go to the Naval Academy and put up with all the rigors of military training, and the military obligation that follows graduation? Their thoughts when they read such a statement?

This kid is either naive or misinformed, and either way, he or she probably has no business in this place.

Neither is it wise to say that you want to go to the Navy Academy because you want to become a doctor or a pilot and you cannot afford to achieve your goal any other way. Those reading such statements are likely to think: "This kid must not realize that the Naval Academy doesn't even have a pre-med program." Or: "If this kid is coming just so he can get free pilot training, does he plan to bail out at the earliest opportunity so he can go fly for Delta Airlines?" Young people have gone into medicine after graduation from the Academy, and quite a large number do go on and receive pilot training. But, in either case, the individual incurs a long-term commitment to naval service and your statement, if it mentions medicine or flying, should include comments to show that you are well aware of this commitment.

Finally, when you think you have finished the personal statement, it is recommended that you have it read by one or more adults who can comment intelligently upon its style and structure. An English teacher whom you respect would be ideal. Also, if you have access to a computer with word processing software, be sure and do a spell check on your essay.

After the Admissions Office receives your application, they will do an analysis and rank you according to a system that determines your eligibility. This is a seven-factor scoring system and here is how it breaks down:

1. Class ranking. According to one admissions official, "A candidate's rank in class is the most important and the most predictable of all our predictors. However, there are some schools that do not give their students a class rank, and while this may help some students get into a civilian college, it is a handicap if you are applying to the Naval Academy. Without a class ranking, we will try to compute a class rank based upon our knowledge, but it doesn't give us a clear picture of where they actually stand." Sixty percent of your rating will be based upon your class rank, so do what you can do to get your school to give you an accurate ranking.

2. Math SAT. The Naval Academy is a technical institution so your math aptitude will be a critical factor determining your success there. Of course, you can major in English, history, economics or political science while at the Academy, but that *does not* excuse you from taking the basic core of math, science, and engineering courses. So your math SAT score is given much more weight in the evaluation process than your verbal score.

3. Verbal SAT. The verbal SAT, though not as important as the math, is still very important. Naval officers cannot be effective unless they are reasonably skilled communicators.

4. Teacher recommendations. Comments from your teachers are important; however, admissions officials place the highest emphasis on what your math and English teachers say about you.

5. Extra curricular activities (ECA). The philosophy of the Academy regarding ECA was explained in Chapter Nine and it might be helpful for you to review that material. Just remember, your ECA tell admissions officials two things about you. (1) If you are involved in a lot of them, it means that you are generous with your time and

are likely to be the type of person who wants to serve others. (2) If you are very active in ECA, it means that you have already had some success with time management, and you will probably be able to build upon this experience at the Academy.

6. Technical vs humanities interests. Although humanities courses are offered at the Academy, it is primarily a scientific and technical institution. Therefore, every candidate is evaluated on the basis of an interest inventory assessment, and those with strong scientific and technical interests are given a higher rating than those whose interests lie purely in the humanities.

7. Career retention. The purpose of the Academy is to supply well qualified officers to the naval services. Therefore, admissions officials would not be doing their duty if they did not try to admit candidates who are likely to go on and make one of the naval services a career. Thus, when your interest inventory is evaluated, they will look more favorably upon those candidates who appear to have potential for becoming career officers.

Your application to the Naval Academy is the first major step in obtaining admission. The second major step in the admissions process is to obtain a nomination.

The nomination is like an endorsement that says you are qualified and should be considered for admission to the Academy. It does *not* mean that you will be admitted to the Academy.

To be admitted to the Academy you must first go through all the admissions procedures and be found qualified by the Admissions Office. Second, you must obtain a nomination from one of several nomination sources, which include the President and all members of Congress. The third step is to receive an *appointment*, which can only come from the Naval Academy Admissions Office. (Neither the President nor any member of Congress can give you an appointment!) The appointment is the formal notification that you are admitted to the Academy.

Most nominations are made by the 535 senators and U.S. representatives who serve in the Congress. Each senator and representative is entitled to have five appointees at the Naval Academy at any one time.

The President is the next largest nomination source. However, all of those nominations are reserved for sons and daughters of career military personnel who move often and cannot establish long-term residence in any congressional district.

The nomination process is explained in the Naval Academy Catalog. In addition, the Catalog describes some of the lesser known nomination sources for which you might be eligible. However, you are advised to solicit as much help as you can get when you begin to seek a nomination. Probably the best person to help you is your Blue and Gold Officer. These officers are familiar with all the nomination sources available to you and can counsel you on every step in the nomination process.

A second person who might help you is your high school counselor. Some are very knowledgeable and may even have visited the Naval Academy and attended a special training session conducted by the Admissions Office. These special sessions are conducted for counselors from all over the United States. [2]

Also, advice may be obtained from parents of Academy midshipmen who supervised the process for their own sons or daughters. Your Blue and Gold Officer can put you in touch with such parents.

In addition to the above, much good advice can be obtained from those who work in congressional offices and those who serve on panels and interview prospective candidates. Comments from those persons are contained in the next three chapters.

[2]Thus author was also advised to warn students that they can receive bad advice from counselors who are unfamiliar with the service academies. The bottom line: be skeptical of dogmatic statements made by a counselor, especially if what the counselor says is discouraging.

ELEVEN
HOW TO GET A
CONGRESSIONAL NOMINATION

"Should I volunteer to work in my congressman's next political campaign?"

"We just moved to this state and everything here is politics, politics, politics. I don't know anybody so my kid doesn't stand a chance of getting into the Naval Academy."

"We're Republicans and our representative and two senators are Democrats. There is no way our daughter can get a nomination."

The above are typical of comments the author has heard from candidates and parents. It seems that most people believe politics is involved, at least to some degree, whenever a candidate for a service academy wins a congressional nomination.

Is that what you believe?

If so, you can probably forget it.

There are 535 senators and representatives (who, in this book, shall be called congressmen) and there is no question that a few of them let politics and friendships influence their choice of nominees.

However, during hundreds of interviews with cadets and midshipmen, parents, Academy officials, Blue and Gold Officers, congressional staffers and panelists, it was rare to hear of any case where a politician was accused of making nominations on the basis of influence.

Almost everyone believed that the nomination process is basically fair--that a very large majority of all nominations are awarded on the basis of merit, not political influence.

A veteran congressional staffer from California was especially adamant about the unimportance of politics. When she was asked how politics influenced her congressman's nomination process, she replied with indignation, "We like to think we are all Republicans in this district, but, hey, I tell the kids, 'I don't care if your parents are Democrats or even if they came from Mars--if you get the points, you're in there.'"

Another staffer said, "If we let politics be involved in the nomination process, we would look very bad to the constituents of this district. Besides that, we would have to listen to a lot of political pleading and that would be worse."

It would not be prudent to completely ignore the possibility that politics might be involved in your state or congressional district. However, the chances are fairly remote. In the opinion of everybody who was interviewed for this book, it would be much better for you to forget politics and concentrate on all the real challenges that you are certain to face in the competition for a nomination.

And there is a lot of competition! Each congressman has a quota of five who can be at the Naval Academy at any one time.[1] Thus, each year, a congressman will typically nominate ten candidates for one upcoming vacancy. Yet, there may be twenty or more candidates in the competition who meet at least the minimum requirements of the Academy.

Each congressman can nominate ten persons for every upcoming vacancy at the Naval Academy. How do they do it?

Each decides upon one of three nomination methods.

One is the principal/numbered alternate method. Ten nominees are selected, then one of them is designated as the principal nominee. If fully qualified, the principal nominee must be given an appointment by the Academy. The names of the other nine are submitted as alternates, but each one is ranked by number and, if fully qualified, the Academy must appoint alternates in the order of their ranking. For example, the number one alternate must be appointed before the number two alternate, etc.

The second method is the principal/competitive alternate method. Ten nominees are selected and one of them is designated as the principal nominee and must be appointed if qualified. But there is no ranking of the nine alternates. They are "competitive," which means it is left up to the Admissions Department of the Academy to decide which, if any, of the alternates should be appointed.

The third method is the competitive method. It is, by far, the most common nomination procedure. By this method the congressman selects ten nominees and makes them all competitive. In other words, the congressman says to the Academy, "For my upcoming vacancy I am giving you a list of the ten most qualified persons from my district/state. Now it is up to you to decide from among the ten who should be offered an appointment."

It should be emphasized that once all congressional quotas are filled by appointment, there are still hundreds of vacancies left that are filled by the Academy. Thus, many alternates are appointed each year and, from a congressman's list of competitive nominations, more than one nominee may receive an appointment. (When alternates are selected by the Academy to fill out each class, they are not charged against the congressman's quota of five who can be at the Academy at any one time.)

In addition, numerous appointments are declined by nominees--because they have changed their mind, or, sometimes, because they have accepted an appointment by another academy.

Every candidate should apply to every nomination source that is available. Sources other than congressional sources and how to apply to them are explained in the Academy Catalog. Also, your Blue and Gold Officer will be happy to counsel you on the different nomination sources that are available.

If you are a resident of one of the fifty states, you will definitely want to seek a nomination from each of your three congressional nomination sources, which are: the U.S. Representative from your congressional district and each of the U.S. Senators

---

[1]Actually, more of a congressman's nominees can be appointed; they are just not charged to his quota. This discrepancy will be explained in more detail later.

from your state. To apply for these nominations, here is what you need to know.

Every congressman has at least one regional office in your district/state. Find the telephone number of that office; then call and ask whomever answers for the name and location of the person on the congressman's staff (called a "staffer") who is in charge of the service academy nomination process. That responsibility is always delegated to a staffer and it is this person whom you should get to know, if not personally, at least well enough to converse informally over the telephone. (It is rare for a candidate to even meet the congressman.)

You will find that a few staffers operate out of the congressman's Washington, D.C. office. If so, they will probably do the complete nomination procedure by paperwork alone--with no interviews. If this is the case, the person at the regional office should give you a toll-free number (800-number) that you can use to call that staffer. If you are not given the number, ask for it.

If the staffer who handles service academy nominations is in the regional office, which is typically the case, you may be put through to her immediately (usually the staffer is female).

In either case, here are the things that you should ask the staffer. First, ask for a brief description of the congressman's nomination process. Find out which of the three methods are used, whether or not you will be interviewed and, *most important*, the date when applications are accepted and the date when applications must be in the congressman's office.

The congressional offices usually begin accepting applications in late spring or early summer. The deadline may be as early as September 30 or October 1, but it is more commonly in November or early December.

When should you make your call? If possible, try to call during the spring of your junior year. Give yourself as much time as possible.

When you speak with the staffer, she will probably ask you some questions to determine your eligibility. And she will probably ask if you have contacted the Naval Academy and have submitted the Precandidate Questionnaire.

Also she will probably explain that she has a packet, which includes all of the instructions and forms that you will need in order to begin the process of applying for a nomination. However, before sending out this packet, many--perhaps most--staffers will ask you to submit a letter formally requesting the packet. You may also be asked to explain in the letter why you want to attend the Naval Academy.

Why do many require such a letter? Why do they not just send out the packet of information when a person calls?

One reason is to see if you are serious. It is easy to pick up the phone and make a telephone call. That can be done on a moment's whim. It takes more thought and effort to write a letter, especially one where candidates have to explain their reasons for wanting to go to an academy. So the requirement for a letter deters those who are not seriously motivated.

But there is another reason for requiring a letter from potential candidates. Staffers get many calls from parents who ask how their son or daughter can get a nomination. They are very leery of these calls. They know that there are parents out there who, for a variety of reasons, tend to push their kids into applying for one of the academies. They also know that the record is absolutely horrible for those who have gotten into an academy but who were there mainly because of parental pressure.

In other words, candidates who go to an academy for ANY reason other than their own, deep, personal desire are almost certain to drop out or fail. No congressman wants that, of course. No congressman wants to see such a person take a slot from a candidate who is truly motivated and will stick it out and graduate from an academy.

So, that is another reason why the staffer may want to receive a letter and, perhaps, a statement of desire from you. She is trying to find out if it is you or your parents who are most interested in a nomination to the Academy. If a student writes a good, persuasive letter, it is a good indication that going to the Academy is the student's idea.

Keep in mind that you have *three* staffers to contact and *three* packets of information that you will receive.

Be sure to treat all three packets individually, for they represent each congressman's own personal philosophy on what a candidate should do to get a nomination.

You should keep separate files for each congressman. Also, you should read the instructions in each packet very carefully and do exactly what the instructions ask you to do. If the instructions say that you should submit two letters of recommendation, do not convince yourself that three or four would be better. If the instructions ask for two letters of recommendation from educators who know you, do not try to "puff" your application with letters from a general or a company president who might know your father.

And above all, do not send one congressman something that some other congressman asked for in his or her instructions. Said one staffer, "It makes me madder than hell when I get something from a kid that I know was requested by Senator ____'s office. If a kid can't follow instructions, why should we waste money sending him to an academy."

Letters of recommendation sometimes cause problems for candidates. One potential problem is the way they are solicited. You should take care to do it correctly, and here is what you should do.

If possible, you should talk to the person whom you want to write a letter. But, before asking the person to write a letter for you, first ask whether he or she thinks it is a good idea for you to apply for the Academy. The answer will tell you a lot about the person's enthusiasm for you.

If there is hesitation, or the person begins to speculate how you might have trouble with this or that, let that be a warning. The letter that person will write is likely to be uninspired or filled with qualifying phrases. This happens. Said a panelist on a congressman's board, "I have seen cases where they [the candidates] have been damned with real faint praise and we can read between the lines."

You do not want an unenthusiastic person writing letters for you. Most staffers and panelists who will read the letters usually do not pay a lot of attention to them because they expect all of them to be good. So a bad one, or even one that is just average, is bound to stick out like a red flag if it gets into your file. Do not take that chance. Make sure that whoever writes a letter for you really believes in your potential, and the surest way of finding that out is during a face-to-face discussion.

Give three things to each person who has agreed to write a letter for you.

First, give them a summary sheet with all pertinent information about you. This should include your college board test scores, your grade point average and rank in class, a list of the extra-curricular activities you have participated in--including any offices or positions of responsibility (e.g. chairman for prom decorations), your out-of-school activities--including volunteer work and job experiences, if any.

Why do this? Because it is doubtful that any one person is going to know all of these things about you. Yet, those who will write the letters will want to write the best letter possible (you hope) and to do so, they need facts--facts that you can conveniently supply with a summary sheet.

Second, give them stamped, addressed envelopes for each letter. This is a minor courtesy, but one that is always appreciated.

Third, give them a written deadline that is at least two weeks before the real deadline. You might clip a note to each envelope with the deadline written there. Or, if the writer might be confused by three different deadlines, clip all the envelopes together with one note and one deadline. Also, hand the envelopes to each writer and explain, verbally, where the deadlines are written and how important it is that the letters should be sent on time.

You should be sensitive to the deadlines of each of the congressmen. Many candidates procrastinate. Doing all the paperwork required in the nomination process is distasteful to many candidates and they put it off as long as possible. But you should fight that tendency. Set a deadline for yourself *at least two weeks* before the congressman's deadline. Put that personal deadline on a calendar or somewhere else where it will not be overlooked. Then meet it. Get your application in before the congressman's deadline.

Here is why you should do that. It is common for ACT and SAT scores to be missent, like to Winslow, AR instead of Winslow, AZ. Also, it is common for high schools, even those with excellent reputations, to fail to include your class ranking or grade point average on your transcript--or to fail to send some other document that has been requested. In addition, it often happens that those who are supposed to write letters of recommendation either forget to do it, or they procrastinate past the deadline. (One staffer said that high school principals are always the worst procrastinators.)

So, to be on the safe side, you should always assume that something will be missing from your file in the congressmen's offices. By getting your application in early, you give yourself time to follow up and correct such problems.

But there is another reason to follow up. As you will learn shortly, the staffer often has considerable influence over the whole nomination process. If you follow up with the staffer, once, twice or even three times, this is a good indication to the staffer that you are a person who is truly serious about going to the Academy.

Remember, the staffer and her congressman are looking for several qualities in their candidates but the most important thing they are looking for is *motivation*. You tell that staffer that you are motivated when you get your application in early. And you repeat the message each time you call to follow up on your application. So don't let the latter opportunity slip by. Let that staffer know you are motivated. Follow up!

Now a word about staffers. Some will openly admit that they have a lot of influence over who does and does not get nominations. For example, there are staffers who not only handle all the paperwork, but who, by themselves, interview each candidate and rate them for their congressmen. Such types wield a lot of influence; they know it and you know it.

But for every one of the above, there are many other staffers who put down their own role at every opportunity. "Oh, I just do the paperwork; the congressman makes the actual decisions." That is a typical type of comment likely to be heard from many. But do not believe it, although in some cases it may be true.

For the most part, the staffers are very dedicated to their task of getting the best people into the academies. Many have visited one or more of the academies. They have seen firsthand the kind of rigors the cadets and midshipmen have to endure. Also, many believe strongly that the country deserves the best military leadership possible.

With this kind of dedication and motivation, you can bet that many staffers want to give input to their congressmen when the nominees are being selected. They may not want candidates to know that, and they may go to great lengths to convince candidates (and parents) that they are mere paper shufflers. But they also want good people nominated. For that reason they would be less than human if they did not try to bring some influence to bear on who gets a nomination and who does not.

So, to be on the safe side, it is highly recommended that you treat each staffer as though she is the person who is going to decide whether or not you are going to get a nomination.

Now it is time for the staffers to speak for themselves. Over thirty of them were interviewed and all were asked to describe the ways candidates create problems for themselves during the nomination process.

Following is a sampling of their comments, and while they are mainly negative in tone, realize that they were selected for that purpose--so you can be aware of the kinds of things *not* to do when you seek a nomination.[2]

A staffer from Iowa: "My biggest problem with the kids is the way they procrastinate. There is always a big interest just before school lets out in the spring; then during the summer they forget. After school starts they rush and try to get everything done but they have a lot on their mind and they make mistakes--mistakes that hurt them. But I'm afraid they aren't going to change."

Another staffer from Iowa: "They should try to be more timely because I won't even consider anybody who doesn't get their paperwork in on time. How could they be a successful cadet at an academy if they can't do that?"

A staffer from Nevada: "Many wait until the last minute. Don't do that. Don't

---

[2]To be fair to staffers it should be emphasized that they generally gave candidates high marks for their attitudes and intelligence. Many said, directly or indirectly, that they considered it an honor to have the opportunity to work with so many fine young people.

wait until September of your senior year. I can pick out the serious ones and the spur-of-the-moment-types. I can tell the difference and it means something to me."

A staffer from Arkansas: "They make mistakes with their paperwork and many don't complete their files. Lots just duplicate their paperwork for some other congressman and send it here. That is a mistake and they get a little upset when we tell them that. We recommend that they keep separate files and that they photocopy everything they send off so they can keep a record of everything in their own file. When they can't follow directions, it is a warning flag for me."

Another staffer from Arkansas: "They put things off till the last minute and don't realize that I have responsibilities other than handling academy nominations. We have deadlines to meet, too. When a kid pushes me because he has procrastinated, it is going to affect his overall rating.

"Also, don't let the parents get involved with the congressman's office. You do everything yourself. By doing so, you are giving this office an opportunity to know you can handle a stressful situation. If you don't have a letter from a law official [verifying that the candidate has never committed a felony--an endorsement that some offices require], don't have your mom call and ask what kind of letter we are looking for. You call me and I'll explain it to you. If you have mom call and mom go out and get the letter, that isn't showing me that you are responsible."

A staffer from Pennsylvania: "My biggest problem is that kids do not follow up on their application. They think once they have sent it off, that's it. I do my best to contact the kids but I know that the senators get so many applications that they can't do that. Those kids get hurt just because they do not follow up."

The staffer from Nevada: "Leadership is what it is all about and they should be able to demonstrate leadership from the moment they start the application. I am not impressed by the child if his parents call me and say, 'What else does Johnny need for his files?' I always wonder what Johnny can do."

A staffer from Ohio: "We get a lot of calls from parents and I'm not saying that is wrong. But, if young people are serious about going to an academy, they should make the calls themselves. They should learn how to do this on their own and they should call again if they have questions. This shows maturity and I will remember a kid like that."

Another staffer from Ohio was more adamant about parent involvement: "I get these calls all the time. 'My Freddie is interested in going to the Naval Academy, etc,' and I say, 'That is well and fine but let us hear from Freddie.' I guess the initial call is fine, but from then on it should be the kid who calls. And to the kid I would say, 'If you don't have the wherewithal to do things for yourself, you don't belong in an academy.'"

The same staffer also had strong feelings about the letters of recommendation candidates submit: "It is really dumb when they submit a whole pile of letters--one had sixteen sent--another had twenty and I was about to kill him! I have to write and acknowledge all of them! We ask for just three and we specify that they should be from persons who know them, who have been in contact with them, know their abilities, know their leadership potential, truly know them as a person. It is not going to impress me that honorable Joe Schmo who knew the kid's parents in the forties writes a letter--I'm not even going to put those kinds of letters in the file--I have to make four sets and I'm not going to duplicate all of those. Then there are those from the neighbor and Aunt Tillie that tell what a fine person the boy is. I won't put those letters in. Our panel who reviews them doesn't care if your Aunt Tillie says you are a sweetheart and you mow her lawn. They are looking for leaders, not sweethearts."

An Arizona staffer who complained about the same problem said: "...you know what I do when the applicant doesn't follow instructions and has a whole batch of letters sent? When I get to the Xerox machine to duplicate the letters for the committee, I take the first three letters, no matter who they are from, and I duplicate them. Those are the only letters that the committee sees and the candidate might be hurt if those aren't the best letters. I'm sorry, but that's the way it is. If the candidates can't follow the simple instructions that we give them, how can they expect to get by [at an academy]."

Another Ohio staffer probably summed up what most staffers think when they get extra letters of recommendation: "It is annoying to us and actually silly to do that. What the person is really saying is that my application demands much more attention that somebody else's--that I am worth more than somebody else. To me there is an inverse relationship that is being revealed here. Those who are the tops do what we ask them to do. The others are more nervous and might not be as qualified--they are the ones who try to get a lot of impressive people to send letters."

Another Ohio staffer said: "Being too persistent can also be a problem. Some think they are impressing us by sending something in every week. We don't need a constant weekly update...we don't like stuff trickling in and instead of helping your case it shows that you are disorganized. Also, we are not impressed with attendance awards or twenty page essays on why you will make a good cadet. We don't request that and we don't want it...we had one kid who put a whole book together--that and fifty cents would get him a cup of coffee."

Said still another Ohio staffer: "They often leave out the thing that impresses my congressman the most. He likes to see evidence that they have done part time work even if it is only delivering newspapers or baby sitting..."

An Iowa staffer mentioned a problem that probably confuses a number of candidates: "I think many of the candidates feel that if they get a nomination, they will automatically get into an academy. The problem with this attitude is that some have low or just average board scores and rather than take the test over again and try to improve them, they assume that because they got a nomination that their scores will be overlooked. Then, when they don't get an appointment, they are upset. Get this point across in your book. Tell them to pay attention to their scores even if they do get a nomination. The nomination definitely does not mean that their scores will be overlooked."

A Nebraska staffer makes another point: "Parents may think they are helping the kid by calling the Academy. They are wrong. Advise them not to call about an application. The Academies are much more anxious to deal with the kids. For example, one kid from here was considered medically unqualified by an academy, but he took matters in his own hands. He left here and drove all night to the academy and proved to them that he was okay. It blew the academy officials away when the kid did that and they were so impressed that they gave him a waiver. They want to see desire, but they want to see it on the part of the kid."

One final point was made by an Ohio staffer. She was commenting about all the excuses that parents make for kids--excuses that never impress her. But there was one excuse they make, which they think will help the son or daughter, but which actually turns out to be a very condemning statement that can hurt the candidate.

Said the staffer: "When they make the excuse that the son or daughter freezes up on tests and therefore is a better student than the ACT or SAT scores show, that is a very bad thing to say. After all, they give tests at the academies--hard tests. And they are under terrific pressure all the time...they are tested in a hundred ways. Can parents really believe that we would send somebody to an academy who can't stand the pressure of a test?"

Filling out the forms, writing essays, meeting deadlines, soliciting letters of recommendation--those are the main tasks that are involved in obtaining a congressional nomination. But for many congressmen, there is an additional hurdle that the candidate must clear--a difficult one. That is the personal interview, usually before a panel of adults from the community or region. Advice on how to get over this hurdle successfully is the subject of the next two chapters.

TWELVE
INTERVIEWS: WHAT THEY
ARE GOING TO ASK YOU

Many congressmen enlist the help of persons from their districts/states to evaluate candidates for nominations to the service academies. Usually such persons serve on panels which examine candidate's files and conduct interviews. For some congressmen the panelists have an intermediate role. They rate the candidates; however, the ratings are turned over to staffers and congressmen who make the final decisions.

Many other congressmen stay completely away from the decision process. In those cases the responsibility for selecting nominees is delegated to the panelists. They make the final decisions, including the designation of the principal nominee and the ranking of the numbered alternates when that method is used.

What kinds of persons serve on congressional panels?

Often they are professionals--educators, lawyers, accountants, judges, engineers, doctors and dentists. Retired military professionals--often graduates of a service academy--are found on many committees. But there is no way to categorize some of the others who serve. The author interviewed more than thirty panelists and they included a farmer, a former anti Vietnam protest leader, a social security administrator, the writer of a column for women, and the owner of a Mexican food restaurant.

When you go to be interviewed, you can expect that most of the panelists will have had anywhere from several days to a few weeks to study your complete file. They will have read your letters of recommendation, noted your academic achievements and test scores, evaluated your extracurricular activities and read any personal statements that you might have written. In short, they already know some things about the "paper" person. What they will be looking for in the interview is a chance to verify what has been said about you and the opportunity to measure certain personal characteristics they cannot evaluate on paper.

Like motivation. What is the motivation behind your desire to attend the Naval Academy? Are you going for the right reasons or the wrong reasons? Some are skeptical about what you might have already written on paper about your reasons for going. They will want to dig deeper, with a variety of questions, and will be trying to uncover the truth, whatever it is.

And like attitude. What is your attitude about handling the rigors and loss of personal freedom at the Academy? Do you want to try it and if you do not like it, come home? Are you going to stick it out all four years? Do you believe in sacrificing some of your personal freedom in order to serve twenty or thirty years in a military career? Are you going to the Academy for a good education so you can "take five and dive"-- serve the minimum five years, get out, then take advantage of the high respect the business world gives the Naval Academy graduate? Do you care about what is going

103

on in your country and the world?

And like poise, level-headedness, humility, potential military bearing and honesty. Is this the kind of person who will be able to lead people into combat? Is this the kind of person who will remain calm when subordinates are paralyzed with fear. Is this the kind of person who, when in a position of command, can spend lives judiciously when some lives have to be lost? Will this person be able to engender trust in superiors and subordinates? How will this person handle authority and power; will he or she exhibit humility or arrogance?

Those are some of the things the panelists will be looking for. But, some will try to get their answers indirectly. They will ask questions, but what you reply may not be as important to them as HOW you reply. The purpose of several questions will be to give panelists a chance to evaluate you on the *way* you can express yourself and the *way* you can handle yourself under the pressure of questioning.

Now for the questions. Every panelist who was interviewed was asked to name, (1) questions that cause the most trouble for candidates, and (2) questions they personally like to ask or which they believe are important in evaluating a candidate. Here are some of those questions, along with comments on what the interrogator is seeking when the questions are asked.

1. WHY DO YOU WANT TO GO TO THE NAVAL ACADEMY?

It is practically guaranteed that this question, or some version of it, will be asked. And, of course, you would have expected this question, right?

Candidates may go into interviews expecting this question, but you might be surprised to learn that most panelists said this was the one question that was the most difficult for candidates to answer. Said an attorney from Pennsylvania: "Part of the problem is that their answers are so predictable. They'll say, 'It is something I have wanted since I was a child.' That doesn't tell me why--it just says that I want it. Or they will say, 'I have read about it somewhere and I've always wanted to do that.' That isn't any more helpful.

"Another predictable but useless reply is, 'I think it would be a challenge.' That doesn't tell me anything, either.

"I think they have to dig deeper for the answer to this question. They should relate their answer to their own personality--they should personalize it a little more-- they have to talk about their goals and ambitions. They have to express their feelings to the extent that they are telling something about themselves. It is these personal kinds of answers that are impressive."

Said a retired Navy captain from Ohio: "When I hear them say, 'I want to go to the Naval Academy because I like to sail and like ships,' that really turns me off. The Academy is basically an engineering school and having a career as a naval officer doesn't mean that the officer is going to serve on ships for thirty years--he is going to be doing all kinds of things. Another one that turns me off is, 'I have always wanted to fly airplanes.' They have to want more than that. If they just want to fly, they can go to a flying school someplace."

Said another attorney from Pennsylvania: "When they say they want to go because it is an opportunity to get a tremendous education, that turns me off--I don't want to hear that. Likewise, I am not impressed to hear that a guidance counselor has told them about it and it seems like it is a good idea.

"I like to hear things that indicate a strong motivation and commitment. I like to hear them talk about the Academy and tell what they like about it--what they observed if they went there for a visit--what they heard from midshipmen or naval officers-- things that show a depth of knowledge--things that show they have made an effort to learn about it.

"I am also impressed when I hear things like, 'It has always been my dream to have a military career because...,' or 'I know myself well enough to know that I like a disciplined environment,' or 'One of my favorite things to do is to read about battles and wars,' or 'I have grown up hearing my father, a retired officer, and my uncle who spent 30 years in the Marine Corps, telling about their experiences. I liked those stories and I would like the opportunity to experience some of the kinds of things they experienced,'--those are the statements that show motivation on the part of the kid-- they show that the kid knows what he is getting into. They are personal and you know that they aren't rote, pat answers--that the kid is not just giving a canned response to the question."

Still another attorney from Pennsylvania: "I'm looking for strong motivation when they answer that question. I am not impressed by someone saying that he wants to get a good education, or that I can't afford to go to a regular college and this is going to pay my way. Service academies are something special and if your purpose is to be a doctor, there are other ways to do that other than with a military education at an academy.

"What I do like to hear is a kid who has personal reasons for wanting to make a career out of the service--'I really love the discipline of the Marines; I have read this book and that book about them, etc.' This kind of a kid isn't just looking for a free ticket to a graduate school. He is going to have an advantage in the voting from our panelists."

Said an elementary principal from Ohio: "If I were giving advice to a relative going before our panel [a hypothetical situation posed by the author], I would remind him that we are looking for someone who is interested in what he can give his country and he does not want to come across as a person looking for a stepping stone to get an education. In other words, it really needs to be something that he wants to do with his life."

Said a former high school teacher, counselor and retired high school dean of students from Washington: "So many say [in response to the question], 'I want to go because I can get a good education free.' They haven't thought through the whole process--they haven't checked out the details. When we come back and ask, 'Do you realize this or that?' they can't respond. Of course, we see the con artists all the time-- those who try to impress us but everybody sees through them immediately. I would advise kids to really think deeply about why they want to go to an academy and it is always impressive if they know a lot about it."

Said a retired navy commander and Blue and Gold Officer from Wyoming: "When they say I want to go because my dad or brother went, I put them on the back burner because I don't think that is reason enough. I remember I asked one kid if he thought he could hack the mental and physical pressure and he said, 'Oh, yes, my father was a major in the army and I know I can succeed.' I didn't recommend him to the Naval Academy but he ended up with an appointment to West Point and beat his parents home--he dropped out right after he got there. I don't put a whole lot of credence in kids whose only reason for going is because their parents were military people."

2. WHAT ARE YOUR ALTERNATIVES IF YOU DO NOT GET INTO THE NAVAL ACADEMY?

This question is usually asked to determine two things. First, has the candidate done enough research to know that there are alternate ways to become a naval officer--ways such as NROTC which might be much better for the candidate. Second, when the candidate says that his reason for going to the Naval Academy is so he can have a career as a naval officer, the strength of his motivation can be verified by evidence of alternate planning.

Here are some of the panelists' comments on the question:

Said a high school counselor from Pennsylvania: "It is unbelievable to me how most kids who come before our panel have thought so little about alternatives. When they answer, they say they have two or three other schools in mind but not two or three other careers, so I strongly wonder how interested they are in a military career. I believe if they are of academy material, they will have firm plans already made--plan b, which is NROTC, or plan c, which is OTS [Officer Training School]. On our panel we really look at thoroughness of preparation--if they have alternate plans, that tells us that they have done lots of thinking and that they are not going just for the prestige or because they can save their parents a hundred thousand dollars."

Said a retired Army general from Ohio: "We ask that question because we believe that candidates who are really interested in a military career will give the impression they will get into the uniform any way they can. They may not say that in so many words, but that perception exists when they talk intelligently and convincingly about their alternate plans for a military career."

Said a female author and women's columnist from Nebraska: "We are all impressed when, after we have asked if they have explored the ROTC alternatives, they say, 'Oh, yes, I have already signed up.' That says they are serious, that they really want to be in the service."

3. WHERE DO YOU SEE YOURSELF IN FIVE, TEN, FIFTEEN OR TWENTY YEARS?

This question is more specifically designed to elicit the intentions of the candidate regarding a career in the naval service.

Panelists' comments:

Said a dentist from Texas: "Kids really have trouble with that question because it is so hard for them to project themselves into the future. A bad answer would be that they would be practicing medicine--if that is their ambition they need to go some route other than a service academy. A good answer is that they would stay in the military as long as they are needed and as long as they have something to offer.

"What is most important in answering that question is to be truthful. We all agree

106

after the candidate leaves on those who are not sincere--those who are telling us what they think we want to hear. I think you should stress to candidates how easily we can tell who is putting us on. Tell the candidates to be truthful, especially with this question, because we know how hard it is for anyone of that age to make a true commitment or know exactly what they will be doing."

Said a university professor from Pennsylvania: "When they say, 'I have decided that the military is going to be my career and I want a good career education,' that is a bunch of malarkey. He is trying to sell me. He can say, 'I'm thinking about a military career, but I don't know for sure that is what I'll be doing. That's okay, but anybody who tells me at eighteen that he knows he is going to be a professional soldier, that is malarkey. He has to be a lot more mature than the kids at the university where I'm teaching because they are never that sure about their future."

Said another retired Army general from Ohio: "When we ask that question, a career commitment isn't that strong a factor with us. We do get a little concerned with a Rambo attitude and when they say they want to serve in the military for the rest of their life. We have no problem with a kid who says he wants to serve a number of years then evaluate. Frankly, we get concerned when they don't say something like that. We sense that they are telling us what we want to hear and that is a bad mistake. All of us can see through that."

Said a contract negotiator from Ohio: "I'm skeptical of someone who says I am going to make it a thirty-year career. The best answer is: I think I want a career at this time but I might get a wife and kids and they may hate that life. I do think if a candidate says he definitely wants a career he should also give two or three reasons why--I want to do this and that. That means that he has given some serious thought to the career and that means that they also have given serious thought about the Academy. That means they are motivated."

Said an accountant from Iowa and a Vietnam veteran: "We have never looked favorably at those with real staunch attitudes on what the military should be--we are not interested in Rambo types. We are leery of those types."

4. HOW ARE YOU GOING TO HANDLE THE PRESSURE AT THE ACADEMY?

The aim of this question is to learn how extensively candidates have researched the Academy. Will candidates respond in generalities or discuss specific kinds of pressures that midshipmen face. Candidates who can be the most specific about the pressures and their own feelings will be the ones who have the most knowledge of the Academy, and the ones who have done the most thinking about it. Indirectly, this shows strong motivation, which is the ultimate characteristic any panel is looking for.

Panelist's comments:

The high school counselor from Pennsylvania: "As they sit there looking sharp with their 1200 SATs and athletic awards, I say, 'How can a person used to being at the top survive when they put you at the bottom of the heap and rub your nose in it? What makes you think you can take orders?' A lot of them squirm and have a difficult time answering. The best answers come from athletes who have been used to high-level competition. Some will cite experiences with their coaches where they had to take orders and when they were chewed out in front of others. Others tell how they learned to keep cool when everybody was shouting at them and while referees and umpires were making calls that went against them. If a kid shrugs his shoulders and says, 'Well, I just know I can take it,' he might as well stop now because I know he hasn't thought about it."

Said a retired school superintendent from Pennsylvania: "Lots of the kids don't know how to answer that question, probably because they haven't done enough research and don't know what they are getting into. To pass off the pressure and discipline casually as some do, saying, 'Oh, that's not going to be hard to handle,' they are giving us a bad answer. Those who give specific examples of how they have handled stress such as telling how their football coach is very tough and how they had to do what they were told, or if they give examples of difficult situations when they could have quit but did not--those would be good answers."

5. HOW ARE YOU PREPARING PHYSICALLY FOR THE ACADEMY?

This is a straight-forward question designed to see if the candidate truly understands the physical nature of the midshipman's life.

Panelists' comments:

One of the attorneys from Pennsylvania: "We always ask that question and many times we don't get good answers. For example, one girl said that she was prepared because of her cheerleading. We jumped on that--it didn't seem relevant at all. The ones who impress us are those who explain their fitness plan, how far they are running and what they are doing to develop their upperbody strength. That is much better than just telling us about their sports activities."

One of the retired Army generals from Ohio: "I am very concerned about the physical condition of the candidates. If a candidate is obviously overweight, I will not grade that person highly because military life is very demanding physically. If the person is real flabby, obviously that person doesn't have a great deal of personal interest in being a cadet regardless of which academy. It is true that they are going to get into a physical conditioning program, but if they are not in shape, they may never get there."

The retired Navy commander from Wyoming: "We always try to pin this down [the physical preparation] because we have had young people drop out of the academies because they cannot be at the top of the class academically or physically. They discover that there are many better than they are and they cannot handle it. In Wyoming they were wonder women and super studs. When these types come before our panel, they want us to think that, because they are athletic wonders, they are physically prepared."

6. TELL US WHAT YOU THINK OF THE BOSNIAN SITUATION?

The above question is just one example to illustrate the kind of current event question a panel may ask. They know that young people do not always keep up on such things, and they are not expecting detailed answers. One thing they are looking for is how candidates handle themselves when they do not know an answer. Do they try to cover up this lack of knowledge? Are they obviously embarrassed? Do they make excuses?

If you have not been keeping up with current events, do not worry about this question. Be honest with the panel and keep your poise.

Panelists' comments:

The retired Navy captain from Ohio: "Generally the questions aren't hard. We just want to see if they are well rounded and know something about world affairs."

The elementary school principal from Ohio: "We talk about current events and try to draw out what the candidates know about what is going on around them. If they do not know the answer, they usually stumble around and try to give an answer. It is better when they say they do not know. It is all right to say, 'I don't know.'

"There may be other questions that they cannot answer, but the panel will admire the guts of one who can say, 'I don't know.' That shows confidence and the ability to make decisions--that the candidate knows when to say what."

The retired Army general from Ohio: "When we ask, 'Are you up on current events, international and domestic,' we get everything from a 'yes' to a doubtful 'no.' Often we will ask, 'What single event in the news today do you consider to be most important?' You can anticipate a complete spectrum of replies. The majority will give some kind of answer and a few will give outstanding answers. But it is not only the substance of their answers that we are looking at, but in the way they deliver their answers. We are looking for self confidence in the way they answer. There is a difference between someone who shuffles into an answer compared to one who says it in a way that makes you want to believe him."

7. WHAT SPARK GOT YOU INTERESTED IN THE NAVAL ACADEMY?

Throughout the interview you may get a variety of questions designed to find out whether it is you or your parents who really want the nomination. This is a typical question of that type. Sometimes the panel will be more direct and ask: What do your parents think of you going to the Academy? They want to know if you have your parents' support, which is almost essential, but they are also probing to see if they can pick up any signs that your parents are pushing you.

Also the panel is looking for spur-of-the-moment types of candidates--ones who decide that it would be a neat idea to apply while in their senior year.

Panelists' comments:

A teacher from Iowa: "We always ask that question. We are always trying to flush out whether it is dad and mom or the kid who wants it."

The dentist from Texas: "We really look favorably on those who have read a lot about military kinds of things, leaders, etc. It shows motivation. What we don't like to see is a kid who just decided during his senior year that an academy sounds like a good idea but who has done none of this background reading. We'll ask them what got them interested just so we can find out how long they have had the desire to go."

8. WHO IS YOUR HERO, OR WHAT PERSON DO YOU ADMIRE THE MOST OR WHAT PERSON WOULD YOU MOST LIKE TO BE, AND WHY?

Some version of this question is asked by many panels. It is often a difficult

109

question for candidates because they are not expecting it and they often get flustered trying to come up with a person who they think would be acceptable to the committee--they might admire a currently popular rock singer but think the panel would not be impressed--which is probably true in many cases. Also, discretion should be used. In some cases the philosophy of the panelists reflects the political philosophy of the congressman. Therefore, if Ronald Reagan or Barry Goldwater or Bull Halsey happened to be your hero, that might play well with the panel for a conservative Republican congressman; it might not go over so well with the panel of a liberal Democrat.

Candidates also have trouble explaining why they admire a certain person so much. In preparing for this question think about your reasons and be ready to explain them.

Panelists' comments:

Said a chemistry teacher from Ohio: "That is my favorite question and I find it interesting how kids react. One said Superman because he can help everybody. Another said Ronald Reagan because he liked to be in a command position. They also have trouble with it. For example, one kid said Gandhi, then everybody wanted to know why he was interested in the military because Gandhi was a pacifist."

Said a retired Air Force Lt. Colonel from Pennsylvania: "Other panelists always ask that question and I don't agree with it. I would rather see a kid say, 'I would not want to be somebody else; I want to be the best that I can be and do whatever I am capable of doing. I want to be the best pilot or soldier or whatever. I respect a lot of people and I would like to take the best traits of everybody or some from each, but not to be somebody else. I would still want to be myself.'"

The dentist from Texas: "Lots have a strong father image and the father may be the driving force rather than the individual himself. When we ask that question, we are trying to decide who the driving force really is--is it the individual or is it engineered from home?"

9. WHAT IS LEADERSHIP AND WHAT MAKES YOU THINK YOU CAN BE A LEADER?

This is a difficult question for many candidates, probably because they haven't thought much about it even though they been leaders in their high schools. One panelist, a retired Army general from Ohio, expounded on this question at great length. He started his career as a private, landed on Normandy Beach in World War II as a corporal, received a commission while his unit was suffering 85 percent casualties, then went on to a long career highlighted with many leadership challenges. His comments about leadership, which follow, are based on extensive experience and are very appropriate for a candidate who is trying to measure his own leadership potential.

"What I am trying to get out of them [when asked about leadership] is to see if they are self-motivated--that is the most important leadership trait. You can't motivate others, which is what a leader does, unless you have the motivation yourself. Real enthusiasm is contagious and if you have it, somebody else is going to get it from you.

"We have a tendency to blend management with leadership and the two are different. Management will get the tools of battle, the people and equipment to the

110

right place at the right time but leadership will determine who will win the battle. Leadership is emotional and management is technical--the latter involves calculations and logistics--it means putting the numbers together so the formula works out.

"Leadership gets people charged up so that they do things they don't want to do. The right kind of leadership will get the job done without being told and the leader will enjoy doing it. If your enthusiasm is such that it takes you three hours to stop vibrating after you come home, you have created a disease that is contagious.

"Many kids confuse leadership with popularity--I can tell that from the answers they give us. They equate leadership with the kind of people they associate with, and that is an artificial feeling because they are with people who feel like they do about things. I am looking for the person who is self-motivated enough that his enthusiasm will become contagious and motivate others. Often that kid is not one who worries about popularity, but is an independent youngster who sets his own standards. That independence is very important to being a leader."

10. EXPLAIN HOW YOU HAVE HANDLED FAILURE OR VERY STRESSFUL SITUATIONS IN YOUR LIFE.

Many who apply to the Naval Academy have been high achievers in their high schools--top students, top athletes, tops in popularity. To such students the idea of failure is either repugnant or is completely excluded from their minds. They are winners, period.

The winning attitude is very important, of course, but anyone thinking of going to the Naval Academy has to realize that they are very likely to fail something. The pressure created by the upper classmen almost guarantees that the plebe will fail inspections or fail to memorize things assigned. The upper classmen want to teach plebes to pick themselves up from failure and to keep going. They have to make sure the plebe is not one who quits when the going gets tough.

The panelists know all of this, of course, and they are aware that some young people just cannot accept failure of any kind. When they ask you that question, they want to hear of specific examples where you have picked yourself up after a failure and carried on. They want to see genuine humility. They want to see a young person who has a winning attitude but who is not afraid to fail and try again.

By asking about your most stressful situations they want to hear of specific experiences and how you handled yourself. That does not mean that they expect to hear that you have always handled stress well. Many young people handle stressful situations poorly. But some learn from those experiences and improve; others do not-- they continue to handle stress poorly. The panelists would like for you to cite specific experiences that enabled you to improve the way you handle stress.

Panelists' comments:

The retired Navy Captain from Ohio: "This is a very hard question for some of them, sometimes because they either haven't failed significantly or because they do not want to admit it. When you ask about stressful situations, you can get into things that are very hard for kids to talk about. For many kids the breakup of their family by divorce and all the consequent problems is a common source of stress. They will be impressive if they can explain how they coped and how they learned from those kinds of experiences."

Said a psychologist and former Vietnam War protest leader from Arizona: "One kid came in and explained how he had lost his father when he was a freshman and how he worked forty hours a week to help support his family--all the while being an honor student and excelling in sports. I was really impressed at the way he could talk about all of that stress and I rated him very high."

11. WHAT ARE YOUR BEST AND WORST CHARACTERISTICS?

This question is frequently asked and it bothers a lot of candidates. Just be careful when discussing your worst characteristics. The panel is not looking for a confession of sins--they do not want to know all of the bad things you have done. Rather, they are trying to find out if you have evaluated yourself, identified your weaknesses, and are making some attempts to improve them. If you do discuss a weakness, you should be prepared to describe the specific things you are doing to correct it.

Panelists' comments:

The chemistry teacher from Ohio: "When you ask a kid to describe his strengths, or ask him, 'Why should we pick you instead of someone else?', the kid will respond in one of two ways. One will respond in a way that we can see that he is proud of what he has done--that he is telling us all the good things he has achieved. He does it in an honest, straight-forward way.

"The other kid comes off as cocky and as one who brags. This kind is more defensive, more insecure and it shows."

Said a retired teacher from Ohio: "When we ask a kid to talk about his weaknesses, his answers don't make or break him. We just ask those questions to spark a monologue from the kid. We just want to see how he can handle himself while talking about his weaknesses."

The author and woman's columnist from Nebraska: "When we ask the kid to tell about his greatest strengths, they have problems. They have trouble blowing their own horn. We have taught them humility for so long they have trouble saying, 'I was the top science student.' But they have to do it--there is no advocate there who is going to tell us what a great person they are. If they don't give us information, we will never know it. And that is bad because their competition is made up of other top students just like themselves. I know some might think they will come across as being cocky. But don't worry about that. Just talk in a cheerful, smiling manner--you would be amazed what a smile can do to a committee--and be honest and sincere."

The contract negotiator from Ohio: "If you don't toot your own horn, nobody else is going to do it for you. But it is how it is said. You can phrase it like bragging or you can describe it in a way that does not appear to be bragging. But if that panel member asks that question [describe your strengths], he is asking you to open up and you should go into detail on everything--we're ready for that."

12. WHAT DO YOU KNOW ABOUT THE HONOR CODE? COULD YOU TURN IN YOUR BEST FRIEND IF HE WAS CAUGHT CHEATING?

This is a very popular question among panelists and one that can create some problems for you if you are not ready with an answer. What they are trying to determine is how much research you have done on the Academy and how much thinking you have done trying to project yourself into the Academy environment where you have to live honorably.

One of the best ways you can impress a committee is to explain that the Naval Academy does not have an honor code; it has the Honor Concept, which is quite different. If you will read Chapter 21 in this book, you will be able to impress any panel with your knowledge of the Honor Concept.

The preceding questions are the ones that are most likely to be asked during an interview. They are also the questions that create the most problems for candidates. But there are other questions that panelists ask, which are of lesser importance and which are probably asked less frequently. The following are some examples:

DO YOU HAVE A GIRLFRIEND/BOYFRIEND? IF SO, WHAT DO YOU PLAN TO DO ABOUT HER/HIM SHOULD YOU GO TO THE NAVAL ACADEMY?

Some panelists who mentioned this question also disagreed with it, saying that it a personal matter of the candidate and none of the panel's business. Others felt that it was a legitimate question because a serious romantic commitment might undermine a midshipman's determination to remain at the Academy. In either case, if you are asked the question, you will have to give some kind of answer.

WHAT BOOKS HAVE YOU READ LATELY? WHAT IS YOUR FAVORITE BOOK? WHAT MAGAZINES OR NEWSPAPERS DO YOU READ?

These are straight-forward questions designed to find out how well rounded you are as a person. If you have been reading a newspaper and a news magazine, it might help convince the panel of your motivation if you explain that current events knowledge is required of plebes and that you are getting a head start by reading this or that magazine and newspaper.

DESCRIBE YOUR EXPERIENCES WITH PART TIME EMPLOYMENT.

Some panelists sincerely believe that any candidate for a service academy should have some experience working in the real world--and they do not fail to ask each candidate to expound on their experiences. If you have not had such experience, it is recommended that you be ready with a good answer for why you have not.

WE NOTICE THAT YOU RECEIVED A C IN CHEMISTRY. WHAT MAKES YOU THINK YOU CAN GO TO THE NAVAL ACADEMY AND PASS PLEBE-KILLER CHEMISTRY?

Some panelists will look over your academic record and will question any academic deficiencies or discrepancies. You should be ready to explain anything of this nature. One panelist suggested that this is an occasion when self-deprecating humor might be appropriate. She mentioned one young man who had a cumulative GPA of 3.85 and a panelist asked out of curiosity, "What did you get the "B" in?" The young man replied with a smile, "In boys home ec," and the panel laughed. In the same tone, you might defend a low grade by saying, "That was the semester I fell in love but I learned my lesson and I will never do that again." Of course, in your own case, humor might not be appropriate, but however you answer, you should reply confidently and not appear defensive.

YOU SAY YOU HAVE NEVER BEEN AWAY FROM HOME FOR MORE THAN A WEEK. THEN HOW ARE YOU GOING TO COPE WITH HOMESICKNESS IF YOU GO TO THE NAVAL ACADEMY?

Some panelists are aware that homesickness is a serious affliction for plebes, so serious that it is a contributing factor to many dropouts. It will help your case if you can describe anything specific that you plan to do to combat that affliction.

YOU ARE A GREAT BIG GUY. HOW ARE YOU GOING TO REACT WHEN A LITTLE FIRST-CLASS FEMALE STARTS YELLING AT YOU?

Some panelists, both male and female, have strong feelings about sexism in the military services and they do not want to send persons to a military academy who harbor sexist beliefs. If you get such a question, you should indicate that you are prepared to respect and obey your commanding officer regardless of sex, race, or other personal circumstances.

Along that same theme, one panelist also cautioned candidates not to speak deprecatingly of their mothers by saying that they are just housewives. According to the panelist that kind of answer can really antagonize a feminist who might be on the panel.

Another panelist remembered a humorous answer given my a big male candidate. He said, "I can't see any big deal about that; my mother has been doing that for years!"

WHAT VOLUNTEER WORK HAVE YOU DONE IN YOUR SCHOOL OR COMMUNITY?

That question is designed to find out how generous you are with your time and how important service to others is to you. The implication is that those who have not been generous may not be the best persons to give service to their country. If you have not done much volunteer work, you should be ready with specific reasons why you have not.

This concludes the discussion on *what* you will be asked to discuss in your interviews. The subject for the next chapter is *how* you should perform while you are in them.

114

THIRTEEN
INTERVIEWS: HOW YOU SHOULD
CONDUCT YOURSELF

Congressional staffers, as well as panelists, passed on a lot of advice on how candidates should conduct themselves in interviews. This chapter is based primarily upon that advice and is mainly a collection of their "do's" and "don'ts."

To begin, we will assume that you are at home preparing for one of your interviews. What should you be doing?

Several persons, including some cadets and midshipmen at the service academies, recommended that you practice before you go before any panel. They recommend that you arrange one or more mock interviews, and that the person or persons who conduct them should ask the types of questions that a congressional panel would ask.

Who can conduct such interviews? One possibility is to get one of you school counselors to do it--possibly with the help of another counselor or teacher.

But probably the best choice, if you can manage it, is to recruit one or more retired military officers. During a service career any officer will have served on numerous panels and interviewed hundreds of officers and enlisted persons. They know how to ask questions like a congressional panelist and it would be unusual to find one who would not be delighted to help a serious candidate.

If you practice, it will pay off. Numerous cadets and midshipmen have commented on how much better they handled themselves in their second or third interview. Even if you are thoroughly prepared to answer a panel's questions, unless you have actually done it once, you cannot be sure that your answers will be given effectively. And you do not know but what your *first* interview might be the one most critical in getting a nomination.

So try to arrange one or more mock interviews. And if you are mentally debating whether or not you might do this, remember a comment made by a cadet at West Point when one of his friends recommended the mock interview. "Naw, that's no good," the cadet said. "What kid is going to go out and arrange something like that?" Just remember: *the cadet is right.* Most candidates will not go to the trouble of arranging a mock interview. So take advantage of that fact. Do it, and get ahead of your competition.

Assume now that you have experienced one or more mock interviews. You have been critiqued; you have rethought some of your answers; now you are ready for the real thing. What next?

You should begin to plan what you are going to wear to the interview. Every panelist and staffer who commented on this subject said something like the following: Be sure to advise the young men to dress well. A sport coat, nice shirt and tie with shoes well shined would be the ideal dress. But if they do not have those kinds of clothes, they should make sure they wear the best they have.

Said one panelist: "Do not wear faddish clothes, loud clothes, jeans or warmup suits the way some who come before us do. I know some kids cannot afford real leather shoes and if this is perceived as the result of economic consequences, running shoes or tennis shoes will be overlooked.

"The really important thing is to be neat and color coordinated. And if you have any doubt about the matching or mismatching of clothes, get advice from someone who understands those things. There is nothing worse than to see a kid come in wearing a coat with a shirt and tie that clash with it. Also, if you have an expensive Rolex watch, leave it at home; few panelists like to see wealth flaunted."

The basic advice is much the same for young women. Dress conservatively in blouse, skirt and sweater or in a blazer-skirt outfit--or a nice dress. Most panelists specified that young women should not wear slacks or pantsuits, should not wear excessive makeup and should not wear party-type clothes such as they might wear to a dance. Said one panelist, "I'll never forget one girl who came in teetering on three-inch high heels; the panel was not impressed."

You should be notified well ahead of time when and where the interviews are to be conducted. Do not procrastinate until the last minute to arrange transportation if that might be a problem for you. And if you foresee a problem, for example, getting from Coon Rapids to Des Moines, Iowa, begin working on the problem early. Call the staffer or your Blue and Gold Officer or talk to your school counselor. Somebody will help you. Just do not miss an interview or be late for one unless there is a very good reason.

Let us move ahead. It is the day of your first interview and you are in the congressman's outer office, sitting among twenty or thirty candidates, all hopeful and ALL nervous. All nervous? Yes, absolutely. The only difference in the candidates is that some manage to hide their nervousness better than others.

And you? Are you ready to go in, poised and confident? Perhaps. But do not psych yourself into playing a role or of pretending to be somebody that you are not. Panelists are not impressed with actors. They can see through any act that you try to perform. You will not fool them so do not even think of trying.

You must be yourself. If you are nervous and you think it may show, do not worry about it. *The panel knows that everyone is nervous.* They expect that and they want you to come in and be your natural self. They are well aware that going to the Naval Academy may be a lifetime dream for you, that you might have worked hard for the last six years preparing for it. They will be sympathetic and likely to ignore some signs of your nervousness if you are trying to keep them under control.

However, there are some nervous affectations that panelists have mentioned that you should avoid if possible. Wringing of hands is one that was mentioned quite often. Place your hands in your lap or on the arms of the chair and keep them under control.

Excess fidgeting was also mentioned by panelists. You should avoid twisting and turning in your chair and repeatedly crossing and uncrossing your legs.

Slumping also was mentioned. The panelists will not expect you to sit ramrod straight, as you will learn to do if you become a plebe at the Naval Academy, but they do expect you to sit upright and in an attentive position.

But we are ahead of ourselves, because we have not yet taken you from the congressman's waiting room into the room with the panel. And, according to many

116

staffers and panelists, that transition, including the first minute of the interview, is the most difficult for candidates.

First impressions are lasting impressions--that is an old cliche, but an important one for the candidate to keep in mind. So here is what you should do to make a good first impression when you enter the interview room and meet the panel.

Typically, you will be escorted and introduced by the staffer. As this is being done, you should concentrate on one person, the chairperson of the panel who will most likely stand to greet you. Look the chairperson in the eye and, if it seems like the natural thing to do, advance and shake his or her hand *firmly* (a limp handshake is repugnant to most men--and probably women, too.). If in doubt whether you should shake hands or just sit down, take your cue from the chairperson. That is his or her job--to guide you and to try to make you comfortable.

Somebody--the staffer or the chairperson--will introduce you to the rest of the panel. You probably will not remember all their names, but try to remember at least the name of the chairperson. You can make this easy for yourself if you will ask the staffer for the names of the chairperson and panelists when you first arrive. You can copy their names and memorize them while you wait.

You are seated now in the "hot seat"; you have center stage all to yourself. What should you do and not do?

What you should do is *maintain eye contact* with the panelists, including the one who asks the question and the others as you make your reply.

The above recommendation is very important according to many of the panelists who were interviewed. Said one panelist, "That is the single, most important thing that you can tell a kid who is going before a panel. Have him make eye contact and keep it. Now I don't mean that he is to look at my hairline or at my chin or at my nose. I want the candidate looking at my eyes! I watch for this with each candidate. The ones who are insecure and lack confidence don't do it--at least that is my impression. Those who have poise and confidence in themselves do. And which do I want to send to a service academy? No way am I going to vote for a kid who doesn't have confidence in himself because he'll never make it."

The above statement was the strongest made by any panelist but you should realize that any panel could have someone who feels just as strongly. So now, before you even have an interview scheduled, practice looking into the eyes of the people you talk with. Do it with your teachers. Do it with your parents. Most of all, do it with strangers with whom you will have a tendency to drop your eyes. Also, this is one more reason why a mock interview can help you. You can practice making eye contact while answering questions when your performance is not being graded.

But now you are facing the real panel and one of them has just asked you a question. Here are some of the do's and don'ts that were passed on by panelists.

Do listen to the questions carefully. Panelists say not listening is one of the common faults of candidates.

Do answer each question if you can. That might seem like advice for an idiot but panelists say that many candidates stray from the question and end up discussing subjects that are not even relevant. Some panelists suspect that candidates do that just to avoid answers that are embarrassing. Others believe candidates stray because they did not listen carefully to the question. Still others believe that the candidates move to subjects they think they can use to impress the panel. But do not do that yourself. Stick to the question that is asked and answer it to the best of your ability.

Do not give short answers. Panelists are not likely to be pleased with candidates that they have to prod to talk with them. One reason you are there is because they want to hear how well you can communicate. They learn very little about you when you answer each question with just a few words. Of course, they might be turned off just as much by those who ramble on and on and say nothing. But there is a happy medium and you should find it. Also, when in doubt and you suspect that you might not have said enough about something, do not hesitate to stop and ask: "Would you like for me to go on and explain....." That way they will tell you if they wish to hear more.

Do not use high school slang or useless phrases. You must face the fact that most panelists will be impressed if you speak well, use good grammar and come across as a sincere candidate. They will not be impressed with the opposite. The use of bad grammar is a deadly sin for a candidate. But almost as bad are candidates who lace their conversation with "you knows" or "umms" and "uhs" or with teenage slang expressions that are currently fashionable.

Do be courteous. Look for genuine opportunities to say "thank you" and "please." For example, if the staffer has escorted you into the room and introduced you to the panel, thank her as she leaves--if that seems the natural thing to do. If a panelist has asked a question you do not quite understand, ask politely: "Sir, I am sorry but I don't quite understand your question. Would you please...."

Some candidates will wonder about addressing panelists as "sir" or "ma'am." In some parts of the country it is routine to address older persons that way whereas in other places the terms sound strange and foreign. If the latter is true where you are, just remember, should you go to the Naval Academy, every officer, every professor and every upper classman will be addressed as sir or ma'am, and you will continue using those terms with your superiors throughout your entire career--even if you become an admiral! So why not start now and get accustomed to the habit?

Do not make negative comments about other people. A few panelists mentioned that they were bothered when candidates made negative comments about teachers, coaches or others whom they thought had wronged them. Be positive when you can and if you must be negative, pick your statements carefully. You do not know whom you might be offending with a negative comment.

Don't feel you have to answer immediately. Candidates feel pressured when they sit before a panel and they often respond by blurting out answers that are not well thought out. There is an old expression for that. It is said such a person's tongue starts moving before the brain is in gear. Do not let that be said of you. Restrain yourself and take a moment, if necessary, to think over an answer before you give it. If you need longer, say to the panelist who asked the question, "Be patient, please. I need a moment or two to think about that." The panel will respect a candidate who can do this. It demonstrates that the candidate wants to be thorough and accurate, and it demonstrates poise and self confidence.

At the conclusion of the interview, the panel usually will ask candidates if they have any questions of them. Numerous panelists said that they were always impressed when a candidate does ask an intelligent question--something other than, "How soon am I going to know something?," which is what most candidates ask. Keep this in mind. If you cannot ask a good question, you should not ask something that you can find out from the staffer after you leave the panel.

One panelist suggested that candidates might use that opportunity to ask the panel if they had any advice for them.

Another panelist suggested that candidates should use that time to bring up points about themselves that the panel overlooked in their questioning. In subsequent interviews the author asked other panelists, "What if candidates use that time for their own questions to discuss something about themselves that the panel overlooked? For example, suppose a candidate said to the chairperson, "Sir, rather than ask a question, would you mind if I told you something about myself that might help my case?" Would the panel be offended? Would they be impressed?"

It was unanimous among the panelists who were queried: they believed that a candidate should do that. They believed that any panel can overlook things and if candidates do not take the initiative, the panel will never know something that could be important. As an example, one panelist recalled a candidate who had very few extracurricular activities listed but nobody questioned the candidate about that. Luckily, at the end of the interview the candidate said, "I think you should realize, when you look at my extracurricular activities, that my mother and father were divorced during my sophomore year and after that I had to work during the evenings to help support my mother and three sisters." According to the panelist, that statement, given at the end of the interview, was significant enough to persuade the panel that the candidate deserved a nomination.

Now the interview is over. The chairperson stands up and you stand up. What should you do?

By all means, thank the panel for giving you the opportunity to come before them. Say it with feeling and, if it seems like the natural thing to do, shake the chairperson's hand and perhaps the hands of the others. Then make your exit and thank the staffer.

That is it. If it is your last interview, you wait.

If you have other interviews coming up, sit down when you get home and critique yourself. What did you do right and what did you do wrong? Put those things down on paper and use those notes to prepare for the next interview. If you will do all of this, you are guaranteed of one thing. You will be far ahead of most of your competition because they are not going to be that analytical about themselves.

POSTSCRIPT:

A highly successful Blue and Gold Officer with 27 years of experience spoke with the author about this chapter and said that he would like to give some of his own advice. He has outstanding credentials--he is a graduate of the Naval Academy, served twenty years as a corporate vice president, taught graduate school business courses at a major university, and has served on hundreds of interview boards. His comments both reinforce and supplement the general advice given in this chapter. He said:

"They should definitely get some practice before they appear before a board even if it is only practice before a mirror. Stand before a mirror, stick out your hand and practice introducing yourself. Say your name, but say it proudly--I want to emphasize that--speak your name proudly, but watch yourself in the mirror. Do you look confident when you say it? If not, keep practicing. Now, practice smiling. Are just your lips smiling? That won't work. You've got to make your eyes smile. Check yourself in the mirror. Are your eyes smiling? If not, keep working on it.

"Now you are going before a board. The secretary or the staffer will introduce you. Next, I want you to walk to each member of the board and introduce yourself. Stick that hand out and give a firm handshake--I mean firm--there is nothing worse than a cold-fish handshake. When you're doing that, you look the person in the eye and you say your name just like you did when you practiced before the mirror. You say it proudly and your eyes should be smiling. Also, you should say the name of the panelist when you do this, "Mr So and So, I'm Jeff Jones." Do that with each and every person serving on the panel. You have to get their names before you go in--that's important.

"Next, when you sit down in your chair facing the board, scoot your back firmly against the back of the chair. This will keep you from squirming. You can sit there for twenty minutes this way. Practice this at home until you feel comfortable doing it.

"Now, when they ask you a question, look them firmly in the eye. Eye contact is extremely important--many will be like me; they will be looking for it. Also, when they ask you a question, answer it completely but do not elaborate on things they didn't ask you. Remember, they are asking the same questions to all candidates and mostly they are looking for how you handle yourself when you answer the questions. So they are as much interested in your body language as they are in how many math courses you took in high school, or whatever the question is.

"After they are finished asking you questions, *always* have at least one question for them. And don't ask just a dumb question; go in there with a good question in mind. Frankly, most of the boys I have seen come in and just sit there like bumps on a log. Do something creative to leave a lasting impression on the panel.

"When the interview is over, get up, walk over to each panelist and shake hands again. And I mean, shake hands with everybody! Don't fail to do this. Even if they don't stand up, go over to them and shake hands and repeat your name like you are damn proud of it. 'Jeff Jones, it was a pleasure to meet you, ma'am.' 'Jeff Jones, it was nice to meet you, sir.' 'Jeff Jones, I would appreciate your support, ma'am.' 'Jeff Jones, thanks for the interview, sir.' These are just some of the ways you can sign off.

"The most important thing: remember that a smile sells. I know, you're going to be jelly inside, but if you have what it takes, you can overcome that with a sincere smile."

FOURTEEN
ALTERNATE ROUTES TO THE ACADEMY

You have submitted all the paperwork required by the Naval Academy.

Your files are complete at all of your nomination sources and you have completed all of your interviews.

And now you wait, and wait. Weeks pass. Then you start getting the bad news. You are not nominated by your representative. You are not on the list of either senator or the vice-president.

Or, there was good news to begin with; you got a nomination. But then came the bad news; you did not get an appointment.[1]

Then what?

From that time on is it gloom and doom for you? Do you see yourself as a failure and with a dream that is over? Are you feeling sorry for yourself because you will never be a midshipman and will never be a graduate of the Naval Academy?

If you give up that easily, you probably should not have applied for the Naval Academy in the first place. The Academy is not for quitters. It is for those who have the mental capacity to fail and pick themselves up again and to continue pursuing their goal with even more determination.

This chapter is for those with that kind of determination. If you fail to get in the first time you apply, ask yourself one question. Am I really qualified for the Academy or can I become qualified in the future? If you can honestly say that the answer is "yes," and if you truly want to go to the Academy more than anything else, *do not give up!*

Here is why. In each entering class more than 300 of those who are appointed do not come in right out of high school. Roughly one-third of the new plebes get into the Academy by alternate routes. If you are determined to keep trying, one of those routes might be the right one for you.

So, how should you proceed?

You should first try to find out why you did not get a nomination or an appointment. To do this, telephone or, better, go in person to see the congressional

---

[1] Several persons have said that the Naval Academy is the slowest of the service academies to notify candidates of their appointments. Admissions personnel commented that they will sometimes wait as long as possible before rejecting a very close alternate until all issues, like medical tests, are resolved for the candidates just above them. If you receive notice of an appointment to another service academy, but your first choice is the Naval Academy, you are advised to hold off on accepting the appointment from the other academy until the deadline, which is usually around the first of May. Some have accepted the first appointment only to be sorry later when the Naval Academy appointment finally came through.

staffers who handled your nomination application. Speak with the staffers and tell them you need their help and advice. Ask them to give you some of the reasons why you did not get a nomination. Or, if you got a nomination but not an appointment, ask them if they would examine your file and give you an opinion on why you did not get appointed. Be courteous with your requests and emphasize the positive rather than the negative. Emphasize to them that you need this information so you can go on and improve yourself. If you will do all of that, it would be an unusual staffer who would not help you.

Also query your Blue and Gold Officer. Use the same approach that you used with the staffers. Ask the Blue and Golf Officer to counsel you and suggest reasons why you did not get a nomination or appointment. Then ask for advice on how you can improve yourself and thereby improve your chances of getting into the Academy the next time you apply.

Then sit down and analyze your case. List the problems and what can be done about them.

Is the problem low or average ACT or SAT scores? This is a common problem and one you might be able to do something about. You can prepare for the tests with books or special classes and retake them.[2] Also, be realistic with yourself. If your math score on the SAT is below 450, test books and special SAT prep classes may not allow you to bring your score above 600. That score is not a firm cut-off number but it is a score that thousands of your competitors have already made.

Is your problem low grades? For example, did you not work as hard as you could have during some of your high school career? This, too, is a common problem and there are several things you might do about it.

One alternative is to enroll in a summer college program where you can take courses in math, chemistry and English. And while you are taking the courses, study harder than you have ever studied in your life. Learn the material. Master it. And if you do, you will get good grades and you will have some teachers who will be pleased to write letters of recommendation for you. After the summer term you may want to take the ACT or SAT tests again. Also, you will need to reapply to the Academy and to all of your nomination sources. With another year of maturity, with better academic preparation and with all your experiences from the previous year to build upon, you should be a better candidate and stand a better chance of getting a nomination and an appointment.

---

[2]There is a school in Santa Barbara, California called the Northwestern Preparatory School, which specializes in helping service academy candidates raise their scores on the SAT. This is the school where the Naval Academy Foundation sends candidates when test score augmentation is the main preparatory objective. For information write: Northwestern Preparatory School, 3821 South San Francisquito Canyon Road, Green Valley, CA 91350. Their term is from July to December and for students without learning disabilities they routinely raise the SAT scores 100-125 points. However, the course is quite expensive and the minimums they will start with are 450 Math and 400 Verbal.)

But do not count on the appointment. You should always have an alternate plan to fall back upon and it should have been worked out during the early part of your senior year.

A good alternate plan is to apply for admission to one or more colleges or universities that have a Naval Reserve Officer Training Corps (NROTC). At the same time you should apply for an NROTC scholarship. Your Blue and Gold Officer can help you with the latter, or you can contact the officer in charge of scholarships at each institution.

You may or may not get an NROTC scholarship. If you do, you can go to the college or university, work as hard as you can, then reapply for the Naval Academy after you have completed your first year. With good grades and the recommendation of your unit commander, you might receive one of the appointments available to outstanding NROTC participants who want to switch to the Naval Academy.

Candidates may perceive one disadvantage of the above option. Even though one or two years of college credit will have been earned, the candidate will still have to complete four full years at the Naval Academy. The same is true for those who have completed all four years of college, except that a midshipman with this background would have more options for course selection at the Academy.

But there also are advantages, which are better explained by a midshipman who went that route:

"I got rejected at the Naval Academy during my senior year but won an NROTC scholarship to Georgia Tech. It was tough there and at first I got C's because I had not learned to study in high school. But that was good preparation for this place because I was used to coming up empty no matter how hard I tried. Others in my class here were not.

"It also helped that I knew what college life was like. Lots of my classmates got letters from their friends who went on to civilian colleges. They bragged about their girlfriends and parties and how great a time they were having. That really bummed out these guys here because they were missing out on all of that. I didn't have that problem because I knew the score--I knew that it wasn't all that big of a deal.

"Also, many of my academy classmates were suffering from homesickness because this was the first time they had been away from home. I was already over that problem so I didn't have that to worry about, either."

If you do not get a scholarship but you do get admitted to an institution with NROTC, another option is to enroll and try to get into NROTC on your own. After all, most of the officer candidates in NROTC are not on scholarships.

But what if you can only go to a college that does not have an NROTC unit? The next alternative would be an institution with an Air Force or Army ROTC unit. Your training would be much the same during the first year, and if you do not get into the Naval Academy after that, you might want to reevaluate your goals and think about continuing with the Air Force or Army program--or apply to their academies.

Some candidates will have a problem with the latter alternative. The problem is money; there is not enough available to attend a college with an ROTC program. If that is your problem, you still have at least two other alternatives.

One is to attend an inexpensive junior college or community college while living at home and, perhaps, working part time.

The other is to join the Navy or Marine Corps. There are several Navy admirals who started their careers by enlisting in the Navy, then going on to the Naval Academy. The same can be said for some of the high ranking officers in the Marine Corps.

There is a risk with this alternative. There are only 85 appointments reserved for active duty personnel and there is always competition for them. It is possible that you could enlist for four years, fail to get into the Academy, and have to serve the complete enlistment (usually four years).

If you should enlist, your mind should be programmed to excel at everything you do. You should do an outstanding job during basic training, get high marks at whatever technical school they send you to, and, in general, be an exemplary sailor or Marine.

Also, you should become familiar with the Navy Regulations and procedures that you must follow in applying to the Academy, and you should always let your commanding officers know of your goal. You will be much better off in the competition if your commanding officers are aware of your desire and if they are strongly supporting your application.

Most active-duty personnel do not go from the Navy or Marine Corps directly into a plebe class at the Academy. Most need a year in the Naval Academy Preparatory School (NAPS), which is located in Rhode Island. Each year at NAPS prospective candidates take concentrated courses in math, English and science along with some military training. The purpose of NAPS is to bring candidates up to an academic level where they can compete as a plebe at the Academy.

Often the Academy will receive applications from candidates who are well-rounded, have excellent leadership potential and who look like fine officer material. But the candidates have one problem--they have academic deficiencies that would prevent them from competing effectively with the incoming plebes.

The Naval Academy believes that candidates of the above type are a valuable resource who should not be turned away without a chance to prove themselves. Consequently, some of them are offered the opportunity of spending a year at NAPS in order to correct their academic deficiencies.

Officials say that candidates who are offered the NAPS alternative usually react in one of two ways. Some jump at the offer and are grateful to have the opportunity to have a year to strengthen their academic potential. After all, the education is free and they get a salary and allowances while they are studying. Others react as though they are offended at the offer. "You mean I have to waste a whole year of my life? Why then it would take me five years to graduate," is the typical negative reply.

You might be thinking how you would respond to such an offer if it is made. But you should know that the author interviewed numerous midshipmen and officers who went that route and they all recommended it very strongly. A typical comment: "When I reported to the Academy, I already had 200 friends in the plebe class and it helped just to wink at each other while we were going through the hassles of that year. It was a lot easier for us because we were more mature and knew more about what we were getting into."

Midshipmen who have prior naval service get to wear the service insignia and ribbons they have earned. Often, those that attend NAPS end up as leaders at the Academy.

Courtesy USNA Photographic Branch.

Several other mids said flatly: "No way would I have made it through the plebe year if I had not have gone to NAPS."

One of the officers in charge of minority recruitment said that candidates sometimes look at a NAPS offer as sort of a put down. He advised candidates who might think this way to think of such an offer as a compliment. "They want you as a naval officer, or they would not offer the NAPS alternative. You should feel complimented with such an offer, not put down. They think you have the potential to be an officer and a leader. That is definitely a compliment."

The Naval Academy has a very active minority recruiting program and many of the students at NAPS are such recruits. They are there because of academic deficiencies that would otherwise keep them out of the Academy. If you are a minority person and believe NAPS might be a solution to your own academic deficiencies, call the Admissions Office at the Academy (410-293-4361) and ask to speak to a Minority Admissions Officer. There are several of them in that office and their sole duty is to work with minority candidates and counsel them on how to get into the Naval Academy.

Also, if you are an African-American female and feel that you have leadership potential, be sure to call and speak with a Minority Admissions Officer. Not many such females know of the opportunities in the naval services and your interest will attract lots of attention.

Worthy candidates with academic deficiencies might be offered an alternative to NAPS. Each year several hundred candidates are recommended for private

125

If you go to NAPS, you will be way ahead of those right out of high school when you start Plebe Summer.   *Courtesy 1/C Jimmy Parker.*

preparatory schools scattered throughout the country.

This program is not administered by the Academy. It is a private effort of the Naval Academy Foundation, which is made up mostly of Academy alumni. Candidates for the program are recommended by the Admissions Board to the Foundation and the Foundation, in turn, contacts the candidate.

With the Foundation program there are scholarships available for needy candidates but these are awarded on a case-by-case basis, based upon a financial statement submitted by the candidate's parents, and candidates must agree to pay the money back if they quit the program before entering the Academy.   Is it possible for a candidate such as yourself to apply for NAPS or one of the Foundation programs? The answer is no. If you think that NAPS or a Foundation program might help you, go ahead and apply for the Academy in the routine manner right along with everybody else. Just make sure that you write in the "Personal Statement" section of the Academy application form that you would definitely accept a NAPS or Foundation school appointment if it were offered.

In short, you cannot apply for NAPS or a Foundation school. But what you can do is let Academy officials who study your application know that you are very serious about wanting into the Academy--that you are willing to spend an extra year of your life studying if that will help your chances.

Are you really serious about getting into the Naval Academy? If so, keep in mind something that has already been said once in this chapter. Do not give up if you think you are qualified or can get qualified.

The author has encountered several officers, cadets and midshipmen who defied advice and outright rejection and still managed to get into one of the service academies. They cited numerous cases where their high school counselors or Blue and Gold Officers told them, "You had better forget going to any of the academies; to be honest, you just do not have the academic potential."

Others told of how they were given false information by counselors, advice such as, "Oh, you can't go to that academy because you don't have 20/20 vision."

Coincidentally, as the above was being written, a letter came in the mail from a Navy lieutenant who had helped the author on another project. The lieutenant wanted to make sure this point on not accepting bad advice came through strongly in the book on his academy--he is a Naval Academy graduate. The following are some quotes from the letter that the author believes are well worth reading by any serious candidate.

"Reading the book [another of the author's academy books] brought back many memories for me. My application process was pretty much a textbook case. I think I followed virtually all of your guidelines 14-16 years ago. But not everyone is so lucky. My wife, Annette, a mechanical engineer for the Navy, wanted to go to the Air Force Academy when she was in high school. Her 'counselor' at the small, inner-city Catholic high school she went to told her, 'You can't go there, honey; your SAT scores aren't high enough.' Maybe they weren't. But no one ever thought of taking the test again. Now she is a GM-13 (equivalent to a Navy lieutenant commander) at 26 years old, but still regrets having her quest cut short by poor counseling.

"In another case right here, the officer in charge of the detachment is a Navy commander and NFO [Naval Flight Officer]. He told me that when he was in high school his counselor told him that only those with 20/20 vision could get into the Air Force Academy. Since his eyesight wasn't that good, he never gave it another thought. Over 20 years later, now a Vietnam veteran with many combat hours, he regrets having gotten bad gouge [advice]." The Navy lieutenant went on in the letter to tell the story of his sister's problems getting into the Naval Academy. She first had a problem getting a nomination, but that was finally solved. Then, wrote the lieutenant:

"The previous story was a piece of cake compared to the next one. At the same time we were solving Judy's nomination problem, she had a bigger hurdle to overcome. She failed her physical. The level of albumin in her urine exceeded established maximum levels. My understanding is that high albumin in the urine is indicative of potential kidney failure. It is also common in women who are vigorously athletic. At the time of the test, Judy was in peak form in the middle of her senior season as captain of the high school swimming team. My parents panicked and without making any behavioral adjustments, sent her to be retested immediately. She failed again, and the joint services medical operation out there in Colorado sent her a medical rejection. We queried them, of course, but with two failures on record, they were adamant. We sent letters from two different specialists saying she was okay but they wouldn't buy it. In desperation I called out there to Colorado and asked to talk to the head man. The Navy Captain doctor who came on line told the Lieutenant (me) that Judy was disqualified for admission to any academy and his decision was final. I realized that this was the honest to goodness end of the line unless I could do something to change his 'final decision.' I kept him on the line. I said anything, everything I could think of to keep him from hanging up. Forty-five minutes later, the probably exasperated but confident doctor told me we could have one more chance. It destroyed her swimming season, but we put her in bed for two weeks. No swimming, no school, no walking except to the bathroom. Her albumin level plummeted, she passed her physical, and now she's an alumnus--and in every physical since then she's never had a problem."

Try to keep this success story in mind if you are struggling with your own candidacy. While your own problems are sure to be different, note that the lieutenant solved his sister's problem by using creativity and persistence. And, although he did not say so directly, he had to have used tact and persuasion to have kept the doctor on the phone for so long and to have made him change his mind after it was firmly made up.

You probably will not be lucky enough to have such a brother or sister helping you, so you may have to fight a battle like the lieutenant fought all by yourself. And if you do, just remember to use the four weapons that won the lieutenant's battle. Use your creativity. Be persistent. Use tact. Be persuasive.

And hope or pray that you have good luck!

FIFTEEN
THE GOLDEN PARTNERSHIP

Commander John Lopez III, Blue and Gold Area Coordinator for north Texas (fourth from left, front, in civilian clothes) takes six of his midshipmen, who are home on leave for Christmas, to a Mexican food lunch. The officer in uniform is an Academy graduate.

The Blue and Gold Officer is an unpaid volunteer who is an official representative of the Naval Academy. Many are retired Navy or Marine Corps officers, but several have a civilian background and many of those have had sons or daughters attend the Academy.

These officers often refer to themselves as "Blue and Golders," but the wise candidate will forget about the "Blue" part of their name and think only of the last part. It is the "Gold" part of the name the candidate should remember. Why? Because it will help you remember their value. A good Blue and Gold Officer is as valuable as gold, and when you can get one of them supporting your candidacy, you truly have a golden partnership.

Here is an example of the kinds of things they can do. Said a Blue and Gold Area Area Coordinator from Texas:

"I was in my office about nine-thirty one evening and I received this telephone call. It was from a senior in a nearby high school and he said, 'Sir, I was told if anybody could help me, you could.' I started asking him questions and found out that he was near the top of his class academically, that with a cast on his right arm he was able to do 35 pull ups, and that he was holding down two jobs in addition to his academic and athletic responsibilities. I was saying to myself, 'This guy has really got it,' and then I asked him to tell me about his problem. He said that he had been turned down for the Academy because he was colorblind. Immediately, I asked him, 'Where is the nearest McDonalds? I'll meet you there.'

"When I got there, I saw his truck. You couldn't miss it; ever part of it had something Navy sticking on it. I met him inside. He was drinking a coke and had a coffee on the table for me. When I sat down he put a big accordion file on the table that was full of Academy information and he began telling me his story. He started, 'Sir, I have been wanting to go to the Naval Academy since I was in the seventh grade.' We talked for awhile and I said, 'Let's take a ride.' We went out where we could look over the city and I asked him to identify red and green colored lights. He had no problem; he could accurately identify each. We talked for awhile and I promised that I would try to help him. A day or two later I had him tested at the Naval district, but he still could not separate red and green colors on the colorblind test. About this same time I received a call from his mother who admitted she hadn't done the best for the boy. Among other things she explained that there had been different fathers for her four sons and from the conversation, it was obvious that the family was totally dysfunctional. I did more research and found out that this young man, by normal standards, should have been a delinquent or a dropout or a gang person. But he wasn't; he was the cleanest cut kid you have ever seen. About that time I happened to be reading the business section of the newspaper and saw an article on Roger Staubach telling all the wonderful things he had done.[1] Then a light went on. I remembered that Roger Staubach was colorblind but had gotten a waiver to attend the Academy. I immediately composed a long narrative for the Academy head physician, and with it, I enclosed photos of my candidate and the newspaper photo of Staubach. Finally, after they read my letter, and after some telephone persuasion on my part, they gave the kid a waiver. He went to the Academy and did an outstanding job--the only thing that could have kept him from being a brigade commander was too much enthusiasm. After graduation, he went to the Supply Corps because of this colorblindness, and then I received a wedding invitation. I was so enthusiastic about this young man that I called the father of his bride-to-be and congratulated him because of the great son-in-law he was about to acquire."

One could say that the young man from Texas, the subject of the above story, lucked out in turning a depressing failure into a fine education and a potentially bright career. But "luck" is not the right word. The young man saved his future by his own initiative. After being rejected, he did not just give up. Instead, he went looking for a partner to help him, *and he was able to convince* a potential partner that he was worthy of help. Note the action word, "convince." That is the key word for you to keep in mind as you think about finding your own partner.

In an earlier chapter you were advised to contact your Blue and Gold Area

---

[1]Staubach was a famous quarterback at the Naval Academy and went on to become a Hall- of-Fame quarterback for the Dallas Cowboys.

Coordinator to find the name and telephone number of the Blue and Golder nearest you. (The phone number of your Area Coordinator can be located in the Academy catalog.) Your next step is to contact that Blue and Golder and convince him or her that you are a worthy partner.

How do you do this? You do it by being honest and sincere. As one Blue and Golder said, "We've been conned by the best. We can spot a phony a mile away. Tell them to be totally honest with us when we ask a question. Tell them we can see right through them when they try to puff themselves up making themselves into something they are not. But also tell them not to be bashful about telling us of their accomplishments. It's the whole person we're looking at. The only tangible things we get are grades, test scores and some letters. The rest of the things about them we have to learn from the candidate."

Several Blue and Golders also mentioned the negative things that candidates do to turn them off--things that are unconvincing. Said one Blue and Golder: "Lots of times I'll talk to kids and they'll be putting on a good show. Yeah, boy, are they motivated. They really want to go back there and get a good education and be a naval officer. Yes, sir, they sure do. But then I start asking questions. 'Have you talked to any mids to find out what it is like back there?'

Answer: 'Well, no...but I'm going to.'

"Well, what about a Naval Academy graduate? Have you talked to one of them?"

Answer: 'Well, uh, no, uh, but I'd like to.'

"Tell me, have you checked out the service obligation if you go there? Do you know how long you have to serve in the Navy if you graduate?"

Answer: 'No, I guess I don't.'

"How about Plebe Summer? Do you know how long it is?'

Answer: "No, I'm not sure, uh..."

"So I get a completely different picture when I start asking questions. I'll get this type, who is just blowing smoke about wanting to go back there--the type who has done nothing that shows a real interest. But I'll also get the ones who answer right back, 'Yes, sir, I talked to so and so graduate, and I went back there with my parents and visited, and I talked to a mid who told me all about Plebe Summer and PEP, etc.'

"There is a world of difference between those two types. The first one...I don't write him off, but I'm guessing I'll never hear from him again. But sometimes they'll surprise you. Somebody like that might take the clue and really get informed. But the other types come right across. They've taken their own initiative to find out about the place and they're anxious to learn more. You feel good about those types. You want to help them."

However, most of the Blue and Golders have been burned at one time or another. Most can tell stories like the one told by an Area Coordinator from Ohio. Said he: "About six or seven years ago I talked with a young lady who seemed determined to go to the Academy. I spoke with her several times and noted that her parents were very supportive. However, she was more frail than a typical woman athlete, but I thought, okay, she wants to do this and seems motivated, so I'll make the recommendation to her congressman and the Academy--although I did qualify it by saying that they might need to watch her--she might have trouble with endurance.

Captain (USN Ret.) M.R. Byington, Jr., a Blue and Gold Officer in Florida, introduces two of his midshipmen to a meeting of potential candidates. He strongly urges potential candidates to talk with midshipmen before they seriously consider the Naval Academy.

Courtesy Richard C. Rapson, Jr.

"I just happened to be at the Academy near the end of July that year, and they told me one of my plebes was in Tango Company and would I like to talk with her? Tango Company is the holding company for those who want to quit. I said, 'Yes, I'd like to talk to her.' It was the girl I had recommended. When I saw her, I said, 'You're wanting to leave before the six weeks is up; why don't you give this a chance?

"She said, 'Hey, I don't like it here.'

"I said, 'Yes, but when we talked, you said that this was your idea and that you could withstand everything. Now you're not even giving it a chance. Can't you give me a year?'

"She said, 'I don't want to be here.'

"I said, 'You haven't given it a fair chance. You have already taken the place of two or three others who would give their right arm to have this chance. Why can't you give it a year? You told me you could take anything.

"Then she confessed. 'Well, I guess I didn't tell you everything,' she said. 'My mother and dad were the ones who wanted me to do this.'

"After that I knew it was hopeless. She wasn't going there for her own reasons and there was no way she could do that first year there without her own motivation. But it really made me angry because she had screwed some good kid out of that slot when she knew she wasn't going to stay. After that experience, I really started trying to ferret out the motivation--is it the kid who wants to go, or is it mom and dad?"

Practically every Blue and Golder who has been at the counseling business for a

132

few years can tell similar stories. But what you, the candidate, should know is that once one of these officers has been burned, they are going to be cautious in the future.

As a candidate you should also know that these officers take great pride in their reputations. It is their reputation that is at stake if they ever do call an admissions official and say, "Hey, you've written my candidate a discouraging letter, and I just want you to know that I have gotten to know this candidate personally. She is a highly respected leader in her high school and I believe she would make a fine naval officer. Couldn't you look the application over again and give it a second consideration?"

Think about such a request. How is it going to be thought of by the admissions official?

One of the first thoughts of that official is to evaluate the Blue and Golder. What is his or her reputation? Has this officer consistently recommended candidates who have done well at the Academy? If the answer is, yes, then there is an excellent chance the candidate in question will get a second look and, maybe, a second chance before the Admissions Board.

So, you, as a potential candidate must keep all this in mind. It is one thing for you to want to forge this wonderful golden partnership with your Blue and Golder. It is a totally different matter whether the Blue and Golder wishes to form a golden partnership with you. The officers, of course, will do whatever is necessary to help you with your application. They are dedicated professionals; they *will* do their job to the best of their ability. But is the officer going to lay his or her reputation on the line for you if you are having problems? Is he or she going to write or phone a congressional staffer or an admissions official to plead your case? In most cases the answer would be, no, if there is the slightest doubt that you are motivated enough to go to the Academy and prove what you are saying about your motivation. They will not jeopardize their reputations, because they want to save their influence for candidates who are in the 100 percent category--the candidates whom they know in their heart will go there and *stay there*.

The application process for any service academy involves numerous hurdles that can trip a candidate. The first is the precandidate questionnaire, and, especially, the personal statement--the essay you must write explaining why you want to go to the Academy. Your Blue and Golder will gladly advise you on questions you might have about the application. Also, you can probably get advice on certain things you might or might not say in the personal statement.

But there is also the candidate physical examination, the physical aptitude examination, one, two or even three interviews before congressional boards, and, of course, the personal interview with the Blue and Golder, which will be placed in your admissions file. There are lots of potential problems you may encounter with any of those steps in the process and you should think of your Blue and Golder as the single, best person to counsel you on your problems.

However, there are things that some Blue and Golders will not do. For example, one said, "When a candidate calls me and asks how he can get in contact with his congressman or his two senators, I give him an indirect answer. I tell him where he can go and find their phone numbers and addresses; I don't give him the numbers

Captain Wendell Suydam, USN (Ret.), a highly respected Blue and Gold Officer in the San Diego area presents a certificate of appointment to a candidate from Torrey Pines High School.

directly, nor the staffers' names. I look at this as a little test of their motivation. If they want to know that information, will they take the trouble to do the research? If not, that tells me something."

Neither do many Blue and Golders like to be bugged about little details that you could figure out for yourself--or find out from another person. For example, they are not likely to look favorably on candidates who ask them to check the grammar and spelling on their personal statements. Many would tell you to go to an English teacher if one of your parents cannot do it.

As counselors the Blue and Golders are at their best when they are dispensing advice. Therefore, the author asked a selected group of them for advice on some of the most common problems, mistakes and misinformation they have encountered while working with candidates--advice that could be passed on in this chapter. The following, in no particular order of importance, is a digest of their comments:

"Get your application in early--I mean during the summer before your senior year or by September at the latest. The Academy has early boards that meet and I will guarantee you that you will have a much better chance to be selected by an early board than by one that is meeting the next February or March.[2] The old saying that the early bird gets the worm applies here. Those who get their applications in early stand a better chance of getting in. And don't worry about the nomination. That process can come later. If they offer you an early acceptance, which is common, that means that they want you. After that, there are all kinds of ways you can get a nomination."

"Kids who have 700 scores on their math and verbal [SAT] and no extracurricular activities are shooting themselves in the foot. The Academy doesn't want scholars; the Academy wants leaders."

"If they're worried about interviews, why don't they call us? Many times we'll not only know who is on the interview boards, but we often know the kinds of questions they are going to ask. We may even be on the boards ourselves!"

"Many wait too long to contact us. If we know they are viable candidates during their junior year, we might be able to get them back to the Academy for one of the Senior Science Seminars, which are held in June."

"Some think they have to have political pull in order to get a nomination. That's mostly nonsense now days. What the congressman wants to know is: Does this kid have the right stuff?"

"I run into kids who don't want to take the tough courses because they might get a B and that would look bad on their transcript. They may even have had a counselor who has said that. That's crazy if they want to go to an academy. No one wants a kid who has not taken the hard courses."

"I find some who try to second guess the system. A well qualified kid may see another candidate who is equally good or better and think, 'I don't stand a chance to beat this guy and get into the Naval Academy. I guess, I'll just apply to West Point.' This type of cleverness is wrong. You have to let the system do its magic. *If you are good enough, the Academy will find a way to get you in.* It's your job to get yourself competitive; it's the system's job to get you in."

"I have found examples where Navy or Marine Corps recruiters have been asked for advice about the Academy and the candidate was given bad advice. The recruiter may have had the best of intentions, but, frankly, a lot of them don't know squat about the Academy. My advice: be very leery of advice from recruiters. Actually, the same can be said for a lot of high school counselors. But they are an additional problem. Besides not knowing much about the Academy and giving kids a lot of misinformation, some are liberal, anti-military types and will do their best to discourage or steer kids away from going to an academy. The latter is frustrating because we have to work

---

[2] A key admissions official swore to the author that this advice is excellent; candidates who do apply early have a competitive edge.

135

through those types when we call on high schools, and, when and if we ever get to the kid, we really can't come right out and openly cut down the kid's counselor."

"Some kids don't know what to do about the interview that the Blue and Gold Officer is required to conduct. Sometimes the Blue and Golder will be a bit negligent and the interview will not be conducted on time. Often, the kid who is dependent upon this interview will sit back thinking that the Blue and Golder has everything under control--that there is a good reason for the delay. That is bad thinking. The candidate must take the initiative. If the interview isn't done in a timely manner, pick up the phone and bug the Blue and Golder. This shows initiative. The Blue and Golder won't be offended; he will be impressed."

"This advice concerns the physical exam. We always advise our candidates to also apply for an NROTC scholarship so they have a fall-back position if they don't get accepted at the Academy. Some candidates won't do this, but one good reason why they should is because the physical for NROTC is scheduled before the one for the Academy. In more cases than you would think, a candidate will encounter some problem that either requires more tests or even a waiver. So there is a definite advantage for getting the early physical; the candidate has more time to take another blood test or see a specialist for another opinion--options that can save their candidacy. Also, a bit of advice on the physical itself. They ask a hundred questions on the forms they give the candidate. 'Have you ever wet the bed?' 'Have you ever walked in your sleep?' 'Have you ever had leg cramps?' Things like that. I don't advise dishonesty, but I do tell candidates: 'Be honest, but use some judgement. If you haven't been bothered by some of these problems for five years and you truly don't feel they are a problem, write, no.' I've seen some kids really get tangled up trying to be honest--a kid is asked about leg cramps and he says, yes, but he has no chance to add that this was after running in a hard cross-country meet. Well, who wouldn't have leg cramps after that? Let me emphasize, I'm not telling them to be dishonest. I am telling them to use some judgement and to be cautious about their answers."

"Never submit a personal statement with your application without having somebody check it over for spelling and grammatical errors. I know of one candidate who wrote that he wanted to attend the *Navel* Academy. When asked about the misspelling he pleaded that he had used the spell checker on his computer. But that isn't foolproof. There are words "naval" and "navel" and the computer will tell you that both are spelled correctly."

"Kids who don't get accepted the first time they apply because of low SAT scores often get discouraged and give up. I tell them to go to a college, take hard courses, get good grades, then reapply. The reason: the purpose of the SAT is to predict the first year college performance of a student. If the student goes on and is highly successful the first year, then the real impact of the SAT is negated; by being successful, especially in hard subjects, the student has proven the SAT score invalid."

"I think candidates make a big mistake by not prepping for the SATs. I have found that they can take 10 practice SATs at home and raise their scores 50 points. I have a handout listing the publications and computer programs that I give to candidates. I strongly advise them to practice as much as they can."

"I would say one of the biggest misconceptions out there is the belief that, 'If I get

136

a nomination, I will then get accepted by the Academy.' Kids don't realize that all the congressmen together can give out more than 5000 nominations for about 1100 openings. Emphasize this: *just because you get a nomination from your congressman, that does not mean that you will get an Academy appointment.*"

"Kids who are turned down for the Academy and for an NROTC scholarship should not be discouraged. If they look like viable candidates, I advise them to go a college with NROTC and sign up without a scholarship. If they'll do that, and do an excellent job in their unit as well as with their academics, their NROTC commander can nominate them for an appointment. The Academy leaves slots open just for those kinds of people."

"More often than you might think, candidates get turned down by DODMERB [Department of Defense Medical Examination Review Board] and they think it's all over. I tell them, 'If you get a turndown, call me,' because they're not going to look at the fine print on the turndown that says you can disagree and have your own doctor give his opinion. I have had phenomenal success getting boys and girls in after a turndown but the key is to take both proper action and prompt action. Too many get the turndown from DODMERB and just accept it."

"A common mistake is for candidates to take their teacher evaluation forms in to a teacher, slap it down on the desk, and say, 'Hey, can you fill this out for me?' then leave. That is not the way to do it. A teacher looks at that form and it is easy to get spooked. The form calls for an evaluation rather than a recommendation. I counsel candidates to talk with the teacher first. Find out if the teacher is supportive and, also, convince the teacher that you are highly motivated and that you are competing with the top 10 percent of other students. Make sure the teacher knows that you are keenly interested and that his or her evaluation is extremely important."

"There are certain things a candidate can do to convince me that he or she is highly motivated. First, I want them to keep me posted on all their actions. When I first meet with them, we will work out a plan of action. I want to know that they are following that plan and I can't know that unless they contact me. Second, I watch their eyes when they talk to me. If their eyelashes flutter, I know they are lying. It's body language they can't hide. So the more they talk to me and show me they are sincere, the more I get sold on them. The third thing that helps is for them to send me a snapshot. I want to have a face in mind when I speak to them over the telephone. The fourth thing that impresses me is if they get their paperwork done when they say it will be done. If they procrastinate, that raises a caution flag."

"My advice concerns the Blue and Gold interview. The first thing I write down in my notes is whether the candidate is early, on time, or late. And you don't have to guess what I say about a candidate who is late. Another very important thing I look for is eye contact. I look for it when I first meet a candidate, and I especially look for it during the interview. The lack of eye contact means to me that the candidate lacks confidence--and that is a bad sign. Also, some candidates ask me how they should dress for their interviews. I tell them to look at the mids in the Academy catalog. I explain that the interviewers are going to try to picture what a candidate would look like in a midshipman's uniform. Personally, I recommend for candidates to wear church clothes. But, I know many don't own good clothes. The key phrase I use in my own notes if the candidate looks good in other clothes is 'casual, but neat.'

"From my experience boys are reluctant to seek out mids and talk to them about the rigors of the Academy. Girls don't seem to have this problem. Maybe it is a testosterone thing, but my advice to the boys is to get over your reluctance. You're in competition and you need every edge. If you've talked to a mid and know what you're getting into, you are a notch up, at least with my own evaluation."

"Sometimes kids have trouble at home with parents that don't want them to attend an academy. My advice to the kid is to ask the Blue and Gold Officer to please contact the president of the local Naval Academy Parents' Club and have that person call the parents. The club president is well experienced on all matters on the Academy and can do as good a job as anybody talking to reluctant parents."

That's the advice from the Blue and Gold Officers--advice learned over many years of working with candidates. Now it is up to you. Can you forge a golden partnership with your own Blue and Gold Officer? If so, and you are otherwise qualified, you will have a powerful new friend.

138

HOW TO SURVIVE

SIXTEEN
WHY UPPERCLASS PRESSURE?

It is a well known fact that the plebe year at the Naval Academy is a long, difficult year. It is also well known that the upperclassmen are the "bad guys"--the ones who deliberately make the plebes' lives miserable.

Why is that necessary?

Is it because the Academy wants to weed out the weak and the fainthearted? Is the plebe year a survival-of-the-fittest exercise, where the fittest go on to become officers and the others are cast aside like rejects from an assembly line?

By taking the oath during the swearing-in ceremony, you are voluntarily committing yourself to one of the great challenges of your lifetime.   *Courtesy USNA Photographic Branch.*

That may be what many candidates believe, but it is a long way from the truth.

The truth starts with the attitude of the officers and midshipmen toward the young men and women who arrive each year and become plebes. The officers and midshipmen are very proud of those young men and women. They feel lucky--even flattered--that more than a thousand of the finest young Americans in the country want to join them at their institution and, later, want to serve with them in their airplanes, ships, submarines and Marine Corps units. One key official who is involved in the selection process put it this way: "When we look over those applications, we really fall in love with some of those kids. We want them badly; we want those kinds of youngsters with us."

139

Now, if the officers and midshipmen feel lucky--even flattered--that so many fine young people want to attend their institution and serve with them, does it make sense to think they would try to drive them away?

Absolutely not. They do not want to drive them away. They want to keep them.

And they have a good record of success. About 78 percent of the recent entering classes go on to complete all four years and graduate.

But what about the way the plebes are treated? From the day they arrive they are harassed and pressured until they are ready to drop; and, occasionally, some will even be told with insulting language that they are not officer material and that they should pack their bags and go home.

Is that any way to treat someone whom you genuinely like and admire? Is that the way to treat those whom you want very badly to keep in your institution? Is that how potential friends and future comrades should be treated?

It is if you have very high expectations for the incoming plebes. It is if you see them as unpolished diamonds.

So it is a matter of perspective.

To the plebes who, during Plebe Summer, are required to memorize pages and pages of material in *Reef Points*, that task is often viewed as a form of punishment and harassment.

But the officers and midshipmen see it differently. From their perspective they are seeing all of those plebes with fine minds that have never been challenged--minds that are like Porsches and Corvettes that have been driven at 30 miles an hour for the last twelve years. They want to see those minds on the fast track where they belong, where they can operate to their true potential.

When the upperclassmen are criticizing the plebes, their actions are interpreted by the plebes as mean, hateful, obnoxious behavior.

The officers and midshipmen have a different view. They see the plebes as future officers who have to learn how to remain calm when there is chaos everywhere around them. In their minds the plebes may someday be directing fire-fighting efforts on a ship--or officers leading airplanes to a target through deadly antiaircraft and missile fire--or officers trying to track a submarine loaded with enough missiles and warheads to kill half the people on the East Coast. Their job is to see that the plebes learn how to remain cool under pressure--that the plebes have ten months of experience learning to control their emotions and their tempers.

Many of the plebes think it is unfair when they are punished for a mistake made by someone else--a mistake that was not their fault.

The officers and midshipmen see that kind of punishment in a different way. They see it as a way to teach the plebes how important it is for a group to function as a single unit. They are thinking ahead when plebes will be monitoring a submarine's nuclear reactor--or as an officer in the radar room of a ship who must decide if a low-flying airplane is truly an enemy and must be fired upon before it gets close enough to release its missiles and destroy the ship--or a Marine lieutenant who is

Are you the kind of person who can become a stickler for details? Will you become obsessed with doing things the right way? That is the attitude upperclassmen are trying to instill.

Courtesy 1/C Jimmy Parker.

responsible for bringing enough ammunition for a battalion going into combat. In each case, if the officer fails to do his or her duty, all the others in the submarine, the ship or the battalion will suffer. The officers and midshipmen want that point driven home during the plebe year when actual lives are not at stake.

When the upperclassmen get down on their knees to find specks of dust under a plebe's bunk, or when they look in a blouse pocket and find a loose thread, the plebes shake their head and think of the harassment as useless nitpicking.

The officers and midshipmen think differently. They see the plebes coming in from a civilian culture where individuals can be sloppy and careless, where just getting the job done is more important than how well the job is done. Those kinds of standards cannot be tolerated anywhere in the naval service. The plebes will become nuclear officers who will supervise the maintenance and operation of nuclear reactors; they will become maintenance officers responsible for repairing all of the critical engine and communications equipment for the naval air fleet; they will become intelligence officers who must interpret every tiny bit of intelligence that is available in order to keep their fleet at the proper level of readiness for an enemy. In short, future naval officers *must become nitpickers* or they will not be able to do their jobs properly when they get to the fleet. That is why the upperclassmen look for dust under beds and loose threads in the pockets. They want to build that nitpicking attitude into every plebe.

Then there is the Honor Concept, where plebes must swear that they will never lie, steal or cheat. To some plebes it may seem demeaning to be forced to swear not to do things they never intend to do. Others may question the oath they must take, wondering, "What is the big deal?"

The value of the Honor Concept is much more clear cut to the officers and upperclassmen. They know that the plebes have come from high schools where cheating is routine. They know that some plebes will come from street cultures where those who lie, steal and engage in other forms of lawbreaking are respected.

They also know that the naval service can never tolerate officers with that kind of behavior. An officer has to be trusted, 24 hours a day, 365 days a year, in all ways and in all things. And this tradition has deep roots at the Naval Academy. Probably nothing is more sacred on this earth to Naval Academy graduates than their honor. Therefore, it should not be surprising when the officers and upperclassmen at the Academy expect the plebes to start living honorably shortly after they arrive.

Another thing that frustrates plebes is for upperclassmen to give them multiple tasks but about half enough time to get them done. "That is stupid," thinks the typical plebe.

That practice might seem stupid, but there is a solid rationale behind it. The practice is designed to teach plebes time management. This involves learning how to evaluate multiple tasks and learning how to establish priorities. Given three things to do in a short time, plebes must learn to recognize which task is most important and should be done first--and which task is least important and may have to be left undone. This leads the plebes to become systematic in the way they undertake new jobs--instead of doing them in the random, haphazard way many of them are used to working.

You may have been a high-school all star, but at the Academy you *will* experience failure and develop humility. *Courtesy USNA Photographic Branch.*

Many plebes, who have been conscientious all their lives, who have always done everything they have been asked to do, suffer greatly when they fail some of the tasks given by the upperclassmen. Failure in front of your peers is a humiliating experience and often a new experience for plebes. And for those who are extremely conscientious it can create real, gut-wrenching, emotional trauma.

Then why humiliate the plebes?

There are at least two reasons and one has to do with arrogance.

Of all the undesirable traits that an officer might have, arrogance is probably the one that is most feared. General George Armstrong Custer was the classic example of the arrogant officer--the officer who believed he was infallible enough to ride through the whole Sioux and Cheyenne Nations with a few undermanned companies of troopers armed only with single-shot rifles. His action, and the action of other arrogant officers have cost lives needlessly--that is why they are feared. The officers and midshipmen want the plebes to be humiliated--note that word because the result that they are seeking is its root.

After failure and humiliation comes *humility*, which is a trait the Academy believes is essential in all leaders. Officers with humility have learned to know and respect their limitations, and, consequently, they are not likely to lead those under them on frivolous adventures that can cost their lives.

When plebes fail to memorize an assignment or when they fail an inspection (both are typical kinds of failures), the officers and upperclassmen are after something else as well. They want to develop plebes with tenacity--plebes who will hang on like a bulldog when the going gets rough.

Occasionally some overzealous first classmen will even tell a plebe that he or she is not officer material and does not belong at the Academy. Those kinds of comments are heard occasionally and they are discouraging to plebes who are struggling with all their other problems. But they are not meant to be discouraging.

It is a mental defeat for plebes when they are told they do not measure up to the upperclassmen's idea of what an officer should be. But do the plebes give up and quit? That is not what the upperclassmen want even though they are probably putting on a convincing act. What the upperclassmen really want is for the plebes to *prove them wrong*--to ignore that mental defeat and hang in there--to persist despite all the negative comments.

Many young men and women in our affluent culture have never encountered true adversity and failure; therefore, they have had no experience coming back after suffering a defeat. (Serious athletes are exceptions and that is one reason why many of them do well as plebes.) Yet, almost every upperclassman and graduate who was interviewed for this book, in one way or another, praised the plebe indoctrination system for creating the kinds of adversity and failures that caused them to develop into better, stronger, persons. So the system works. What is important is for the candidate who goes to the Academy to believe that it works.

To summarize, the plebe indoctrination system is not meant to be a weeding out process or a survival-of-the-fittest exercise. Instead, its purpose is to take carefully selected young men and women with outstanding potential and build upon that potential. It is a system designed to strengthen the plebes mentally, physically and morally so they will develop the attitudes and traits that are essential for naval officers.

Said the Marine Lieutenant Colonel in charge of the Plebe Summer Program (who went through the program as a plebe, as a supervising upperclassman, as a Drill Officer and, finally as the supervising officer): "We think the admissions process is thorough--that the plebes bring the right tools and equipment when they come here. But what is hard is to predict motivation and the desire to succeed. One of our big jobs is to motivate desire to succeed no matter what the circumstances.

"Personally, I feel like we bring in a precious nugget and we need to treat it that way. We don't want to pulverize it into a quivering mass of Jello. What we are trying to do is smooth off the rough edges and to polish the sharp corners. These nuggets come in all sizes and shapes and we are trying to get them to a uniform size so they will fit into the Brigade at the end of Plebe Summer. We don't want to tear these kids down: we want to build them up."

However, before the plebe year is over, approximately 150 of the plebes will have left the Academy. Of those, about half will have left voluntarily. They mostly will be those who were at the Academy for the wrong reasons or those who were naive when they arrived and did not realize just how rigorous a program they had gotten into.

The others are dismissed for a variety of reasons. Some are for misconduct, including honor violations. Some are for poor military performance. But mostly they are the ones who get themselves into such deep academic trouble that no amount of counseling and tutoring will save them.

Unfortunately, it is mostly the stories from those who leave the Academy that perpetuate the idea that the plebe indoctrination system is a weeding-out process. But let those stories continue to entertain the weak and the fainthearted. And you, the candidate, read on. For it is now time for the midshipmen themselves to speak of the plebe indoctrination system, to tell you how they personally managed to survive it, why they wanted to survive it, and how you, the potential plebe, can do the same thing.

SEVENTEEN
PLEBES TELL HOW TO
SURVIVE THE SYSTEM

The plebes who survived the system can tell you what they did right, and what the nonsurvivors did wrong.

Hundreds of plebes were interviewed during numerous visits to the Naval Academy. Most were interviewed in late winter and spring--after they had survived eight to ten months of plebe indoctrination. Some were interviewed just days before "Herndon," when one of them, with the help of classmates, would climb the Herndon Monument--the ritual that celebrates the end of the plebe year. The same general comments were made to all of them. You are here. You have survived, yet 150 or more of your classmates are not here. They did not survive. Why? Why are you here and why are they gone? And what have you learned from your experiences this year that could be passed on as advice to future plebes?

Virtually every plebe stressed the fact that survival was largely a matter of having the right attitude. However, there were many opinions on what that "right attitude" should be. Here are some of them.

Said one: "The key to my success were the attitudes I had learned in wrestling. When you're on the mat wrestling, you have to believe that you are never going to give up--so when someone is in your face yelling at you, you throw up a wall and you pretend you're on the mat and say to yourself, 'I'm never going to give up no matter what he is saying to me.'

"The other attitude is to keep an open mind. I had no idea when I came here what it was really going to be like and I had to change plans. You have to be flexible. You have to fit into situations you don't expect. You have to be ready for surprises."

Get used to the idea: no matter how well you perform, you *will* be yelled at.

Even if you do not see any reason for marching, you should be prepared to give it your best effort.   *Courtesy USNA Photographic Branch.*

Said another: "The biggest mistake I saw was the attitude of so many who thought they were the best. You come here and you'll find out you're not the best. You might have been a big shot in the town you came from, but here you are in with a thousand other people who were big shots just like you. The kinds who tried to be big shots here got cut right down to size and they weren't prepared to handle that at the beginning."

Said another: "You have to have the right attitude, especially during the summer when you are made to do things that seem stupid. You have to realize that you're not going to see the meaning of what they're making you do--you have to have an attitude where you take everything on faith."

A first classman who happened to hear the above comment added: "You have to take it on faith that there is a reason for everything you are made to do. Take marching, for example. Nobody likes it because the Navy doesn't march. But you should still give it one-hundred percent. If you are not trying to do your best, you are wasting your time--but if you give that effort [one-hundred percent], you will make it here. As a first classman, I'm always looking at the guy who is trying the hardest. In my mind those who try the hardest--even if they don't do as well as some who try less--are better people."

Said another plebe: "You have to have the right attitude or you won't survive. You have to be objective and have an open mind. You can't take things personally. Also, you must be determined--people at home told me I wouldn't make it and that stuck with me and kept me going. Things aren't always going to be to your liking but once plebe year gets by, you begin to see the reasons why you had to do certain things--you see that things which seemed trivial and pointless do have a meaning."

Said another: "If I hadn't had the right attitude, I wouldn't have made it. I was overweight--I lost 35 pounds during the summer--and not in shape. I didn't have the endurance like everyone else. Three weeks into Plebe Summer I hit the lowest point and the first classmen were really on me. They said I wasn't fit for this place and they kept on me, saying: 'Why did you come here? Well, you're not going to make it, buddy!'

"That was very hard and if it hadn't been for my roommates, I wouldn't be here now. They got something in my head that kept me going. They said, 'When you start a race, you run it through the tape.' When I got that in my head, I decided I wasn't going to let up and I didn't. With the right attitude you don't get mad when they tell you that you aren't going to make it. You turn all that into motivation and it makes you want it more. You realize that somebody is trying to take your life away and you aren't going to let them do it."

Said another: "I must have read your book [first edition] 15 or 16 times. It helped me so much during Plebe Summer. Everything they did and said--all the game playing, the teamwork exercises--I was ready for all that. But there was one thing I didn't get from the book and wasn't ready for--I lost perspective on why I was here. I was so entranced with the Naval Academy. I thought it was going to make me into a great person and that I was going to serve my country. I did all right during Plebe Summer because I was prepared. But when it started getting rough during the academic year, I didn't understand why I was here any more. I lost my perspective. I think it is hard to gain it back, even now. You are always pushed in some way, even when you are a second or first class. You just want a little time off. Since I lost that perspective, I have been getting by and surviving one day at a time. Not even one day at a time--one hour at a time--one period at a time. If you start thinking, oh, my God, this plebe year will never end, it is going to take forever. You have to take it one day at a time and concentrate on the task at hand and not the goal. When you lose your perspective, you start thinking about your friends. I have a bunch of friends in Santa Barbara [California] and they are having a great time right now. When I wake up at five- thirty in the morning I think, Why am I here? That will go through your head tons of times. You have to have one single, solitary reason why you decided to come here. It can't be some lofty dream that I'm going to become an admiral someday. It has to be a more immediate goal. I want to be an officer. I want to be a pilot. You have to have a reason like that. You have to have the faith that that is why you are here. On days like this--its rainy, its cold, I have tests--I have to grind my teeth and ask: Why? You have to have a reason when you ask that. You have to have a narrow mind set."

Said another: "Don't come here without a confident attitude or you're not going to make it. If you don't have that attitude, what are you going to do when they tell you that you shouldn't be here? You will go downhill and start second guessing yourself thinking maybe they are right. You have to believe that they are wrong. You have to be able to say to yourself, 'I do belong here.' You have to be a fighter. You have to believe you have the right to stay here no matter what they say."

When everything is going downhill for you, can you keep on believing in yourself? You have to be able to do that.

Courtesy 1/C Jimmy Parker

Said another: "Don't come here with the attitude that you hope you can make it. If you just hope you can make it, you will probably not have the strength to do it. You have to have the confidence that you will make it no matter what they tell you or what they do to you."

Besides attitude, many of the plebes stressed the importance of keeping your thoughts focused, and not letting negative thoughts into your mind. The following is one plebe's explanation of how this was done:

"I mentally tried to psyche myself up for Plebe Summer by telling myself it is only six weeks long. I said to myself that I have gone through a lot of six-week periods in my life and I made the decision that whatever happens during that six-week period, I wouldn't quit under any circumstances. I realized that I wouldn't have a clear mind then--that I'd be under pressure--so I made the decision before I came that I would not quit. "Then I got real excited about coming--the whole history and tradition of the place got to me--and when I got here I never thought about quitting once--it never entered my mind. I refused to let it enter my mind. The people back home complained because I didn't call and it's because I threw myself at it completely and had to forget that my friends were at home drinking beer and having a good time--if I had thought about that, it would have gotten me down.

"The main thing is to have a positive attitude and hit the deck running. I had a roommate who was a varsity football player--he wasn't too swift--he barely got through academically. But he had such a positive attitude about this place. He could get through all the military stuff--the rates [knowledge that had to be memorized each day such as menus, days until the Navy football team beats Army, etc.]--even though he didn't have time to study them. He would give rates that were all wrong but he would get by because he did it so loudly and with so much energy. He wouldn't know what we were having for lunch but he would shout out something and they would let him get by because it did it with so much energy. He showed that he had the energy to make it here. That is the secret. Show them energy. Show the upperclass that you want to be here and they will leave you alone.

When you are about to go under, are you the kind of person who can call up your last measure of strength and keep going?   *Courtesy 1/C Jimmy Parker.*

"You have to do this especially at the times when you feel down--they [the upperclassmen] pick up on that and ride it. So you should especially show energy when you are down. I had another roommate who got down and never picked himself up. We could never get him to be positive and eventually the load just got too heavy. His academics went downhill and he was always having problems with the upperclassmen. He always complained that it was everything else and nothing that he could help. In reality, if he could have turned it around and shown them energy, he could have survived."

Another plebe stressed the role of a positive attitude in relation to failure and to the upperclassmen one cannot respect: "Don't be afraid to fail. Be ready to accept failure and you will have your head right when you do fail. Accept failure with the idea that now I'm going to do better. And remember, no matter what an upperclassman says to you, he can't kill you. "You have to be disciplined mentally because you will be yelled at for hours by people who you think are not as good as you. For hours! Accept being crapped on by people you don't respect. Be ready to accept the fact that you are living with a cousin of a KKK [Ku Klux Klan]. But be positive. Stay constantly motivated. Keep a fire inside and keep it lit all the time. Make yourself crazy in a way--when asked a question, don't be afraid to give it as loud as if you were using a knife." Just being away from home and without comforts of your home environment can compound the survival problems. Said one plebe:

The most difficult time for me was the first four weeks of Plebe Summer. I was being confronted with situations where even the things I used to be good at were not good. The pressures, the short amounts of sleep, the complete control of your time-- they were things I was not prepared for. I'd heard stories about them, but the situation was a lot more severe than I had expected. Even things that involved memorization and the learning of facts--the things that usually came very easily to me--in that kind of pressure situation, even those things I lost. I was starting over from scratch and being dependent on other people. That was difficult for me.

"The fact that I was living three thousand miles away from home and without a familiar face was a major part of the problem. That whole separation process was extremely difficult. While just surviving those first four weeks, I was going from one shock to another. Every free second I had I was spending trying to correct the things I knew I was doing wrong. You have to learn this--and get it across in your book. Part of being a plebe is learning to admit that you are going to do dumb things. After you realize that, it is just a matter of buckling down and fighting to overcome your dumb mistakes--and learning from them."

Many plebes had heard stories about how the upperclassmen would be on them, but many confessed that they expected to avoid heavy criticism because they planned to work extra hard and thereby please the upperclassmen. However, they all came to realize that those thoughts were dreams in a fantasy world. To survive, the candidate must take to heart the following comment:

"No matter what, you are not going to come here and get out of getting flamed on. There is no way to avoid it. They have to find something wrong with you. Even if there is nothing wrong with you, they will find something wrong and you have to accept that fact. If you decided to come here, accept it--especially during Plebe Summer, but it doesn't end when you get to the academic year. It slowly goes down but there is no great lifting once you get to the academic year because the upperclassmen outnumber you three to one. You just have to put your head down and plow through it--and then, well, I'm soon going to be shaking hands with those guys."

Is there a way to get back at the upperclassmen when they are flaming you? Actually, there is a way and it is called the loud response. Here are plebe comments:

"So much depends on the way you answer the questions. If you scream it right out, they will take it differently than if you cower down to them. My advice is to yell at them--even if you are wrong. As long as you are loud and you think you're right, it is okay. They may not know if you are right or wrong--they don't know a lot of the

"No matter what, you are not going to come here and get out of getting flamed on."
Courtesy USNA Photographic Branch

stuff they make us memorize--they've forgotten it and they're too busy studying to memorize it again. Even if they ask you the menu, you may know the entre and nothing else. But make up the rest and spit it out loudly and chances are you will be okay."

Another emphasized the importance of keeping your voice confident: "You don't have to answer right away when they ask you a question. Think about it; then draw yourself up and when you say it, say it with force and confidence. Someday you may have to tell some men to go risk their lives to take a hill and your voice has to maintain confidence. That is what they are training you for."

When you are being yelled at, you have to keep in mind that the person yelling at you made it through plebe year. Tell yourself, "If this guy made it, I can make it."

Courtesy USNA Photographic Branch.

"The loud response also is tradition," said another plebe in response to the above comment. "Back in the days of the sailing ships and, later, in the noisy engine rooms, the ability to shout so you could be understood was an important part of being in the Navy. That is where they get a lot of the tradition for shouting. It is hard at first--it seems silly. But the quicker you get used to it, the easier it will be."

Said another: "You can't be the quiet type and survive here. You have to have the self confidence to be loud and project yourself--like people are asking you stuff about some newspaper article. You have to give a summary and it has to be loud enough [so everybody] can hear what you are saying. You also have to have conviction in what you say. A couple of guys in our company had no confidence and no voice projection. One dropped out and the other is tumbling."

One of the most difficult problems plebes have is during Plebe Summer when the detailers do a lot of "in the face" yelling. The plebes were asked how they handled that. Here are some of their responses.

Said one: "I came in right out of high school and my counselor had told me they were going to yell at me. But I didn't know they would yell right in my face. I had a hard, hard time at the beginning because of that. After about the first semester, you learn what is going to be expected; then you know what they are going to yell at you about."

Said another: "I found out that it takes mental toughness. When you have somebody in your face yelling at you, you have to focus on *what* he is asking you, not on him calling you a dirt bag and stuff like that. It takes heavy-duty concentration and you just learn how to keep your mouth shut, and when you have to talk, you say, 'yes, sir, no, sir or no excuse, sir.' No excuse is the best--if you have an attitude problem and you have to give an excuse for everything, you'll get eaten alive."

Said another: "The best advice for me was not to take it personally--that the upperclassmen don't hate you; they are just doing their job--they want to make you a better midshipman." Said another: "It is really tough when you are staring in the face of a guy giving you a bad time, but I got through it by concentrating on just one thought. I kept saying to myself, 'Hey, if this guy made it, I'm going to make it.'"

Said another: "When I laid down at night, I often thought: Is this really for me? Then I would think about my thoughts before I came here and what I thought it was going to be like. I knew it was going to be hard, but I knew if I gave up, I would always wonder if I could have done it. Also, I couldn't think of any place I wanted to be more than here--any other place would be second choice. My dad, every day before I came here, he would say, 'Remember, they can't kill you and if they kill you, they can't eat you.' When I was getting yelled at, or thinking about all the hard times I was going through, I would say, 'I'm not dead yet and they haven't tried to eat me.'"

In every group of plebes there are always one or two whom the upperclassmen seem to pick on more than the others. The plebes and upperclassmen have a name for those unfortunates. They are called "s___ screens," although the vulgar first word is usually dropped and just the term "screen" is used in most conversations. During the interviews, one plebe volunteered his identify as a former screen and suggested that what he learned might be helpful to others who might share that fate.

He said: "I was a screen. During Plebe Summer I ranked 12th out of 12 in my squad. They then put me in a bad squad and I had to start to dig my way out--and I did, eventually. Later, I was first in my squad.

"My problem was that I was quiet to begin with and it took me a while to learn how to yell. I could be just as tough as they were but I didn't have the command voice and they really got on me. You have to be confident in anything you do. When you say, 'I'll find out, sir!' yell it in their face. If you know you are going to get in trouble, get your confidence up and be bold. Don't shake and shiver when being disciplined. Try not to show emotion--if you do start showing emotions, they are going to make it harder. Keep a straight face and if you have to show some emotion, laugh--they will be hard on you but they are going to respect you a lot more.

"But don't laugh during Plebe Summer; some got in a lot of trouble for that. I had learned to handle stress at home by laughing, but never laugh before an upperclassman if you can help it--wait until you get back to your room. Or the shower is a good place to laugh. Just remember to take on your game face in the hall."

Besides laughter, which many of the other plebes mentioned as a good outlet for pent-up emotions, there were many recommendations for relieving stress with physical workouts. The following was a typical comment: "What is hard is when you go back to your room, PO'd, and your temper boiling and no way to get it out of your system. But you have to keep your temper under control and I found that anything you can do physically helps. Wrestling was a great outlet for me and that is what is so great about the athletics that are required here. They help get all the pressure out of your system. And if it isn't your day for athletics, try to find something else to do even if it is just hard running."

Many of the plebes emphasized the importance of keeping positive things in your mind when the upperclassmen are about to get you down. The following are some of their comments:

Said one: "I kept at it a day at a time and tried not to look ahead--that is deadly--do not look ahead or the days will frighten you. Also, I tried not to take things personally, but sometimes I couldn't help it--that is hard not to do. But the thing that really got me through this year was thinking of the positive things about this place. I kept going back in my mind to the goals I had when I came here--I wanted an education and a job that I could be proud of--and a college that I could be proud of. Like now, when I go home, there are adults coming up to me and asking how it is going at the Naval Academy. They don't go up to my friends and ask them how it is going at the University of Pennsylvania. I get satisfaction out of that. I feel secure here. I know I'll have a job after I graduate--other college graduates don't have that guarantee. I have my books and I can concentrate on the things that are important here--I don't have to worry about all the other things most college students worry about. Thinking about all these positive things is what got me through the plebe year."

Said another: "I have always been determined but you can't help thinking about quitting, especially during the Dark Ages [weeks after Christmas vacation] when it is cold, dark and dreary and the upperclassmen are trying harder to make your life miserable. But when I started thinking about quitting, I always came back to the good things about this place and the reasons why I came here. And when you ask yourself, 'Do I really want to quit?' you have to think, 'What am I going to do when I quit?' Then you begin to realize that you have the security--you know you have a job when you get out. It's a big security blanket and having it makes everything more enjoyable, especially knowing I'll get a job that I will enjoy.

"I see my friends and all of them are working over the summer. I can relax because I don't have to worry about making money. During summer training I go to foreign countries--my friends can't say, 'I went to Spain this year.' That's a benefit and I would tell anyone who is thinking of quitting, 'Hey, think of what you would do if you weren't here. It may be rough but if this place can get you what you want, it's worth the extra effort to stay here.'"

Another said: "I never seriously thought about quitting because I am always looking to what I am going to get at the end. My father counseled me for a long time. He convinced me that once I made up my mind to accept the appointment, that I should enjoy the hell out of it, that I should look past all the negatives and enjoy the excitement and the adventure. I know it sounds corny, but how many others are able to do all of this--travel in the summer, learn to sail, you name it. My friends--they're all going to school getting ready for a boring nine to five job. When I get out of here, I'll have more responsibility than they'll have; I'll have more action; I'll see the world--all of these things keep me from thinking about quitting."

Another said: "I had an ROTC scholarship but after a year at this place, I am really glad I didn't take it. This place is steeped in tradition and I know I am following men like Chester Nimitz and other great leaders. If you go to a regular college, you're just another college student. Here you know you are something special--and the girls know it, too! Also, there are things you can do here that you can't do at any college. I'm planning on going to airborne school and places like Pearl Harbor and Rotterdam. And I'm going to Bermuda on a sailing ship. After being here just one year, I already know that I don't want to get out after five years."

Another said: "I agree that all the positive things about this place help keep you here, but the greatest thing of all is the network of friends that you develop here. They are the key to survival. And you know that you will have these same friends for your whole career--wherever we go in the world we will meet old friends--the same network of friends that we have right here.

"It is amazing how you come here in the summer and get with a group of guys, how you learn to depend upon each other--and the whole group against the other classes--that gives you the strength to survive.

"I had heard a lot of horror stories about this place before I came here, and although what I found here was not a letdown, it was not as hard as the stories. I also think many of the plebes now feel that it isn't as tough as they thought it was. But it was the friends who made it all worthwhile, and they sure make up for the lack of fraternity life at the regular colleges."

The final quotes in this chapter are selections recorded when some plebes were asked to give the kinds of tips they would pass on to a younger brother who was coming to the Academy next year. Here are some of the them:

"Know what you are getting into before you get here and accept it before you start--that is a huge thing. Also, keep your sense of humor about everything--laugh in your room with your roommates when you screw up."

"Expect the mental pressure to be tougher than you think and don't worry too much about the physical stuff--just be in decent shape. I didn't expect the memorizing and all that business. I didn't think it was going to be as bad as it was. "Also be ready for the heat and humidity during Plebe Summer. Drink lots of water when you get here--three glasses every meal. There were several days when it was over a hundred.

Keep that glint of humor in your eyes. It is a game. It is competition. It is a contest to see whose will is stronger. And always remember: in just a few years after you are going through the hell, you will be partying in Singapore and Hong Kong and Naples with those who are giving it to you.   *Courtesy 1/C Jimmy Parker.*

It was so hot in the open that shooting with a rifle against your face was painful. The humidity never gets below 94 percent around here during the summer and it usually stays around 90 degrees. This is very hard on westerners who live where it is dry."

"Keep in mind that this place isn't perfect. I came here with stars in my eyes, thinking how nice it would be living in honor with people who want to serve their country. But you look around after awhile and you see upperclassmen that you can't respect--they're pushing the system and getting by with as little as possible. This was a shock for me and I was cynical for awhile. But I finally realized that I was just naive. This place isn't perfect and it never will be. Be realistic in your expectations. As soon as I accepted the fact that this place isn't perfect, then I began to appreciate all the great people here even more."

"I'd tell my brother to keep a clean room. I was told that, but I couldn't believe that the upperclassmen will get dirty looking for dirt--they will get down on their knees and get under the bed to find a speck of dust."

"Also get ready for lots of nitpicking. I never expected their pickiness about the uniform--they can always find something. They tell you to get the strings off your white works [the white fatigue uniform worn by plebes--the strings are called Irish Pennants] and I got some of them off. But at the first formation they looked in my pockets and pulled some strings out. They can find anything wrong so don't be surprised at how picky they are."

"At home they sent us an exercise sheet on running and other stuff--how much we should do. After I got out of school in May, I worked all day, then ran at home about five or six o'clock. That was nothing like running here at eleven o'clock in all the heat. To train properly I would recommend running in the middle of the day just to get used to the heat."

"I would tell him to learn to swim before he comes here. I never swam in my life and it gave me the most trouble of anything here--and I mean *anything here*. If a person can get good and validate [be excused from] swimming, that would give him two extra periods a week. That doesn't sound like much, but if you can get them before lunch, it really helps a lot."

"Realize that things are going to change drastically. Here you are, just out of high school and you are going to live the best month of your life. You feel good about yourself; you did well in high school; you've won an appointment to the Naval Academy; now you can go to the beach and let your hair down and just relax. But you don't realize that you are about to have your world turned upside down. Suddenly you are away from your family; you won't see your friends--your emotional attachments are severed instantly. Then you will start questioning yourself--you do it the first day. Is it always going to be like this? You start to wonder and you start to question whether you can handle what you got yourself into. An enlisted guy with time off can take a walk and get a sandwich at the corner store. Here you cannot leave. That really bothered me when I got hungry--I wanted to go to a store outside the gate and buy something. We couldn't even walk out in the front yard during Plebe Summer. In fact, you don't even want to venture out of your room for fear that an upperclassman will stop you. These are the things I would tell a younger brother coming here. If he expects all these things, it won't be such a shock and it won't create as much stress." [A graduate who read the above comment said: "During the first summer we used to say that the world we left didn't exist anymore. The town we could see beyond the walls was really just a projection on a screen.]

The final tip came from a female plebe who, with a puckish smile, said: "About all I'd tell my little brother is to be sure and memorize his social security number and not to forget how to laugh."

EIGHTEEN
A FIRST CLASSMAN'S
PERSPECTIVE ON SURVIVAL

Many upperclassmen were also interviewed during the research for this book. However, one of them, a first classman from Ohio not only summarized much of what the others gave in the way of survival advice for plebes, but he also described some of his personal experiences as a plebe himself, and later, when he was responsible for training them. The author believes the first classman's comments will be very helpful to candidates. Therefore, the text of that interview, which follows, is presented in its entirety.

Said the first classman: "I have been heavily involved in the training of the plebes and therefore I have seen it from both perspectives--that of the plebe and that of the upperclassman. "The biggest difference between the two is that I thought as a plebe that everybody was out to get me. Now I see that the upperclassmen are just doing a job they have to do. They have to indoctrinate the plebe into the Brigade of Midshipmen and into our way of thinking. And I can say with a lot of pride that the people we met on I-Day [Induction Day--the first day when the plebes begin their training] and the people who are over there now are totally different persons. In seven short weeks they have become midshipmen. [Note that the first classman calls them "short weeks"--this is definitely a difference in perspective.]

"The rest of the plebe year is just a process of refining what was started during Plebe Summer. They go to classes and they have to learn their rates and they always have a conflict in deciding whether they should study for their classes or study for their rates. For the past year, I have been one of the guys in the company who has had to help the plebes solve some of these problems.

"The biggest problem was homesickness, especially this summer. I had one plebe after just three days who was so down that he didn't know what to do and he wanted to talk to mom and dad [which is forbidden except at certain times]. He was at the low point of his whole life.

"I called him into my room, sat him down, and one-on-one, I told him what the purpose of the Academy was and what we were trying to do during Plebe Summer. But he was bawling his eyes out because he was scared. I was as sympathetic as I could be because I could remember being in the same exact position, but I maintained our professional relationship and let him get it all out. Then, instead of saying it's going to be all right, I turned it around and I made him start thinking about why he was here and what he was going to do. Then I made him set some simple goals that he could do every day--to have a squared away uniform and room, and know his rates every time he walked out of his room. "That's a key survival tool for this place--having goals. Not that this semester I'm going to get a 4.0 GPA or an "A" on the obstacle course or, do a good job with my rates. Not any of that. They have to be realistic and short term. You have to keep the big picture and live just for today--that's what I taught him.

"Then I did let him call home, and it turned out that this plebe was one of the best we had all summer.

"Part of the preparation coming into plebe year is to say to yourself, 'Why am I going to the Academy.' And to survive, your reason should be,'That I am going to become a professional officer in the naval service.'

"Unfortunately there are some who can't say that. I counseled another plebe this summer whose parents wanted him to come here so he decided to go along with them. When he got here, he found that he really didn't want to be here. He wasted our time, his time--he grew a little bit--he got a little bigger, but quitting, which he did, had to be a major setback in his life. "It has to be the individual's own decision to come here. I know, it is a great honor and all that, which is appealing, but you will not succeed if you aren't looking forward to giving nine years of your life [four years at the Academy and five years of required duty]. Maybe the Navy [or Marine Corps] is for you and maybe not; you have to trust your gut feeling. And if you really want to come here, come and work hard and do your best, and if you fail, then at least you tried. If I hadn't come here, the rest of my life I would have been thinking maybe I could have done it. But coming to the Naval Academy was the best decision I ever made in my life.

"I made that decision in my freshman year [of high school]. I knew I wanted higher education and to work with people. I began to look at the options I had. My junior year I made the full commitment because I began filling out all the forms. I was well rounded, had good academics and SAT scores. But my first semester here I got a 1.41 GPA and the first "F" in my life. I went before the Academic Board and was inches from being kicked out. The fear of God was in me--officers sitting around looking me over. But I knew I wanted to be here and I convinced them that I was working hard--I just wasn't prepared. My problem was that I didn't know how to study. I got the "F" in English because my writing skills were bad--I had never had any real practice in high school. I had studied more than most of my friends in high school but not enough for this place.

"I got all kinds of help after that and the things that kept me here were the upperclassmen who tutored me and helped me learn to study and the Writing Center. When someone is in academic trouble, the amount of counseling here is tremendous--everybody starts helping you--your squad leaders, the company officers, your professors--the professors are required to give extra instruction to any student who requests it. Also, if I ever had a question on any homework assignment, I could knock on any upperclassman's door. No matter what they were doing, they would drop it and help out. They would never harass you for that--academics are sacred here--they are the number one priority. "I learned a lot about studying that year. I learned that I was a procrastinator and my upperclass tutors made me learn and believe what they call the "seven P's," which are Proper, Prior, Planning, Prevents P..s, Poor Performance. And all it is is time management. It is being able to look at the big picture and say, okay, I have these daily assignments and I have to plan out when this project is due and when the quizzes and tests are going to be. And if a paper is due or a test is coming up, don't go out on the weekend. You have to sacrifice to get

Academics are sacred at the Naval Academy, and it is the smart plebe who takes advantage of the extra instruction (EI) that every professor is obligated to give.

Courtesy USNA Photographic Branch

success--by coming here you sacrifice things that are now privileges.

"In high school I was able to pay attention in class, study formulas and look over notes right before a test and do well. The number of papers and projects [in high school] can't even begin to compare to here. In one semester I had 11 papers due because I had economics, history and English all in the same semester. I had never written that much before in my life.

"My advice is to come in here with good keyboard skills for word processing. Also try to learn how to study more efficiently. When I was a plebe, I studied 35 to 40 hours a week. That is incredible, ridiculous. Now I can study 25 hours or less and get twice as good results. But you have to plan things out. You don't sacrifice a course you know you are good in--you adjust your study schedule and learn to get all the work done.

"Note taking is very important. You should come in here with the idea that you are going to take copious notes. And remember, the classroom is where you get your education--not in the room later, reading a textbook. The best advice for a plebe is to

161

pay attention in class--make use of that time so you don't have to learn the same thing back in your room. And do not study your rates in class, which I have seen plebes do because they feel under the gun. Instead, pay attention and interact as much as you can. I also recommend that plebes should try to sit in the front few rows. Your attention span is less when you are at the back of the room. Go into every class like you really mean business.

"To make it through here you also have to have a positive attitude and confidence in yourself. I know lots of people who got the first "F" they ever got in their life at this place. But you have to grow from that. You have to look at yourself and say, 'I did my best and failed; now what did I learn from that;' then go on. And always try to remember, nobody is trying to weed you out. On the contrary, the system is designed to build people who are strong and can handle pressure--people who have the guts to hang in there when the going gets tough. That's what this place is about--and the positive attitude is what is going to help you make it. I was once at the ultimate low, ready to be kicked out. Now I have the class ring; I'm starting my senior year; I'm well respected by my peers and subordinates; and this is because I hung in there and trusted the system.

"And what would I tell a candidate if he asked me what is the best thing about this place?

"I would tell him that it is a place where you will find out who you are."

NINETEEN
ACADEMIC SURVIVAL TIPS

Upperclass pressure is not the only problem the plebe has to solve. For many there is also academic shock to overcome.   Who is most likely to suffer academic shock? After discussing the problem with the midshipmen, it seems that the ones most likely to have problems are those who do well in high school with little effort. Those types will have problems because they have not learned to study efficiently; in high school they got good grades just by listening in class and by cramming before tests.

Those who had to work hard in high school for what they learned do not experience as much academic shock say the mids. Some in this category were from demanding high schools with high standards, where students were held accountable for most assignments.

Others developed good work habits for other reasons. One said, "Hey, school was never easy for me and I always worked for what I got. So it wasn't all that much more difficult when I got here."

You will rarely have enough time to do all your homework. The corollary of that is you will always have to take some "hits" because, in the small classes, your professors will know who is prepared and who is not.   *Courtesy USNA Photographic Branch.*

Another said, "I lived out in the country with nothing else to do and I just got into the habit of outlining every book as we went through them. I had no idea then how much that habit would help me when I got here."

But forget about academic shock for the moment, since you already know that you will suffer from it to some degree. The subject of this chapter is academic survival and its goal is to give you information from the midshipmen--information learned the hard way--which will help you, not only to survive the shock, but to put you on the right road for solid academic achievement.

The comments that follow represent a wide assortment of advice, mostly from midshipmen who initially had to struggle to pull themselves out of the academic quicksand. As you read these comments, think how you might adapt some of their techniques and recommendations to your own study routine.

When you are in chemistry class, think only of chemistry.   *Courtesy 1/C Jimmy Parker.*

The first comments are from the varsity quarterback, a first classman who remembers how he had to surmount not only the academic and upperclass pressures, but the athletic pressure as well. He said:

"Actually the pressure in sports helped me because it forced me to do the things that are most important.

"And the most important thing of all is so important it should be a rule that is

164

adopted by every plebe. It is this: *Always put your mind where you are at.* That means when you are on the football field, think only about football and nothing else. Then, when you are in chemistry class, think only about chemistry and nothing else.

"That might seem simplistic to a plebe, but it is really not that simple, especially when you have so little time and so many demands upon it. But if you follow the rule, you will focus 100 percent on whatever you are doing, and you will try to achieve as much as possible with that time. In chemistry class, focus 100 percent on what is going on and learn as much as you can in the class. Don't just say, 'Hey, I'll listen to this guy and pick up what I don't understand when I get back to the room.' That is a trap. Do not let anything go by you in class that you do not understand. Ask questions and stay alert. Give it your best concentration. Then when you go on to English class, do the same thing.

"I have one other important recommendation but it is very difficult to get plebes to do it. I will use chemistry again as an example. When you are back in your room and you start to study your chemistry, do not go directly to the assignment. Instead, review your notes from the last class and make sure you understand everything that is in them.

"I know this seems like a waste of time--it did to me, too, and it was very hard for me to start doing it--you always want to charge ahead and get the next assignment out of the way so you can go on to something else. But what you'll find is that the next assignment probably requires knowledge that you are supposed to have learned already. When you charge ahead, you spin your wheels without that knowledge and end up spending more time on the assignment and, to do it right, you have to go back anyhow. This is very inefficient and you cannot survive here, with time as limited as it is, without developing an efficient study routine. Another thing I would recommend for a candidate trying to get ready for this place is to get rid of all distractions when you sit down to study. Forget that you are going to call your friend. It goes back to the same rule; put your mind where you are at. If you are going to study chemistry, then study chemistry and do not let anything distract you.

"Another thing--it isn't the quantity of time that you spend studying; it's the quality of the time. And here, you must prioritize because you will often have twice as much work for the time that is available. You have to decide that this assignment has top priority and this other assignment just may not get done. Of course, in doing this you have to be ready to take your lumps in some classes. But that is the system here. Everybody has to learn it sooner or later and you might as well come in here ready to make those decisions.

"I know it is difficult doing that--it was difficult for me to go to a class knowing that I would probably do badly if the guy hit us with a quiz. Those who have been conscientious students really fight this, but I would tell any candidate to get it in your head that you are rarely going to have enough time to do everything that you want to do, especially that first year when the upperclassmen are pressuring you to learn your rates. If the plebes could just get over this mental hurdle quickly, they would be so much better off. There are little things, too, that would help them. For example, don't sit down to study without all the things that you are going to need. If you need a book from the library, get it ahead of time so you don't waste those precious moments that they have set aside for you to study. That is YOUR time--those hours are sacred and the upperclassmen cannot bug you then--but it has to be used efficiently.

"One final tip--when you have things that require a lot of memorization, work with one or two others who have to learn the same things. Memorize; then test each other; then memorize some more. That kind of group study helped me and a lot of others." The next advice comes from a third classman: "I didn't have to study in high school and it took me the whole first semester to get into the groove. But I learned some things that I would pass on to [new] plebes.

"First, do not be timid in class. The system here makes you that way and as a plebe you tend to carry that meek attitude into your classes. That is a mistake. Forget you are a plebe when you get inside the classroom. Be aggressive. Ask questions. Start discussions. Not only will you learn more, but some of the professors grade on class participation and you need all the points you can get.

"Next, realize you will never have enough time to do all of the studying you need to do. Get your mind prepared to blow off one assignment in order to get another one done. It's called prioritizing and I guarantee, you will fight it. But it has to be done and the sooner you accept that, the sooner you can start juggling assignments to keep from going under in everything.

"Another thing, take notes intensively in class. It is real easy just to sit and listen. You say, 'oh yeah, I understand everything he is saying.' You do, but two days later you have forgotten; then you have to dig it out of the book. Also, while you are taking notes, listen carefully and the prof will tell you the questions that are going to be on the next test. Now, he doesn't actually say, 'This is a question I'm going to give on the next test,' but he always hints at it. They all give it away in some way or another. You just have to figure out how they do it.

"Another advantage of taking thorough notes is that it keeps you awake. You can't imagine how tired you get around here and it's easy to fall asleep. Some mids get up and walk around in order to stay awake--the profs are used to that--most would rather you would do that than sleep at your desk. But when you take good notes, it keeps you alert and that is important."

A plebe, after hearing the above comments, wanted to stress the importance of prioritizing:

"You have to be ready to take the hit. Say, I've got an English assignment due tomorrow and also a quiz in chemistry. I have to decide, maybe, to study the chemistry and to blow off the English assignment and take the hit in English the next day. Those are the kinds of decisions that you're always having to make.

"Also, always try to take one course where you can learn everything in class--where you are not going to get the hits if you don't read the assignment. That was history for me--I took good notes and paid attention in class and got by except at the end. We had four books to read and I ditched them, then, before the final, I had to read all four in one week. But I had that extra time all semester and I didn't take any hits."

The next suggestion comes from a second classman, but it was repeated by several others who have had special counseling to improve their study routine:

"It is very important to keep separate notes on everything that you are supposed to do. I was told that at the beginning but just passed it off. When I got into trouble, that was the first thing they asked me: 'When you sit down to study, do you put your notes in front of you so you can see what you have to do?'

"So I started doing it and now I can't believe how much it helps. On the notes I say, do this, and study extra on that--I use the little yellow noters--the kind that are on a pad--the kind you can stick up. At night, when I start to study, I pull the noters off the pad for the things I need to do that night and I put them out in front of me on the desk so I won't forget anything. That is what is important--you don't ignore things that are staring at you."

One of the main problems for the plebes is the conflict between learning the professional material assigned by the upperclassmen--the "pro stuff" and "rates"--and the regular academic homework. Several of the mids commented on this conflict and gave advice on how to resolve it.

Said a second classman: "The problem is that the upperclassmen give you these assignments like, 'Be prepared to give a ten minute oral report on a hand grenade.' Well, you are living with them [the upperclassmen, not hand grenades] and the profs are over in the other buildings, so there is always that extra pressure to do the pro stuff or to know this or that rate rather than study for the academics. The upperclass threat is right there, while the academic threat is down the road. Many plebes get themselves in trouble because they forget to balance it out--they work too much on their rates and not enough on the academics because they are frightened.

"What you have to do is follow the study routine like a slave. Use the pro time from seven to eight for learning that stuff; then use the time from eight until eleven for the academics. And if you get behind, you've always got the weekend to bail yourself out of whatever trouble you are in. It's a juggling act."

Said another mid, a third-classman: "The pro stuff is a problem but it is also the most interesting if you came here because you are interested in ships and airplanes and guns and missiles. It is a lot easier to memorize things that are interesting--it is much easier than the stuff during Plebe Summer--stuff out of *Reef Points* like John Paul Jones' 'Qualifications of the Naval Officer.'"

Said another third classman: "A lot of that stuff [pro stuff] could be learned before you come here. Learn all you can about the different ships and airplanes in the Navy--even learn their number designations if you can. But don't flaunt that knowledge when you come here--keep it cool that you know all that."

A plebe who was listening to the above said: "Yeah, but also tell them it will help if they take a public speaking course and they know how to research. They'll [the upperclassmen] give you an assignment to give a ten to fifteen minute report on a certain kind of ship. For that, you have to search everything--I mean really research to get enough for that long a report. Then you have to stand up in the hall, maybe on a chair, and you have to speak loud and clear."

The final comment is from a recent plebe who was trained to study at the Naval Academy Prep School (NAPS). He said: "What I really learned at NAPS is to follow a routine. They had me programmed. I studied the pro stuff from seven until eight. Then I knocked it off and hit the books at eight o'clock.

Academic survival for those who are admitted to the Naval Academy boils down to just one word: motivation. If you have the motivation, you will survive the academics.

Courtesy 1/C Jimmy Parker.

"And we learned that you don't mess around during that time. You don't go visiting or BS with people in the company. You never go to the other side of the building to see somebody. You sit down and you study.

"You have to discipline yourself to do that. Because of what I learned at NAPS--and I dreaded going there originally--I had very little problem with the academics here because I knew how to study. I was disciplined when I got here. By Christmas last year I was twelfth in the battalion and had a 3.25 GPA--it later dropped to a 2.95 but I'm happy because I probably wouldn't have survived without the discipline I learned at NAPS."

A word of caution is appropriate for a conclusion to this chapter. Throughout this book you have read statements from mids that tend to exaggerate whatever predicament they are describing. Over and over you have read statements like the one above: "I probably wouldn't have survived without..." These kinds of statements are quoted to alert you to potential problems--to get your attention. But do not take them all literally. Mids might say that they would never have survived unless... But, in most instances, they are saying that for effect--to get your attention.

It is a fact that the Naval Academy is a rigorous academic institution. It is also a fact that the professional demands upon a midshipman's time makes going to the Naval Academy roughly the equivalent of going to a Stanford or a Yale while holding down a part time, very demanding job.

But despite all of that, it still should be emphasized that roughly 78 percent of those who make it into the Academy also make it through all four years. Also, it should be emphasized that a large number of those who fall by the wayside do so because they are not strongly motivated.

So, as a candidate, and as you ponder your chances of academic survival, just keep in mind two things, which have been said in earlier chapters.

First, if they give you an appointment to the Naval Academy, it is almost a sure bet that you have the potential ability to survive the academic challenge.

Second, after you get into the Naval Academy, surviving everything--upperclass pressure and academics--is primarily a function of your motivation. If you truly want what is available at the end of the four years, namely, a career in the naval services, you do not have to worry because you will find ways to survive. There are tens of thousands of active-duty Academy graduates who are doing everything from piloting jets to commanding submarines who suffered as many frustrations as the midshipmen whose comments you have been reading. They made it and they are successful now because they wanted to make it--and you can, too, if you have their kind of desire.

TWENTY
GETTING ALONG WITH CLASSMATES
AND ROOMMATES

During interviews the midshipmen were sometimes asked to describe the worst and the best things about the Naval Academy. Most agreed that the worst thing about the Naval Academy is the loss of personal freedom.

Most agreed that the best thing about the Naval Academy is the extraordinary friendships that are developed.

If you put iron in a hot fire, then hammer it, it becomes stronger and harder. In a way, that is how the friendships are forged at the Naval Academy.

On I-Day about 1200 strangers get shuffled off and sorted into companies, platoons and squads. And one of the plebes' assignments that first day is to memorize the name and hometown of each person in their squad. And the second day, they must learn the same information for each person in their platoon. Those are the first steps in converting strangers into friends.

At the same time, roommates are assigned, with each plebe normally sharing a room with two others--of the same sex, of course.

Then plebe indoctrination begins in earnest, and, as a part of that indoctrination, certain concepts, which are the raw materials for the forging of friendships, are hammered home to the plebes day after day.

"Never bilge a classmate or a roommate."

"Never leave your classmates or roommates behind."

"Work together and survive together."

"Always inspect each other first."

But what do the above concepts really mean? And how are the extraordinary friendships that the midshipmen speak of forged out of this raw material?

As in the three previous chapters, the explanations are best given by those who have had the experiences. Here is how the midshipmen explain them.

Said a third classman: "The rule here is that you never bilge a classmate or a roommate. That means you should never try to make yourself look better than a classmate or roommate.

"As an example, when the upperclassmen are grilling one of your classmates in the hall and she doesn't know a rate, you would never step up and say, 'I know it, sir!' then give the rate. That would be an example of bilging. You would be trying to make yourself look good at the expense of a classmate. "Another example is when three roommates are standing an inspection of their room. Your bed might be made perfectly and so might the bed of another roommate. But if the upperclassmen find that the third bed is not up to the standards of the other two, it is the other two plebes who will catch hell. The beds that were well made are ripped up and the two plebes are hacked. The reason? If you know how to make a bed that well, why haven't you helped your roommate learn the same thing? You have made yourself look good at his expense--you have bilged him."

Said another third classman: "Another thing you never do is leave a roommate behind. Even when you have uniform races where everybody tries to change from whites into PE gear in two minutes, you never step outside that room without your roommate. That means even if you are going to be late for a formation. If you show up without a roommate, that is a bilge--you are making yourself look good at his expense.

"Sometimes this is a problem, like when a roommate isn't as fast or maybe is not motivated as much as you are. But still, it is better to be late and take the hit than to show up without him. Of course, when you are asked why you are late, you have to say, 'no excuse, ma'am!' and take your lumps. Then you try to work it out with your roommate later. If you start blaming your roommate, you really get into hot water.

"It's the same thing when you are doing something with a bunch of your classmates. If someone is dragging, you go help them. You carry something for them or you encourage them. You're bilging your classmates if you go off and leave them."[1]

The importance of working together was stressed by midshipmen. Said a first classman: "Classmate and roommate loyalty is preached from day one--I just gave a lecture to plebes this summer. In the lecture I stressed the importance of always looking around to see what needs to be done, especially in the rooms. And when you see something that needs done, do it. Don't wait. Don't think, 'Well, that's not my mess; it's the other guy's so he can do it.' That is the wrong kind of thinking for this place. Here, classmates and roommates can't keep a balance sheet, yet everybody comes here with that in their head--I do this and he does that and we keep track so neither of us has to do too much. That is the wrong attitude. Get the balance sheet out of your head and do what has to be done. It will equal out in the long run, and if it doesn't, so what?"

Said a second classman: "It is also important to open up with your roommates and communicate. You run into trouble when one of them is unhappy or thinks something is wrong with the others but won't communicate the problem. If you have a problem, you have to get it out. You can't keep it to yourself. You should always let your roommates know how you are feeling and they should do the same. When you get it out in the open, you can compromise and get along. When you keep it inside, pressure builds up, then hard feelings, and sooner or later, something will break down and you all will pay the price.

"Just remember, you never know who you are going to have to room with, but you make the best of it by working together side by side. Of course, it helps if you make

---

[1] In the movie, *An Officer and a Gentlemen*, the actor Richard Gere played the role of a classic bilger. According to the midshipmen who discussed this movie with the author, the fictional character played by Gere would never have survived the Naval Academy or the Air Officer Candidate School at Pensacola--the fictional setting of the movie.

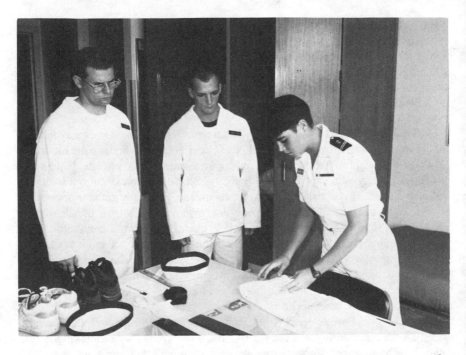

You and your roommates will be shown how to fold clothes and maintain your room. After that, in the everyday time crunch, room maintenance has to be a cooperative effort.

Courtesy USNA Photographic Branch.

friends easily."

Said another first classman: "Roommates have to work together or it is very difficult to survive. If I don't feel like cleaning up the room, you are going to have to do it if you are my roommate. That is bad, because when the upperclassmen come by, you can't bilge me; you just have to say, when asked why the room is dirty, 'no excuse, sir!' even though it is your lazy roommate's fault. Sometimes this is a real problem that you can get into just by the luck of who you get stuck with. But the philosophy here is basically, 'suck it up and get the job done,'--in other words, if you won't work together, we will make it so hard on you that you will."

Said a second classman: "Everybody learns sooner or later to do the big things in the room--cleaning and making the beds, etc. But it is the little things that make the difference between good and bad roommates. A good roommate anticipates problems and takes steps to solve them. If my roommate sees that I am late getting to the room, yet I have a formation, he anticipates all the things that I'm going to need. He lays out my uniform and checks it for lint, or he checks my shoes and if they need it, he shines them. It is these kinds of things that mean a lot. When roommates look out for each other like that, a close bond develops. That's how really close friendships develop. And that attitude, which is common throughout the brigade, is what I love about this place."

Said another mid: "It also helps to divide up the workload according to who does things best. Like before an inspection, one guy who can do a good rack [bed] does all three of them. Another, who can wax the deck well, does that. What you don't want is a guy who is a slob--who is messy with everything. But, if you get one, you just have to communicate and work it out."

Another mid, commenting about the previous statement: "That's right, but it can get so bad that you never can work it out. I ended up being a screen during Plebe Summer because I had this roommate who had seen [the movie] Top Gun and was just

Even when you think you are ready for inspection.....

...the upperclassmen can always find something that is not up to their standards.

Courtesy USNA Photographic Branch.

here to put on a uniform for awhile so he could go off and fly an F-14. Of course, because he was a slob, the upperclassmen got on my other roommate and I because we weren't teaching him to do things right. They said we were bilging him. It is very frustrating when you become a screen for things your roommate won't do--and, of course, there are no excuses. Luckily, at the end of Plebe Summer I got a new roommate and soon afterward I got first in my squad."

Another mid, a female plebe, confessed that she was having problems that were impossible to solve. She said, "I have this problem right now that I can't find a way

174

to solve. As a female you don't have that many choices for roommates--you can't change, and whoever you get to live with, that is who you are going to live with for a very, very long time. So, all I do is suck it up and go on. If you always have little squabbles, that won't help; it just makes both of you upset. You have to wait until things are calm before talking things out."

Another female plebe who heard the above comment, said: "With roommate problems you definitely don't talk right when the problem occurs. You have to let things cool down a little bit, then talk about it. When you're both cooled down, you can see each other's side. It generally works out then. Also, you have to remember that no matter where you go in life you are always going to have to deal with people you don't like--in the business world--in the fleet--it is good to learn now how to communicate with people you don't get along with."

All of the stress during the plebe year tends to make a bad roommate situation even worse. Said one plebe who was experiencing problems at the time of her interview: "I have a roommate who studies 24 hours a day. It is really annoying. She is up studying at three in the morning. I realize that some things I do annoy her, too. Before I get mad and say you are psycho, I just say, hey, look, I've got to think about this and realize I do things that really annoy her. I tell myself that I have to control my temper. If you don't control your temper, you will kill each other. It is easy to get annoyed here. You have so much pressure, so much stress and the last thing you want to do is come in and see the same person every day. When it gets bad, you just have to leave the room and go somewhere else."

You may get lucky and have the opportunity to pick your roommates. If so, take the advice of one plebe who said: "At the beginning of your plebe year your room is a base. You can't spend any time out in the hallway or else you are going to be attacked by the upperclass. You have to get used to living with these people somehow. In my company we were able to pick our roommates right at the end of our Plebe Summer--before the academic year. With that in mind, when you are with the other plebes during the summer, be looking around at the people you are working with and see who you might like to room with--who you are going to be able to survive with. You are going to be spending at least the next semester and possibly the whole year with that same group of people."

Keep in mind that in some companies you may have to share a room with three or even four other plebes. One plebe who had the latter situation said: "You are always going to have some disagreements at times. There is no way around it. But here is the way it works in my room. I live in a five-man room and we are packed in there like sardines. You can't survive unless you work together so you have to learn how to get along. There are times when we have disagreements, but you can't let things build up. If some guy is bothering me...well, I won't repeat what we say, but we lay it to him. We get it out in the open. We've even had some physical scuffles, but in the end you apologize and make up. You have to. You are under so much pressure, you have to let off the steam. It would be much worse if you let it build up. But, I should also say that my roommates are now great friends. I think that's because we're honest with each other and we all know how we feel."

The final comment is from a first classman who stresses the importance of roommates checking each other. He said: "The best roommates are those who are always checking your back--literally. Before anybody goes out of the room, you look each other's backs over for little pieces of lint or thread. If one goes out and I find something like that on his uniform, I will come down harder on the roommate than on the one with the IP [Irish Pennant--a piece of thread]."

What you have read should be enough testimony to convince you how unique life is at the Naval Academy when compared to a civilian college. (If you need more convincing, go visit some college dorm rooms or a fraternity house.) Clearly, you cannot be a loner or a person who is selfish and wants his or her own way. To survive the group dynamics at the Academy, you must be the kind of person who is eager to conform to group standards.

Think about the last statement and honestly try to assess your own feelings about living in a room with two other persons.

Do you need privacy? You are not going to get it.

Do you tend to bottle up your feelings and keep things to yourself? That is not going to work very long.

Do you hate confrontations? You cannot avoid them.

Can you tolerate being repeatedly blamed for mistakes and the sloppiness of other people? This will happen time after time.

Do you have an unerasable balance sheet in your head? If so, you had better find a new eraser because you have to get rid of the balance sheet and quit thinking about what is fair and what is not fair; you are going to have to do what has to be done, period--and if you cannot accept that, you are sure to be miserable. Are you adaptable?

Can you keep an open mind?

Would you like to develop a lot of deep, personal friendships--friendships that will last for the rest of your life? Say, "Yes," to those questions and you are probably ready for your new roommates.

TWENTY-ONE
YOU MUST LIVE BY THE HONOR CONCEPT

The subject of the last chapter was how you must live with classmates and roommates. The subject of this chapter is how you must live with yourself.

Specifically, it is how you must live honorably, both as a midshipman and, later, as a naval officer.

The words of the Academy Honor Concept provide a prescription for your personal behavior:

Midshipmen are persons of integrity: They stand for that which is right.

a. They tell the truth and ensure that the full truth is known. They do not lie.

b. They embrace fairness in all actions. They ensure that work submitted as their own is their own, and that assistance received from any source is authorized and properly documented. They do not cheat.

c. They respect the property of others and ensure that others are able to benefit from the use of their own property. They do not steal.

But the Honor Concept is an idea that is broader and more positive than the words.

A part of the idea is how midshipmen are to be treated by their classmates and their officers. It will always be assumed that midshipmen are honorable persons. They are persons who can be trusted at all times. They are persons who are forthright under all circumstances. They are persons who, if they say they will do something, they will do it because giving their word is the same as pledging their honor.

Another part of the idea is how midshipmen relate to others. Specifically, midshipmen must always be ready to judge honorable and dishonorable behavior when

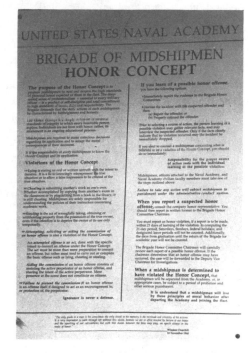

This plaque is mounted where every midshipman will see it and be reminded of the place of honor in every midshipman and naval officer's life.

Courtesy 1/C Jimmy Parker.

they see it around them. They must neither permit behavior of the dishonorable type, nor must they accept anything that results from dishonorable behavior.   In other words, living with the Honor Concept requires midshipmen to take on the responsibility of seeing that everyone else also lives by it.

This requires midshipmen to take action whenever they believe they have observed dishonorable behavior. That action may take one of three different forms.

1. Midshipmen may report the incident directly to the Midshipman Honor Organization. In Academy jargon, this is the "directly turn in" option.

2. Midshipmen may confront the offender and get more facts, including the offender's side of the story, then report the incident. This is the "counsel and turn in" option.

3. Midshipmen may confront the offender and counsel the person. Following the counselling the midshipmen must complete a form that documents the matter and this form is turned into the Brigade Honor Chairman. No further action is taken, but the form is retained should the midshipman who was counselled get into trouble. This third option is called "counsel and drop."

What if a midshipman observes an offense and does nothing?

Doing nothing is also an offense. However, it is a "conduct" offense, punishable by disciplinary measures, rather than an "honor" offense, which could result in separation (being permanently expelled).

And what happens to those who have been turned in for an honor violation?

Their cases are entirely in the hands of the Brigade Honor Organization, which is administered exclusively by the midshipmen.

When a potential violation has been reported,the Chairman of the Honor Committee, an elected first classman, appoints an investigating officer--also a first classman--who investigates both sides, that of the accused and the accuser. The investigating officer also informs the accused of the charges and gives that person advice.

In addition, a first or second classman who is a company honor representative is assigned as an advisor to the investigating officer. The sole job of the advisor is to make sure that the rights of the accused midshipman are upheld.

Once a case has been investigated, it is then given to the Brigade Honor Chairman who must then decide its disposition. The Honor Chairman does not have to send a case to an Honor Board. If Honor Chairman believes that there is clearly no integrity issue involved, he or she has the option to drop the case as a misunderstanding. A second option, if it seems warranted, is to personally counsel the accused and document that counselling. A third option, if it is an integrity issue but not lying, cheating or stealing, is to bring the accused before a Counselling Board, which also must document and file a counselling report. The fourth option is to send the accused before the Brigade Honor Board.

The Brigade Honor Board is made up of a combination of elected and appointed midshipmen who represent a cross section of the Brigade. The Chairman of the Honor Committee also serves as Chairman of the Honor Board.

At the Board hearing the investigating officer introduces witnesses and asks questions designed to make certain all aspects of the case are understood. Those are

178

followed by questions from the Board members. The accused is then afforded the final opportunity to question each witness.

After the investigating officer has called witnesses for the prosecution, it is the accused's turn to exercise his or her options. These include the right to remain silent, or to present a defense, which could include the calling of witnesses who might be supportive.

Then the Board votes and decides guilt or innocence. If the accused is found innocent, no further action is required; the accused is completely exonerated.

If the accused is found guilty, the Board passes the case on to a legal officer who reviews the Board's decision, and then the case is passed on to the Commandant of Midshipmen. The Commandant, after interviewing the violator and reviewing all documents in that person's Academy file (which are not available to the Brigade Honor Board), must then decide whether the midshipman should be separated or retained, and if retained, what the disciplinary action and terms of probation should be.

During a long interview with the Honor Committee Chairman, he was asked to explain why one violator may be separated while another might be retained, albeit with discipline and a probationary regimen. Here is his reply:[1]

"Many things may affect that decision. Usually premeditation is a factor. I will give you two examples to explain what I mean.

"Let's say a midshipman signs out on a Sunday morning to go to one of the churches in Annapolis. She does not have liberty, but she does have the right to go to the church and then return immediately. But let's say she goes as far as the church steps, then sneaks off to see her boyfriend. If she is later asked, 'Did you go to church?' and she replies in the affirmative, then she has deliberately tried to conceal the truth. Technically, her feet did touch the church steps but her act was dishonorable because she was deliberately evading the truth when she told us that. In other words, she was lying. In this case, the decision would probably be to separate the mid from the Academy.

"Why? Because it was a premeditated act. The deception was planned and the accused had plenty of time to decide whether or not she would lie should she be questioned about her actions.

"Another example would be a midshipman who has prepared a 'cheat sheet' and taken it into an examination. This, too is a premeditated act and most probably would result in separation.

"But now let's consider an entirely different kind of case. At a morning formation the company commander walks up to a plebe and, noticing stubble on his chin, asks,

---

[1]The original interview, published in the first edition of this book, was reviewed by a later Brigade Honor Chairman and deletions and additions were made by this individual in order to incorporate changes that have occurred in the administration of the Honor Concept over the years. Hence, the words enclosed with quotation marks represent a composite interview with two Brigade Honor Chairmen.

'Did you shave this morning?'

"The plebe replies 'yes, sir!' but then, seconds later, realizes what he has done--he has lied. Immediately he calls to the company commander and confesses that he had lied--he had not shaved that morning.

"That case, of course, would almost surely end up before the Commandant, but consideration would be given to the relative inexperience of the midshipman--that he was a plebe--and to the fact that it was a spur-of-the-moment lie and not premeditated. Other factors would surely be considered. What is the attitude of the mid? Is he genuinely remorseful and sorry for his mistake? Everybody is human and that needs to be considered. Another factor is that the plebe turned himself in. That shows he believes in the system and that he has probably learned from his mistake. And there could be extenuating circumstances that might affect the decision.

"Just to give some perspective on what happens, last year 110 cases were turned in, and 55 of the alleged offenders were found guilty by the Brigade Honor Board. Of those, 30 of them were separated from the Academy and 25 of them were retained. However, it is pretty standard for those who are retained to forfeit a year's leave--meaning that they cannot go home--and to stand weekend restrictions and other punishments. In addition, they could be on honor probation for the rest of their time at the Academy and they will definitely have to undergo extensive honor training.

"Also, it should be pointed out that the Commandant does not have the final decision. The case must be reviewed by the Superintendent; then it goes to the Secretary of the Navy where the final decision is made."

Generally, the other midshipmen who were interviewed were strongly supportive of the Honor Concept. Several confessed coming from high schools where lying, cheating and stealing was common behavior. They expressed relief to be out of that kind of environment and into one where there is mutual trust of everybody.

It is probably safe to predict that plebes can easily adapt themselves to living by the Honor Concept, especially when they look around them and see how proud the upperclassmen are of living by those standards. In other words, living by the Honor Concept is something candidates should prepare their minds to accept, but it should be the least of all the potential changes in their life that they should worry about. The midshipmen who commented on the matter expressed nothing but pleasure in living with classmates who believed in living honorably.

TWENTY-TWO
PLEBE QUICKSAND: CYBERSPACE, DOOM, PROCRASTINATION AND THE SLEEP PROBLEM

It is a Tuesday morning in early October and you are a plebe at the Naval Academy.

Despite heroic efforts at studying you have just received a bad grade on a quiz in calculus. Your grades are now below 2.0 in your two hardest classes: calculus and chemistry. In addition, you were flamed on during your come-around this morning because you did not know your rates, you haven't received a letter from your girlfriend in over a week, and you are so tired you could lie down right on the sidewalk you are walking on and sleep for 24 hours. But you head to your room. You have a rare break between classes. You have almost two hours you can use to study for your one o'clock chemistry class.

You are in your room now and you are all alone. It is quiet and ideal for concentrated study. But, first, you are compelled to check your e.mail. That is your passport to the outside world. Cyberspace is a breath of freedom when you feel like a prisoner inside gray walls. It is the only warm-fuzzy that exists in your life.

You read the first e.mail letter, an announcement for tryouts for the Academy choir. You have no talent for that and you quickly go to the next letter. It is a note from your little brother telling about his cross-country match. You were a cross-country runner yourself, so you write a reply and send it. You quickly scan your other mail. You have twelve letters already today, and you know, with your average of about 40 per day, that others will come rolling in--letters from mom and dad, and your old friend Mike at Purdue, and your sometimes-girlfriend Jennifer at Wayne State, and your history professor with an update on your assignment, and your two new internet friends at the University of Florida and...

How wonderful. You are a nobody out in the yard and in the hallways of Bancroft, but in your room you are like a busy executive, needed, wanted, even in demand. You continue to read the letters and respond to most of them because those who wrote are also lonely--your replies will make their day just like their letters are making yours. Then you hear the sounds. Fellow plebes chopping in the hallway and shouted replies to upperclass questions. You don't have to check your watch. It is almost noon and you have a formation. One of your roommates bursts into the room, "Come on, man, we've got to get moving," he says. You hesitate. You look at the chemistry text and notebook at the side of your computer. You have to rush now. Every second counts. It is room check, uniform check, chop to formation, a quick lunch in King Hall, then to chemistry and the Henderson-Hasselbalch Equation and acid dissociation equilibrium that you did not understand yesterday, and the assignment on Titrations and pH Curves that you failed to study last night. And you

Your life will be dependent upon the computer, but you have to keep that dependency from evolving into an addiction. *Courtesy USNA Photographic Branch.*

have blown away almost two hours this morning--time that you could have used to help dig yourself out of the chemistry sinkhole into which you are descending.

The preceding scenario, a generalized account synthesized from interviews with numerous plebes, may be hard for a candidate to appreciate. That is because candidates in normal high schools have *always* been somebody; they have always had an identity, even when they were freshmen. And it is difficult to imagine otherwise. It is difficult to form a mental picture of how low and how insignificant you would feel as a plebe at the Naval Academy during the first months of the academic year. Several times over the years the author has heard plebes describe their excited feelings when they found junk mail in their boxes. "Wow, I got some junk mail today!" was how they would describe their reaction. You may wonder: Why the excitement over worthless junk mail? The reason you may wonder is because you have never been a nobody. Therefore, you cannot imagine what receiving a piece of junk mail means. But, to a plebe, the junk mail brings a message that is shouted loud and clear: "Hey, I am important, at least to someone out there. I really am somebody."

However, try to stretch your imagination. Try to picture yourself as a nobody, then try to imagine the power of 40 e.mail messages available on the screen of your computer. Can you sense how compelled you would feel, during a break between classes, or during your evening study hours, to dig into those messages and savor being somebody? If you can grasp this idea, you will have some appreciation for the

182

temptation that awaits you should you become a plebe. You will have a computer and you will be linked to all the friends you made during Plebe Summer--friends that are now scattered into the many different companies of the Midshipman Brigade. In addition, you will undoubtedly be corresponding regularly with members of your family, friends from your high school years who are also at college, and, possibly, interesting people whom you have met while surfing the internet. At the same time you will be under a crushing academic load. If you are like most plebes, you will be struggling in calculus and chemistry, you will be putting off doing the research and writing of term papers in English and history, and you will be frightened by the upperclassmen who are demanding that you learn what seems like mountains of "pro stuff"--and all of this after you come to your room dog-tired after three hours of practice in some mandatory athletic endeavor.

So what do you do? Do you take the hard road and try to unbury yourself in calculus and chemistry, then start research on your term papers, and, finally, before you go to bed, study your pro stuff? Or do you cave into the seductive temptation to light up your computer screen with warmth from the outside world? Do you succumb to the desire to be somebody again and get sucked into the black hole of cyberspace?

These are questions that plebes who survived the first year say you should have answered in your mind before you arrive at the Naval Academy. They say that you must look at all the ways you can lose yourself in cyberspace as a threat with more potential danger than the upperclassmen with their flaming tongues. The latter is a visible threat, there to be received and conquered. Cyberspace, on the other hand, starts out as a non-threatening warm-fuzzy, but can slowly make addicts out of plebe nobodies--addicts who, first, wind up on academic probation, and, if the addiction continues, to involuntary separation from the Academy.

The basic problem, however, has nothing to do with cyberspace. It is a problem with which plebes have struggled for decades. The problem is *time*.

You will never have enough time in your day to meet all of your obligations. Read the preceding sentence again before you continue; somehow you have to get this fact stamped deeply into your consciousness. It is a fundamental axiom.

Now for the corollary. Because you will never have enough time in your day to meet all your obligations, you must always set priorities and do those things first that have the highest priority. This process goes by a couple of names: "prioritization" and "time management." In plebe terms, when you have five hours of work to do and only three hours to do it in, you have to lay out your tasks and decide which ones can be blown off.

But that is just the beginning. The next step is to use the three hours of study time efficiently. But the question you have to ask yourself is: Can I study effectively sitting by a computer that is just waiting to swish me off into cyberspace? Only you can answer that question.

Besides tempting you to take trips to cyberspace, the computer offers other seductive charms. These charms are called video games.

During recent interviews with plebes, they said that the computers they were issued had two video games on the hard drive in addition to the basic software needed at the Academy. The video game, "Doom," was the one the plebes discussed the most. They all knew of Doom addicts and some confessed to having escaped that addiction themselves. They also told stories of Doom addicts who paid a high price for their addiction; they told of bright, academically talented mids who failed classes because they spent too much of their precious study time at frivolous activities on their computer.

Now, for some comments from the mids. Said one plebe: "Doom destroyed my exams last semester. I would sit around and study for about ten or fifteen minutes, and then I would get hungry. I would get up to get some food, then I would come back and decide to check my e.mail. Then I would turn Doom on and two hours later I would study for another fifteen minutes. It was a rough cycle. After awhile I realized I wasn't doing anything so I deleted everything I had on my drive."

Said another plebe: "I played the games once or twice but I don't have any games on my computer now. I deleted the ones they gave us. There is no point to them. I learned that a five minute break turned into like an hour, so I took them off. There was a guy in my company who graduated from high school with a 4.0 and last semester he was always playing games on the Internet. He was really a smart guy. He ended up with a 1.6 last semester. That was reason enough for me to get rid of that stuff."

Said a third classman: "My roommate was kicked out on an academic board this past semester. He wasn't dumb or anything. He came out of plebe year with a 2.18, but coming into this year he got addicted to video games. He started playing these e.mail network games, like role playing where you interact with people in other colleges across the country. He would literally stay up until two or three in the morning on one of those network games. He would be half asleep in his classes and did very little homework. He wasted his entire semester. We kept on him and tried to get him to study. We would get up in the middle of the night and unplug his computer. He's just one example; I have seen a lot of people suffer because of those games. It's easy to get connected with almost any university in the country and you get to doing this role playing and it's hard to log off. You are in the middle of something with somebody else and you say, 'I'll wait until I get done with him and then I will log off.' But it goes on and on, and you stay on because you are hooked."

A first classman who describes himself as a "recovering addict" said: "I have to keep myself from walking by a computer store. I would buy all the simulators in there if I had the money and if I had the time, which I don't. But, I see the problem all the time. I get this academic tracking sheet on this plebe who has been unsatted [given an unsatisfactory academic report] and I go to his room on a Wednesday night. I know what I'm going to find. He'll be in there playing a computer game. I find that pretty hard. Actually, it's stupid. It's a good way to get yourself out of here, and the worst part is that it's a good way to keep me here on my Christmas break because I have to attend his academic board."

A plebe who fought addiction said: "I have two good roommates and we'd helped each other fight the addiction--until exam week. We didn't know it but during exam week they have a couple of reading days where there are no classes. You are supposed to use those days for study. Well, my two roommates had Doom on their computers and they said they would go nuts if they didn't take a break from studying and play a little Doom. But both of them got hit by the Doom bug and they just played and played and they bombed some of their exams. It's easy to say you're not going to do this, but if you have things like that on your computer, it's always a temptation. I cleaned everything like that off my drive. I know my weakness. They [computer games] can snare you for the entire day."

It is easy to get caught up in projects the upperclass want done. Beware: the rationalization you use to justify such activity may be a subtle form of procrastination.

Courtesy 1/C Jimmy Parker.

A problem even more widespread than computer addiction is the procrastination problem. Said one upperclassman: "I think midshipmen, in general, are procrastinators by nature."

Many high school students are procrastinators but they get away with it. They wait until the last minute to do an assignment, but it is usually not difficult, and high school teachers, conditioned to having students who do not bother turning in assignments, are often pleased just to get anything from you, and are not overly concerned with quality. If you are a viable candidate for the Naval Academy, there is a good chance that you "are one of the procrastinators by nature." In high school you probably waited until the last minute to do your assignments and you still got good grades.

Plebes at the Academy usually try to do the same thing. But they make two serious miscalculations. First, they underestimate the amount of time it takes to do an assignment like a term paper. Mostly, they fail to realize how long it takes to do the research for such a paper. If they go to the library the night before the paper is due, they are lucky to get out of there with enough raw material for a paper before study hours are over. And they still have the paper to write.

Their second miscalculation is the attitude of the professors. It is not enough just to turn in a paper and say to yourself, "Well, I've done it." The Naval Academy professors read your paper. They *really* read it. Thoroughly. And carefully. And they expect quality, and will not settle for anything less.

So, procrastination is plebe quicksand, and, to survive, you have to struggle with your nature. You have to be aware of your weakness, then find ways to outsmart it. Here is how some of the mids have thwarted their own weakness.

Said one plebe: "I have always waited until the last second to write papers. I got a C in English last semester. I thought I deserved better so I decided to do something different this semester. Now, as soon as I find out I have a paper due, I make an appointment at the Writing Center. But I make the appointment three or four days before the paper is due. This is a trick. This forces me to have something ready for them to critique when I go there, but then, after I revise it--with their help--I then have extra days to look it over again. That way I can maybe make it better. This has really helped me. I have a B+ on one paper and an A on another."

A plebe who heard the above advice commented: "That's really a good idea. It forces you to get your paper done early because you don't want to go to the Writing Center with nothing in your hand. At least you should have some kind of draft ready. I like the idea. But there is still one thing missing. Nothing has been said about the research. That is the time killer. You can't believe how much time you can blow off on some assignments. My problem was finding time for the research. Every night I was buried in assignments and with pro stuff. I didn't have time to go to the library. My third class [third classmen serve as advisors to the plebes] gave me a suggestion that helped. She said, 'Use your Friday nights for term paper research.' I tried it and it made sense. Instead of blowing off the night, which you feel like doing after a hard week, go to the library. It's quiet and it's amazing how much work you can get done. Then, come Saturday, take that time to forget about academics. Watch TV, go to your sponsor--do whatever to take a break from this place. Then go back to work on Sunday. It's a great day to catch up. I know, that may sound difficult. In high school you can take off the whole weekend. But not here. You have to use some of your weekend time. I strongly recommend it. Set aside Friday night strictly for library research. Even if you are under a lot of pressure, blow Saturday away. But then use Sunday to catch up or get ahead. I'm getting ahead now that I'm using this system."

Another plebe said: "I was the king of procrastinators in high school. I had all kinds of ways to put things off. I would turn things in late all the time, but a lot of my teachers didn't pay that much attention. My third class [mentor] turned that around for me. When I got an unsat [unsatisfactory academic report] she demanded to see my papers two or three days before they were due. I couldn't get out of it. You tend to respond better to the upper class than to the instructors. The instructors are not going to flame on you..."

186

And another: "I use Friday evenings for research and I write my papers on Sunday. I work all day because you are stuck here on the yard...I just started using the Writing Center this semester and that is the best thing you can do. If my paper is due on Monday or Tuesday, I always make an appointment for the Wednesday or Thursday before. They help you so much there. You go in and there is a desk and you sign in. There is a real friendly lady there and she opens the file and she will tell you to sign up for a time slot--I schedule it after English so I don't have to walk back over there. They have coffee in there and there are different people who will work with you. They will read through your paper and pick out grammar things. They also critique it. Afterwards, you correct it and bring it back in and the person who critiques it actually writes a little synopsis of how you did. If you go in there and find somebody you really like, you can sign up for that person again."

Said another: "The first time I used it [Writing Center], I got an A on my paper. The guy really helped me out. Also, if you use the Writing Center, a form is sent to your teacher [the one for whom you are preparing the paper]. Even if your paper isn't that great, your teacher knows that you are putting in the effort to do a good job. It's a psychological thing. Even if you think your paper is great, go to the Writing Center anyway and get a second opinion--plus your teacher or professor will know that you have been there."

Said another: "When I was in high school I didn't have to work very hard to maintain my grades. When I got here, the situation really changed. Once you start seeing your grades slip, it is a natural reaction; you want to make changes. I started out slow and it was because of the way I was working. At the beginning of the year they told us about a study skills class that is available for plebes. Sometimes it is required if your grades slip, but I went to it voluntarily. I knew I was a procrastinator. It was very helpful to me. It is an hour per week. I highly recommend it. They taught me time management. They told us that studying in the daytime is one and one-half times as effective as studying at night. They taught us to use a Day Planner--I bought a little one down at the mid store that fits in my pocket. I keep track of everything now. All my assignments are in there. I keep track of reading assignments. The main thing I'm doing--if something is due Thursday, I'm not going to do it Wednesday night. That came from experience. It's natural to wait till the night before. You have to change or you won't make it here."

Most of the mids either carry a small Day Planner (there are several brands available), or they carry a pad of yellow stick-notes and transfer their day-notes to a larger Day Planner that they keep in their room. If you visit the Academy for an overnight stay, look around and see the different time-management systems used by the mids with whom you will be living. Also, this is a good subject to discuss with the mids during your visit. They all seem to have developed their unique techniques for staying on track. You may find a system you like, or one you can modify, and you can begin to use it during your senior year in high school. If you can get yourself organized before you go to the Academy, it will be just one less stress point to worry about.

During one of the discussions the author was having with a group of plebes, a first classman came into the room and listened for a few minutes. The plebes were discussing how they managed to keep going when they were sleepy, which, according to them, is all of the time. Finally, the first classman interrupted. "Hey, I've got news for all of you. Life here at the Academy is basically four years of sleep deprivation!"

The first classman was right, of course. The sleep problem is not exclusively a problem for the plebes; it is a problem during all four years. But it is one that the plebe has to learn to manage during the first year. The following include a variety of suggestions the author was able to obtain from plebes and upperclassmen.

This photo, taken through a classroom window, shows a plebe who lost a battle with the sleep demon.   *Courtesy 1/C Jimmy Parker.*

Said a plebe: "I was amazed when I first got here because everybody slept in class. I never had a problem with it in high school. The first semester, in my worst classes, I brought a soda just to keep me awake. I also drank iced tea loaded with sugar. They just changed things and now we can't bring drinks to class.[1] Many mids stand up but I don't because I want to take notes. Taking notes helps, but even while doing that, I have found myself falling asleep. Later, when I'm trying to study them, I see places where they start to trail off. Sometimes they don't make any sense at all."

Said another plebe: "With me, a bottle of water has become my best friend. I carry one everywhere with me. I think just playing with the bottle and having it to

---

[1]The ban on drinks in class might be lifted by the time you get there. Historically, sugared drinks were highly effective in keeping mids awake.

mess around with keeps me awake. If it gets bad enough that I can't stay awake, I start writing a letter to one of my friends--it keeps me awake and I am still listening to what the teacher is saying--not 100 percent, but at least 75 percent, and that is better than being asleep.

Said another who heard the above comments: "This really surprised me--I never had trouble in high school. But this sleep problem is more of a brigade-wide thing--it's a problem with everybody. Everyone is too tired from cramming so much stuff into a day, then staying up late at night. The teacher in one of my classes said, 'Go get some coffee,' when some of us drifted off. That can take some time. The caffeine helps, but a water bottle would probably be a better choice--you don't have to waste time to go get it--you can just fill it from the tap."

Said another: "Sleep was really a big problem for me last semester. I would spend all night trying to work, then the entire day I was gone. It really didn't pay off. This semester it is a lot better. Three things helped me. One is slow, deep breathing. I take in ten really deep breaths in a row and let it out slowly. I find that to be helpful. Second, I don't write letters when I get ready to fall asleep, but I do homework for the following class. Third, having something to drink helps a lot. I don't have a drink of choice; I think it is the temperature--I take a really cold drink and that wakes me up. In addition to all that, I recommend going to sleep on time every night. My roommates and I all go to sleep on time now, and if anything, I will wake up a little early and do a little bit of homework that I could have stayed up to do."

Said another: "I had huge trouble with sleeping when I first came here because in high school I was like a freak and went to bed at nine-thirty and got up at six-thirty. It seemed important for me to get nine hours of sleep. When I came here, over the summer, I had huge bags under my eyes and the only thing that has worked for me is standing up. I have probably stood up in 80 percent of the classes I have had. I usually stand the whole period. People make jokes out of it because they will time me and see how long it takes me to stand up--and usually it takes about ten minutes. If I don't stand up and it is a chemistry or calculus class, I'll follow along with the teacher in the book and highlight things as I go. Usually I end up highlighting everything, but it keeps me awake. Also, I think you get used to it. This semester I am not having near the trouble. Still, when I go to the library, I'm afraid I might nod off so I always carry a little alarm clock and set it.[2]

Said another: "I have a big sleeping problem. First semester, I slept through meal formation in a classroom--my watch, the bells--nothing woke me up. I got in big trouble for that. The second class and plebes are arch enemies, so as soon as I walked

---

[2]A universal recommendation by cadets and midshipmen at the three major service academies is to set some kind of alarm--on a watch or clock--when studying outside one's room. The author heard all kinds of horror stories about first-year students waking up late at night in a classroom or library, then having to pay the price for getting to their room after hours.

in King Hall, all the second class looked at me. I knew I was dead. They came down on me for a couple of days. In classes now like chemistry or calculus, I try to do the problems in the books. Trying to do the problems, you are really active figuring them out and that keeps you awake. Once I sit down in history, English or naval science I'm in trouble--I eventually have to stand up and walk around. Also studying for those classes--all you do is read and read. In five minutes I would be asleep if I didn't get up and walk around. I'll go over to study hall and I'll take a book and just walk through the hall reading. It's weird, reading while walking around. But it helps me. In class, if I can't walk around, I'll sometimes start drawing."

Said another: "Before I came here I had to get eight and a half hours sleep a night. Now, if I get six, I am happy. If you fixate on sleep, you are going to make yourself sick. You just have to go with the flow. What I don't do is stay up late. I get up early. If you have more homework than you can do [during evening study hours], go to bed and get up at four if you have to. Don't stay up late at night--it messes up your sleep schedule. In class do whatever you have to do to stay awake. If you don't stay awake in class, then you spend extra hours studying to find out what you missed in class--and that takes away from your sleep time."

Said another: "The first week of academic year I think I slept through all my classes. I thought I was never going to be able to stay awake. You do get used to it. The best thing that has helped me is working out and being in shape. I work out in the morning and in the afternoon. It wakes me up--you would think it would make you more tired--but the break helps--just getting out and breathing fresh air helps a lot. It doesn't make sense but it makes your body more tired but you are more awake. Also, I've found that the better shape you are in, the less amount of sleep you need. If I didn't work out I would fall asleep all the time."

When the plebe was making the above comment, heads were nodding affirmatively among the other plebes who were listening. In a discussion of exercise, fitness and the problem of staying awake that followed, there was a strong general consensus that, indeed, staying in top shape by running every day seems to immunize the body to some degree from the problem. However, they all agreed that the mids all have a "sleep debt" that they never ever pay off. Also in the discussion, some cautioned about sleeping excessively during leaves at home--such as at Christmas. "That really screws you up," one said, and when you get back to the Academy, "you have to adjust all over again."

In concluding this chapter on "plebe quicksand," keep in mind that the threats described here are not things that will hit you forcefully when you arrive at the Academy on I-Day. They are not like the upperclassmen who are obvious threats from day one. Instead, they are insidious threats that can creep up on you very slowly.

The purpose of this book is to alert you to those threats so that you will be aware of them. However, the intelligent candidate will go to the Academy with more than awareness. The intelligent candidate will go with a game plan already in place. If you can say, "When I get to the Academy, I know how I am going to deal with those threats," and you can back up those words, you will be way ahead of your classmates who will be learning their lessons the hard way.

TWENTY-THREE
WHAT FEMALE CANDIDATES SHOULD
KNOW ABOUT SURVIVAL

Females are a small but highly visible minority in the midshipman brigade at the Naval Academy. Each year they comprise about 10 percent of the incoming class of plebes.

It was revealed during interviews with females that they experience a variety of unique problems at the Naval Academy. In an attempt to provide a spectrum of viewpoints and advice, the author has selected the accounts of nine females for this chapter: four who were interviewed while midshipmen, three who were recent

When you are a minority person, you are more conspicuous in everything you do.
Courtesy USNA Photographic Branch

graduates and two who are graduates and were back as staff members at the Academy.
Here is what they had to say.

A third classman from California:

"I went to an all-girl Catholic high school and that had a lot to do with my being able to come here. Throughout high school I was involved with a lot of things and had a good time, but that was not something that was important to me. The structure at the school was more important and in many ways I felt right at home when I came here.

"I did take my studies seriously in high school and I was very thorough. I really worked at it and classes here aren't that much of a problem because I was used to being thorough--I did all I could do for my assignments--I didn't leave anything out. I didn't have outstanding SAT scores--I just was prepared with good work habits.

"I have to think that the social part [in high school] wasn't that helpful--I was president of the student body and the Honor Society. I also ran cross-country and that was much more helpful here because I was able to click into a mode that says, 'I have to keep going.' It taught me perseverance, which I badly needed after I got here.

"I had a horrible plebe year. I was always in trouble with the professional military things. But the worst part of it was that I was taking everything personally. It was extremely hard not to take things that way and I had a very difficult time with military bearing.

"One thing I saw among the other females was how a little more maturity helped. I think those who had gone to NAPS or to a year of college had an easier time of it.

"To prepare for this place I definitely advise cross-country running, not only for what it teaches you, but because it gets you in good physical condition. My physical condition probably saved me with the upperclassmen, because when they look at you and you look physically fit, you have an advantage. The upperclassmen see that and say, 'I want that kind of person in my school.' Things are definitely easier for the females who are in shape when they get here. They will be respected more by the upperclassmen; life will be easier and they will be happier.

"It is interesting to be in such a minority, like in sports I might be the only girl on a team. I found it was easier to try hard and do well because guys are not worried about me being ahead of them--like in wind surfing they are not bothered by being passed. I do feel that my roommates and I do not have as many friends as the guys have. There seems to be a little more distance between the females than between the guys.

"Why did I come here? Well, I could have gone to Berkeley, but is it going to be as exciting as the Naval Academy? And what about when you get out of Berkeley? I even thought of ROTC there, but it doesn't offer the whole new support group--people with values similar to mine. That is important. I like the values here. I like the tradition. I like the broad opportunities when you get out. I am majoring in political science and would like to work in intelligence.

"The best thing about this place? People's attitude. They believe in you here. They have a great willingness to help you. Also I like what is being taught--like the upperclassmen telling you that you have to help people, that you should reach out to help your classmates. I know if I need something, I can ask for it and I like the idea that I can be helpful, too. Here every single person can be your friend--you don't see

It helps to participate in a team sport because the upperclassmen need you and, therefore, treat you better than in Bancroft Hall.   *Courtesy USNA Photographic Branch.*

anything like that at Berkeley."

A first classman from Georgia:

"My dad was a marine and I learned to shine boots in elementary school. My whole life I just wanted to be a marine like daddy. It was a way of life that I liked. I enjoyed it as a kid.

"I applied for the Naval Academy right out of high school. They said I was qualified, but I wasn't qualified enough to get in. I had a lot of extra-curricular activities in high school but didn't participate in athletics and I think that hurt me the most.

"I went to a year of junior college, then someone told me that I could get into the Naval Academy directly from the Navy. So I enlisted and did very well--the military record got me in here. I was top graduate of boot camp and I had the highest grade point average in my tech school. My CO [commanding officer] wrote a good letter for me--she had been in the first class of women at the Academy.

"The hardest thing for me was not the military things because I was used to them. What was hard was the let down after making a 3.89 GPA in high school and straight A's at the junior college. Here I started making straight C's and that depressed me until I got a better perspective and developed better study habits. Why did I survive? Going back to the Navy as an enlisted person was not even a question. I had lots of motivation to make it here.

"But I did lose three roommates. The first one left before Plebe Summer was over. She had a leg injury and was on crutches. That was hard for her. She got behind and everything just went downhill for her.

"The second one was a physical dud, but also she was not impressed with what she saw--all the yelling and screaming turned her off. She didn't want to be like that, ever.

"The third one belonged in a civilian school partying every night. She didn't have the discipline. She stayed through the second summer but then she quit."

"My advice is to know what you are getting into when you get here. Visit the place and learn what it is like. It isn't for everybody."

A third classman from Florida:

"The thing that helped me the most when I got here was my experience on a crew team in high school. I learned how to function as a team member, how to be competitive and how to get along with a group. This helped me prepare for the competition and stress that you get here during plebe year. If you can handle physical rigors, it helps you mentally--your mind can't handle the thinking if you are overstressed physically.

"Every morning during Plebe Summer you have PEP [Physical Excellence Program] and it will drag you down for the rest of the day if you are not in shape. Then the mental stress builds up and it is a vicious circle.

"Upperclass pressure? You have to keep an open mind. I was lucky because I had two older brothers come here and they programmed me not to take it personally when I was singled out--that they are just testing your strength--that they are only doing their job. They don't hate you because they are yelling in your face. I handled that okay.

"They [my brothers] also told me to do my best and to show 100 percent effort--that the upperclassmen want to see that kind of motivation. Also, to try and fit in with the group and to carry my share of the load. They warned me not to try to get out of things and not to expect anything special because I am a girl. The girls with problems asked for them, in my opinion. Some of them came here expecting special privileges just because they were female. That was a bad mistake on their part.

"My personal secret for survival? I had a good outlook this past year because of the crew team. The attrition was much lower for team members. I know I did better because of the physical outlet and because of the closeness of the team. It especially helped me to see a whole different attitude of the upperclassmen toward me [on the

194

You should not expect special treatment because you are a female. Do what you have to do to hang in there with the guys and you will survive.

sporting field as compared to Bancroft Hall where all the mids live and where the plebes are hassled]. We were literally pulling together on the team. I was treated totally different there and that change helped me see the total picture--it helped me forget about the hall. And one big thing! I had a haven with a stereo--we had one in the club house. Plebes are not allowed stereos in the hall, but I had one!

"I strongly advise anybody coming here to get a solid academic background. Take all the AP courses you can and definitely take more than one year of chemistry if possible. I didn't have that much trouble with academics because I had taken several advanced courses and knew how to study. Also, I had a strong algebra background--and you should emphasize that. Algebra is very important, not only in math but in chemistry.

A third classman from Washington, D.C. whose family has a long, distinguished history of Navy service:

"I see being here as more of a calling. But that feeling was a long time coming.

"It may be hard to believe, considering my background, but I never even thought of applying for this place when I was in high school--in fact I would have argued against it. No way would I have considered it. At that time I was so against the Navy

I would not have even considered marrying a Navy officer.

"But once I allowed myself to think about it--near the end of high school--I wondered what I should be doing for the next four years, and then for the ten years after that. And I just knew that I would be happier here and in the Navy more than anywhere else. I just knew that was the truth.

You will see many examples of women who maintain their femininity while performing in nontraditional ways. *Courtesy UNNA Photographic Branch.*

"I like constant challenges and I like being busy all the time. I thought about other colleges but I knew I would get bored with the party life.

"One thing people should think about before coming here is their attitude toward patriotism. Many have the wrong idea and think they should have a patriotic feeling before they come here. That isn't necessary. They do not have to be motivated to serve their country. They will catch that here! Here you feel the pride and the tradition. It's like catching a cold--you can't avoid it. That's the reason why I'm here now. I said it felt like I have a calling for this place. I really feel like I belong here.

"When I went home for Christmas, I heard all my friends talk about their college experiences. It sounded like they were having fun, but I told them my stories, too, and I've had some similar experiences. Of course they have the party life, but I don't need that in my daily life--that's not enough for me.

"My mother worries about all the stress here and about my academic struggles. But I'm making it--I'm not sliding through. I have always had to study hard. I studied

196

very hard in high school and those study habits helped me here. I was used to studying every spare minute so it wasn't a big change when I came here--as it was for a lot of others.

"Physically, you must come here with a competitive spirit. I love competition but I like competing within myself. I did have to psych myself into getting up in the morning and going to PEP. But once you get your head set so you look at it as a challenge, you begin to look forward to it. I ran a lot before I came in but that is not enough to get you in shape for the long, arduous days. But PEP gets you through the day because it makes you alert. Without PEP I would have gone to sleep.

"How did I cope with upperclass pressure? I have always wanted to do better at anything I was required to do. That is an attitude that I have always had and that was how I dealt with it inside. I always knew there was more inside and all I had to do was call on it when I needed it.

"I had heard a lot about Plebe Summer and I came into it really afraid. It didn't turn out as bad as I expected so I was always thinking, 'It could be worse.' That got me through it.

"I also had a big advantage because my family is close by and every Sunday they would come over and we would go to church together. That close family support really helped.

"But there were other things that helped, too. You have to rely on people in the platoon--everybody helps each other. That support--that feeling of working together keeps you going.

"I also have a good sense of humor. You have to have that. You have to laugh--just don't let the upperclassmen hear you! You are always going to have some bad days and some very bad days, but you have to laugh with your friends about the bad things--and in the end the worst things turn out to be the funniest. When somebody was in my face yelling, I kept a straight face and knew I would be laughing about it someday.

"You can't take anything personally. You have to turn off guys yelling in your face calling you a dirt bag and telling you that you are not for this place. You have to know you have what it takes and turn off what they are saying. I knew deep, down inside they were wrong.

"The great thing is having your classmates coming up to you and telling you that the upperclassman was wrong when he told you that. You do that when others need it. One day I saw a plebe really being put down and I went up to him afterward and encouraged him--helped build him up. If one person is falling down--doing badly with rates--the others will try to help him to maintain a positive attitude.

"That's the key--a positive attitude. Plebe Summer is designed to teach you how to respond under pressure. They are really saying to you, 'Prove me wrong that you don't belong here.'

"You get so many examples of leadership here and you see them acutely during the plebe year. Some try to drag you down--that is negative leadership as far as I am concerned. But I also saw great leadership. The new Brigade Commander was in our company and when we were not performing, he quietly said, 'You're not performing like you can and you're letting me down.' I wanted to cry I felt so badly for him. We

197

all wanted to help him and we did. That is a positive form of leadership.

"I'll say this about females here. Some are here to find a husband, to get the free education, etc. That makes it harder for the rest of us. It takes just one person like that to bring down the reputation of all other girls.

"To be honest, there are some people here who think females shouldn't be here and all it takes is just one [a female exploiting here femininity] to ruin it for the rest of us. It makes me mad that I have to prove myself again and again just because of one like that.

"To girls who want to come here I say that you have to want it for yourself--you have to come here for the right reasons. And don't go looking for a relationship with a guy. Dating is not allowed during plebe year[1] and you have to be ready for that. And if you have a bunch of relationships, your reputation can be shot *and it will follow you out to the fleet.*

"So be careful. There are a lot of good looking guys here and lots of opportunities--and lots of pressure. Girls have to have a good attitude about that. One cane get a bad reputation at the drop of a coin here--and when they do, that is just one more way women get a bad name.

An ensign from Georgia, a recent graduate on temporary duty at the Academy waiting for a class in intelligence school: "I was mentally prepared for Plebe Summer whin I came because I had visited the academy and stayed in Bancroft Hall. Three girls [midshipmen] prepared me very well. I knew what I was getting into.

"One thing they told me, which helped, was that a girl has to be emotionally stronger than the men. Also, that it was a very unfeminine environment, but that you should not try to hide or abandon your femininity--that you just have to constantly use judgement as to when to show it and when not to show it.

"One of the hardest things was keeping calm when somebody was yelling in my face. It is hard emotionally but a girl here can never cry.

"The key to surviving the harassment is concentration. When somebody is yelling in your face, you have to think of it as a game. Who is going to win? You or the

---

[1]This policy has been changed recently--dating between classmates is okay. However, plebes must not fraternize, or "frat" with upperclassmen. That is strictly forbidden and can get one into deep trouble.

upperclassman? It is not a silly game. There is a purpose behind it, which you don't appreciate until later.

"You have to keep the right attitude and keep it all in perspective. You must not take it personally. But you must listen to what they are saying. They may be just trying to find a weakness, but they also may be trying to tell you something. So listen, and if something is wrong, fix it.

"They were really hard on me. I'm small and speak softly with a southern accent. They would come at me saying, 'Oh you're just a little southern belle--you don't belong here.' You really have to believe in yourself because they can be convincing. One guy kept telling me that he, personally, was going to make sure that I would be gone from the place. That just made me all the more determined to prove that I could make it.

"You have to go back to your room and laugh with your classmates about all your mistakes and the things they say to you. One thing about the whole plebe year is that it magnifies your flaws. And if you do not have a strong character, it will show sooner or later. When pushed, you can't let it bother you if you fail.

"When you are depressed, you must always keep in mind that if you are selected for this place, you have the tools to survive. You just have to supply them.

"It is also important to be in shape when you come here. To be able to run two miles comfortably would be a minimum. If you are not fit, it looks bad.

"Actually, though, plebe year wasn't the hardest part of it. The second year was the hardest because the new company that I went into had only four women and we were not treated well. Despite what you may hear, there is still some discrimination and bad feelings against us. We weren't treated well and that year I actually thought of quitting. But I talked with my parents and I sat down and made a pro and con list. When I looked at the list, the good things far outweighed the negative things.

"But don't come in here thinking discrimination is not here. You just have to ignore the guys who think that way and get along with the rest. But sometimes it is kind of lonely being a minority.

"Also get used to the idea that the guys will have bunches of close friends while you might only have a few who are as close. Actually I have many more good male friends than girl friends.

"It's like living in a fishbowl when you are a girl here. Everybody is looking at you all the time. The professors always know you first because in some classes you might be the only girl. And dating--be very careful. Girls are watched and everyone knows who you are with. If you go out with many different guys, you are going to be talked about. It is a double standard because nobody cares what guys do. But all the guys care what the girls do.

"There are other things that can help you survive. Bring something that will make you feel at home--like pictures that make you happy. I was very homesick and it was the worst in October. I called home a lot and crossed off the days until Christmas. And it was very tough to come back after Christmas. But there is a saying about the Dark Ages [weeks after Christmas] that is true. 'The days are long but the weeks are short.' You are so busy that those weeks go by very fast.

"What advice would I give a sister coming here? I would say, don't come unless you know something about it--know what you are getting into. Also, I would tell any girl not to come with a chip on her shoulder or come thinking she has to prove something. This is not a place for strong feminists. It isn't a place where a girl should use her femininity to get ahead, either. The most important thing is to get by on your own performance as an individual--not as a female.

"I would also tell her, when somebody's in your face yelling at you, listen with one ear but step outside yourself. Be a good actor, especially if you want to smile."

A lieutenant from Pennsylvania, who, at the time of the interview, was the Flight Schedules Officer at Naval Fighter Weapons "Top Gun" School:

"I was always interested in the military. I read *Dress Grey* and *Lords of Discipline* and started writing for catalogs when I was in the eighth grade.[3] I visited the Naval Academy the summer before ninth grade and again after I got my appointment. I don't know why I had this interest; none of my family had a military background. In fact, my mother was a little scared that her little girl was going off to a military academy.

"It was really hard for me to get used to being at the bottom. Here I was, a hot shot in high school, and now people were yelling at me whether I was right or wrong. It is frustrating when you are trying as hard as you can and when you are used to doing things well--I was used to not screwing up. But they yell at you no matter how well or how badly you are doing; so you have to get used to it.

"It helped me to keep in mind the phrase that was common advice. We were told to "play the game" and that is what it was. It also helps to remember that the plebe year is a finite period of time--it does end. Thousands of others have survived and you will, too.

"And don't take things personally. They don't hate you, although it seems like they do.

"The best thing about the place? For me it was great to have the best of everything. I got a great education. I had great professors. The athletic facilities were fantastic. I was always with high quality people. It was just a great experience being associated with high quality in everything.

"I strongly recommend that girls do everything aerobic that they can before going there. I was in fairly good shape and was running about five miles a day about five days a week--eight and a half to nine-minute miles. I definitely recommend track as a sport for girls. If you have trouble starting on your own, you have a coach saying, 'You will do this and you will run that.' That helps you get started.

"Attitude is what is important. You have to come in here positive in your mind that this is what you want. You also have to be mentally prepared to work hard, academically and physically, for four years. If you have that kind of positive attitude,

---

[3]Do not do this now. You have to have a precandidate questionnaire on file before they will send you one. A way to get around this is to have your school counselor or librarian request one.

you will make it.

"Of course, there are times when you get down. I was extremely homesick at one time. I called home every week and I'm glad now my parents urged me to hang in there.

"The worst thing of all for me was not the upperclass pressure. It was the tower jump. Every semester we had to jump off a ten meter (33 feet) tower into the pool--this is done so we would know how to jump from a ship without hurting ourselves. They teach you to cross your arms and legs, but oh, I had nightmares about it. I hate heights. But I wasn't the only one who was afraid. The first time I got up there the guy in front of me wouldn't jump.[4]

"If there is any secret of survival, I think it is knowing that what you receive at the end is worth it all. That kept me going, and now I can definitely see that it was worth much more than all I put up with. When you graduate, you feel this tremendous sense of accomplishment. Also, you know you have earned something that can never be taken away from you.

"It also helps in so many little ways when you get out on the job. Initially it helps you when you report to a new assignment. There is an initial respect that you feel. Of course, that is temporary; you have to perform. But everybody knows that you just didn't go to a school and pass some courses. They know you had to conform to the Honor Concept and live with a lot of rules. Graduating from the Naval Academy is an accomplishment that I'm proud of--it's not like saying, hey, I graduated from State U.

"If I had a sister, what advice would I give her before coming? I would tell her not to use the fact that you are a woman to make it easier for yourself. For example, when things start going badly, don't start crying. It happens quite a lot--I've seen it--but the men are getting good at ignoring it and going on; however, a lot of times they will back off. But, in the long run, it will not help you. Of course, I've seen guys cry, too, but the upperclassmen ignore it more than with girls. It still hurts them more to make a girl cry.

"The other thing about being a minority is to learn quickly how to be a professional around the guys--learn how to separate your personal life and feelings from the professional relationships. Some girls who are just natural flirts probably don't belong at the Academy. They will create problems for themselves. That doesn't mean that you can't be feminine or can't date. Just be prepared to know when to be a professional and to keep your personal life personal

"The important thing is to enjoy all the friendships that you will make. I have many good men friends and some girl friends who are very close--we keep in touch constantly."

---

[4]Her fear was definitely not sex-limited. The author spoke with several male mids who were terrified of the jump, including one who confessed that he practiced stepping off his desk in his room in an effort to overcome his fear.

An ensign from Indiana, Class of 1996, who was still at the Academy working at a temporary job until she enters a pilot-training class:

"One of the downfalls of this place--and I don't think there are a lot of women who get through here completely unscathed mentally--is what I'd describe as the depletion of feminine self confidence. I don't mean self confidence in terms of handling a difficult assignment--this type of confidence increases dramatically after four years. I'm strictly talking about confidence in yourself as a female being.

"It is difficult to maintain confidence in yourself as a female when you have to dress like a man for four years. That uniform is not flattering; you will never feel like you look as nice as you could if you dressed as a female. Also, there is such a big difference between women and the guys. When the guys get dressed up in their uniforms they look great--they look cool, and when they go somewhere, they'll get compliments: 'Boy, you really look sharp.' You would also like to draw that kind of attention--as a female it's a natural thing. But, when you are dressed up in your uniform, you are not going to attract the same kind of attention; you are not going to look nearly as nice as you would in female clothes, with your hair done, and with makeup. If you come here, this is something you are going to have to accept.

"My recommendation to girls coming here is to find a middle ground whenever possible. Wear *some* makeup; it just has to be moderate. Go ahead and paint your fingernails--just follow the uniform regs [regulations]. The color has to be brown or peach tone or clear--it has to be complimentary to your skin tone.

"Keeping a low profile is the key. If it is important for you to wear makeup and really look feminine, consider waiting until liberty and leave, and your third class year. As a plebe, you don't want to do anything to draw attention to yourself as a female, especially to the upperclass.

"Overall, a mid must find the balance between being professional and military, and feeling good about herself as a female. And there is a balance; it is possible to be professional and feminine at the same time.

"I was a company commander during last year's Plebe Summer so I had a good chance to see the kinds of mistakes the female plebes were making. The one thing that bothered me the most was the way a few of them interacted with the upperclassmen. I saw the flirty batting of the eyelashes and the other little flirty looks, and this just made me cringe because it is so destructive. Let me give a strong warning right here. *Do not do anything to try to win favors from any upperclassmen. Most will be disgusted with that, although it might appeal to the egos of a few. But, the worst thing that happens is that a plebe will be ostracized by her class for that kind of behavior.* If that happens, you have had it.

"Also, a girl has to be very careful that plebe year because it is very easy to be charmed by an upperclass male. You can get in big trouble for frat [fraternization]. When I was a plebe, I had an upperclassman writing me e.mail. I thought it was an innocent thing at first. Then I realized how bad it was. It is against regulations for one thing, but, worse, if word gets around--and it will--you can get a bad reputation. If that happens to you, don't answer the e.mail, or tell somebody. Don't let yourself get involved.

"Push yourself until you think you are going to pass out or die before giving up."

Courtesy USNA Photographic Branch.

"Another thing. They give you a desk blotter and encourage you to keep pictures in it just to ease the homesickness. I have seen girls put in pictures of themselves in a bikini. That is a mistake. The guys inspect those rooms and a girl doesn't want them snickering about a certain room that needs to be inspected more often. You can just hear their comments: "Wow, does this one look like she can lead men into combat!"

"My advice is to keep a low profile. When I was a plebe, I had a picture of me in my high school soccer uniform in my desk blotter. But it disappeared. Some upperclass male got his trophy at my expense.

"Also, during PEP and other physical activities during Plebe Summer, I heard girls in a whiny voice say, 'I've got to stop, I've got cramps,' or 'I have to stop and go get some water.' My advice: don't whine. That's not going to impress anybody. Anything that's tormenting--any kind of complaining that draws attention to yourself is bad. When a girl whines or complains, that is telling the others--your classmates as well as the detailers--that you expect special treatment. That is bad.

"My advice, when it comes to physical things, is to push yourself farther than you think is physically possible before you even consider giving up. Push yourself until you think you are going to pass out or die before giving up.

"Just remember that it takes a lot longer to build respect than to lose it. And the fastest way I know to lose it is for word to get around that because you are a girl, you want special treatment.

"One final word. Do whatever it takes to stay in shape after Plebe Summer. It is easy to get lazy, especially if you elect a soft sport like frisbee football. They put a lot of food in front of you here; the diet is designed primarily for males in their late teens who are still developing. They are getting better with their food choices, but a girl still has to be selective."

A lieutenant from New York who was an instructor of physical education at the Academy:

"I got interested in West Point and Annapolis back in 1976 when the first women were admitted. The New York papers were full of stories about them. I read them all and the more I read, the more I wanted to be like one of those women.

"I was a basketball player and came to the Naval Academy as a recruited athlete. When I got here, it was the academics that were the toughest. There were so many distractions. When you are out for a sport, there are so many things going on and it is hard to sit down in the evening and put all those things aside and concentrate on the books.

"The first semester I got in trouble academically. But I received counseling and they had me take a study skills class the second semester. In that class I learned how to use my time, how to get at the heart of reading material, and, most important for me, I learned that where you study is important. In a three-man room it seems like somebody is always talking or somebody is stopping by to chat. I spent a lot of my time studying in the library where I could concentrate.

"I also learned in the study skills class that your pride can hurt you. That was true in my case. I wanted to tough it out--to do it on my own. I learned what a mistake that was. I learned not to let yourself get behind. Every professor has EI [extra instruction] sessions and the sooner you forget your pride and get help, the less chance there is of falling behind.

"Plebe summer was very physical, but being an athlete, it was not a problem. Swimming and sailing were easy. And I learned how to take upperclass pressure. Everybody is getting yelled at. You just have to let it roll off your back--but also listen to them because they may be telling you something.

"Advice for female candidates? To get in shape physically you should do some jogging and be able to do a few miles at an eight or seven-thirty pace. Also, read the Naval Academy Catalog and see what the exact requirements are and try to meet them.

"The main thing for females to work on is upperbody strength. If they want to get higher than a C in physical education, they have to do one pull-up, where you pull yourself up on a bar, gripping the bar with your palms facing away.

"One of the problems women have is a lower center of gravity than men. We have a machine--it's like an incline board with a bar that you can reach. We start out training girls to pull themselves up using just 30 percent of their weight, then we gradually increase it. [5] Eventually we raise the angle of the board so 100 percent of the weight is lifted. Right now, one chin is all that is ever required.

"I think everybody gets depressed and thinks about quitting at one time or another. I did, but I never lost sight of the ultimate goal, which was graduation. Also, my friendships on the basketball team helped keep me there. It was a feeling that we are all women together--that we were all in it together and we would all graduate and make it.

"What would I tell a sister coming here about dealing with the guys? Any girl has to remember that being in a company here is like inheriting a hundred older brothers. You are watched closely. You stand out and that can be difficult. Many of your actions affect all the women here. How you act may be generalized to cover all female mids.

"You have to remember that Bancroft Hall is not a college dormitory. If you are seeing somebody, you might see him once or twice a week--you meet off the place--you go out to dinner or to a movie. There are so many demands on your time, it can be difficult to get together.

"I think it is also important to go with the guys and just be one of them when you can. I mean, participate in company outings, softball games or pickup basketball. You have to be alert and learn when it is time to be 'one of the guys' and when it is time to back off. But be willing to participate, even when you perceive that what they are going to do isn't all that important. You need to join in and be a part of the group--like on recon raids [group pranks]--sometimes you need to go along even though you are not that happy about it.

"My final advice would be to come and see what it is like here while you are a

---

[5]Other females have recommended a "homemade" way to develop the strength to do chins. Stand on a chair or have someone lift you up to the chinning position--your chin above the bar. Then let yourself down as slowly as you can. Repeat several times daily and this exercise will develop enough muscle strength to allow you to go the opposite direction--to pull yourself up.

high school senior. There is nothing better than spending a weekend at Bancroft Hall. I highly recommend that."

A lieutenant from Pennsylvania, who was on the staff as the Honor Officer:

"We had a boy from our high school go to the Naval Academy--the first one ever--and on the spur of the moment, I decided to try for it. I was lucky and got in.

"At the beginning it was sort of overwhelming because I didn't know what to expect. I thought plebe indoctrination would be over in six weeks, then I'd just go to class like anyone in college. It was a shock when I learned that it would last all year!

"But most of us were blundering around at first. I'll never forget sitting in the field house waiting for them to take us away. Somebody had heard that we had to memorize the names and hometowns of the other plebes so we started practicing. I can still remember them, like _____ from Red Bank, New Jersey--those names and hometowns still stick in my mind.

"You have to keep Plebe Summer in perspective. You are always rushed for time, but that is the purpose of it. Also, I will always remember being sweaty--you never get unsweaty the whole time.

"The yelling in the face? You just have to listen to it and answer the questions the best you can. You should also realize that a lot of people have done it before you. You're not the first one to be yelled at. You have to keep that perspective when they are calling you the name of every insect. They are always trying to attack your weaknesses and always figuring a way they can get to you. After it is over, you laugh about it. You laugh at all the wrong answers you gave. It is frightening at the time, but remember that nothing bad is going to happen to you. The worst is the yelling--they are not going to hurt you physically.

"The hardest thing for me was adjusting to two other roommates. I was used to having privacy at home; then suddenly I was thrown in a small room with two others. And each had her own quirks--one wants the lights off to sleep--the other wants them on to study. Things that seem trivial now seemed like major conflicts at the time.

"But you have to be flexible and adapt. You have to be open minded and make compromises--like saying to your roommate, 'If that corner of the second shelf is really where you want to keep your soap, then put it there,' or, 'If you want the lights on late and need to study, go ahead.'

"The academic year was also difficult. There is so much homework and so much to do, it is overwhelming. Then there is shock, like when I got a "D" on my first history test. I wasn't prepared with good study habits. In high school if you went to class and paid attention, you could pick up the stuff and get good grades. You can't do that here. You have to study.

"You need to prepare physically for this place. But my recommendation is to read the material the Academy will send out to you. It will tell you how much to run, etc. I was in fair shape but I remember some who hadn't run a mile in their lives. The problem is, if you get behind in PEP, it starts you out badly for the day and you get behind. Read the stuff they send you and *do it*!

"Some other advice would be to try not to be overwhelmed when you get here. Just remember that a thousand people graduate every year and they are no different from you--they started in the same place.

"In dealing with the guys, it is very important to come in here with the attitude that you will be accepted by them. If you can think that way, it will show and you will be accepted by most of them.

"Also, keep yourself in shape and don't get overweight--it is easy to do with all the food they put in front of you. If you become overweight, you will look bad in your uniform and it is one more thing for people to make jokes about. Whatever you do, don't draw attention to yourself in a negative way. For example, use enough makeup for your self confidence, but don't overdo it. If you date, just remember that you are not in the high school dating atmosphere. You have to be discreet. You must keep your relationship out of Bancroft Hall. You don't walk to the library together every night--you don't walk to classes together or eat lunch together--none of that is good here. A lot of my classmates dated and married other midshipmen and it worked out fine. You just have to be very careful.

"The best thing about this place? I heard it said many times and I found out that it is true. This is the largest fraternity in the world. Everywhere I went--on ships, in ports--everywhere you seem to run into people you know.

"You have friends everywhere--friends from your class--friends from your company. That is a good feeling when you are in a new place.

"Every time I go on a ship now I always look on the quarter-deck where the roster of officers is posted. I always see somebody I know--somebody from my class or somebody who was in a sport I played.

"Also, when you're sitting in the wardroom, you always seem to be with someone who has been at the Academy. And you know what we laugh about? We laugh about all the things that made us so miserable during plebe year--the memorizing and all the other things. That's what plebes should try to keep in mind when they're going through all that. It gives you something in common with a whole lot of people you are going to be serving with."

PARENT
INFORMATION

TWENTY-FOUR
ADVICE FOR PARENTS

Parents are always concerned when their sons and daughters leave home for college. Many worry about their safety and well being in the new surroundings. Many others worry about how they are going to pay the ten to twenty thousand dollars the education is going to cost each year.

The parents of Naval Academy midshipmen do not have either of those worries. The Naval Academy is one of the safest places a young man or woman can be, and the education does not cost parents anything, at least for traditional college expenses.

That is the good news.

The bad news is that being a parent of a midshipman is much more demanding than being the parent of a regular college student. The demands include time, patience, some money and lots and lots of a hard-to-define subsidy called moral support.

In short, Naval Academy parents have a unique role and it is important to the survival of their midshipman for them to learn what they should and should not do.

That role is what this chapter is about. To define it, nearly seventy parents of Academy midshipmen or recent graduates were interviewed by the author.

The parents were asked to describe the problems they and their midshipmen experienced from the time they became involved in the admissions process through the end of their midshipman's first year, which is, by far, the most difficult year for both the midshipman and the parents.

The parents were also asked to use twenty-twenty hindsight and give advice on how to resolve the different problems they encountered--advice that could be passed on to the parents of candidates in this book.

In addition, numerous plebe midshipmen were asked to comment on parental support and the kinds of things that have helped them and their roommates. In this chapter their advice is interspersed with the advice of parents.

THE ADMISSIONS PROCESS

Getting into the Naval Academy is a two-step process. The candidate must first get a nomination from someone eligible to give one. The most common nomination sources are the two U.S. Senators from the candidate's state and the U.S. Representative from the candidate's congressional district. A smaller number of nominations are awarded by the U.S. President, Vice-President and other sources that are described in the Academy catalog.

The second step, after receiving a nomination, is to get an appointment to the Naval Academy. The appointment is a letter officially admitting the nominee and is awarded solely by the admissions officials of the Naval Academy. Contrary to what many parents will have heard, neither U.S. Senators or Representatives nor the U.S.

President or Vice-President give appointments to the Naval Academy.

Also, parents should realize that candidates who are given nominations do not necessarily get appointments. For example, there are 535 U.S. Senators and Representatives and each one may nominate ten individuals for every vacancy. (Each senator and representative has a quota of five persons who can be at the Academy at any one time.) Thus, in a typical year, the senators and representatives alone can make at least 5,350 nominations. Yet, each year the Academy will only give about 1100 appointments.

The entire process of getting a nomination and appointment is long and involved and is thoroughly explained for the candidate in earlier chapters. The purpose of discussing the subject in this chapter is to define the role of parents in the admissions process. What should they do and what should they not do?

Many parents believe that candidates need help with all the paperwork that is required.

Said a mother from New York: "These kids are under a lot of pressure during the last year of school--they are out for sports; they have leadership responsibilities and they are trying to maintain top grades. They can't always be well organized and that is where we can help. The parent can keep things filed in the right folders and can duplicate paperwork that is sent in so there is always a complete record of everything. Also, the parent can keep track of all the deadlines for paperwork, appointments for interviews, physical and medical exams--and all the other little things. Kids can get messed up if the parent doesn't help them keep organized and it is real easy to miss a deadline."

Parents are also cautioned not to get themselves completely involved in the paperwork. For example, they should not fill out the forms for the candidate, nor should they make calls to congressional offices or the Naval Academy asking questions about procedures.

Why not?

Because everyone involved in the process of screening candidates is looking for those who are applying because of parental pressure. The survival record at the Academy is disastrous for midshipmen who have gone there because it was what their parents wanted. Unless midshipmen are totally committed by their personal desire to be at the Academy, they are almost certain to quit or get themselves expelled.

So, everyone involved in the screening of candidates is suspicious of *any* parental involvement in tasks that candidates could be doing for themselves. And because of the very intense competition between thousands of qualified candidates, there is a strong desire to nominate and appoint those who exhibit the strongest motivation.

And how motivated are candidates who cannot do their own paperwork or make their own telephone calls? Do not let that question be asked about your own son or daughter. Stay in the background. Help the candidate get organized, but stay out of the process yourself. Do not do anything that would make anyone question your son or daughter's motivation.

Besides helping candidates keep their paperwork organized there are other worthwhile things parents can do to help during the admissions process.

One of the most important is to make sure the candidate learns as much as

One of the best things a parent can do for a candidate is to make sure the candidate visits the Academy and spends time with the mids.   *Courtesy 1/C Jimmy Parker.*

possible about the Naval Academy. Help the candidate locate and arrange discussions with local Academy graduates. Do the same with Academy midshipmen who are home on leave during the summer or Christmas vacation.

Graduates and midshipmen can be located in various ways. One of the best ways is through your local Blue and Gold Officer. This person is an official spokesman for the Naval Academy and it is part of his or her job to arrange such meetings for candidates. Instructions for locating your Blue and Gold Officer can be found in Chapter Ten.

Another way to locate graduates and midshipmen is to solicit the help of your state or regional Naval Academy Parents' Club. Your Blue and Gold Officer can tell you how to contact officers of the club (if there is one near you) or you can contact the Parent Club Coordinator, U.S.N.A. Alumni Association, Alumni House, Annapolis, MD, 21402, telephone number: 410-293-4455. (If your son or daughter ends up at the Academy it is *strongly recommended* that you join a parents' club.)

Parents should realize that candidates who select the Naval Academy are not just selecting a college for a four-year education. Graduates of the Naval Academy are obligated for a five-year tour of duty in the Navy or Marine Corps, and those who are making selections for the Academy are strongly biased toward candidates who are likely to remain after that five-year obligation and make the Navy or Marine Corps their career.

For that reason it is also important for parents to help arrange visits for candidates with Navy or Marine Corps officers. Retired officers are especially good resource persons because they often have plenty of free time. They also have the perspective necessary to discuss the pros and cons of a military career. Candidates often see just the glamour and romance associated with the Academy. A good frank discussion with a retired officer can do a lot to give candidates a realistic outlook on what follows after the Academy experience.

Many parents also strongly recommended that candidates visit the Naval Academy. A variety of programs are sponsored by the Academy. Academy Admissions Day, in November, is open to 9th, 10th and 11th graders living within 175 miles of Annapolis. Academy Information Day, held on two Saturdays in March, is open to candidates and their parents.

The best visitation program, offered by invitation only to the most competitive candidates, is the Bancroft Hall Candidate Visitation Program. Held on various Friday/Saturday periods between October and April, this program allows a candidate to accompany a third classman (sophomore) through two days of normal life at the Academy. The candidate attends classes, and eats and sleeps with the mids in Bancroft Hall. In short, the candidate gets a full preview of what lies ahead, while still possessing ample time to prepare for the challenge.

Another visitation program was highly recommended by several parents. It is called the Senior Science Seminar Program. Each summer the Naval Academy hosts high school students who have completed their junior year for a series of one-week academic seminars that parents say are outstanding. The schedule changes each summer, so for details contact your Blue and Gold Officer or the Admissions Office at the Naval Academy. (The Senior Science Seminar is explained in more detail in Chapter Ten.)

Parents also may need to get involved when the candidate hits a snag in the admissions process. For example, a father from Texas got involved when his son was turned down because of bad vision and because the boy had experienced some asthma when he was younger. That father's message to other parents was:

"Don't give up. We had our son's vision tested by our ophthalmologist and he found our son to be within the limits specified by the Academy. Even though he had already been turned down by the Academy, they accepted the letter from our ophthalmologist.

"His previous asthma was more of a problem but I eventually got them to agree to a pulmonary function test that he passed with no problem.

"I think a lot of parents would have a tendency to say, 'Oh well, there's nothing I can do when they are turned down. That is not true. I urge all parents to challenge the system if you believe the child is qualified."

Another father, a high school principal from Indiana, concurred:

"Our son had stress asthma when he was fourteen and couldn't run up or down the basketball floor. We mentioned that on one of the forms and when we got his information back from Colorado Springs [where medical decisions for candidates are finalized], they said he was ineligible. I called out there and they said that his previous asthma was a red flag and that no way could he be admitted. That's when I got our Blue and Gold Officer into the act. I don't know what all he did, but we ended up getting him reevaluated at our expense and the doctor, a specialist, wrote a letter. The high school coach also wrote a letter saying that our son was on the starting five in basketball and that he had no problem on the court. Eventually the case went before the Chief Naval Officer at Bethesda and then we got a call from one of the counselors at the Academy saying that he had become eligible.

"I think lots of people would have given up, and our son would have given up, too, if I had not gotten involved. I kept at it with a lot of phone calls even when people were discouraging me saying that I could appeal but I was wasting my time. The important point was that we knew he had outgrown the asthma and we would not have wanted him to go if he still had the condition."

A mother and father from Connecticut did not have medical problems with their son, but the story of their persistence and success might help some other parents:

"By the middle of April we hadn't heard anything and then we got this letter saying that our son was among 2400 who were qualified. We asked around and found out that this was really a 'kiss-off' letter but my wife and son decided to go down to the Academy and talk to a friend who was there.

"He suggested that they talk to the Head of the Naval Foundation who was very nice but said our son was not on his list of candidates for one of the prep schools. But he stressed the importance of showing commitment and suggested that we knock on some other doors. After that our friend hailed a professor from the math department who looked at our son's SAT scores and said they weren't bad at all. Then he started asking us about some of our son's other abilities. When he learned that our son was an excellent trumpet player and had played in a number of school musicals, he sent us to the music director. This man was very interested in our son, but he explained that he was not allowed to recruit. Yet he was very supportive and said he would make a few calls on our behalf."

Their son got in and the parents are not sure whether the music director's calls were helpful or not. But they believe that they were, and other parents with similar experiences stressed the importance of having an advocate at the Academy--someone there who really wants a candidate.

Parents should keep in mind that there are numerous minor sports at the Academy and the coaches who recruit athletes may not know of a champion 128-pound wrestler from Buffalo, Wyoming or an all-conference cross-country runner from Marvell, Arkansas. Such a candidate, during a visit to the Academy, just might be able to convince a coach to become an advocate on his or her behalf. That is no guarantee of admission, but, according to parents who, through their own intelligence network have gained a lot of information about the Academy, a coach who is a strong advocate for a candidate can be very helpful.

Parents should also realize that some candidates who are attractive to the Academy but who are borderline academically may be offered the option of attending a prep school for a year. The Naval Academy has a prep school of its own called NAPS. It is free to all those who are offered a year's preparatory study there. In addition, the Naval Academy Foundation has contracts with several private institutions around the country. They are not free; however, the Foundation has scholarship programs for needy students.

According to admissions officials and the Director of the Foundation, some candidates and their parents react negatively when the prep school option is offered.

That is a big mistake according to midshipmen who elected that option and were interviewed. They said they were very glad they had taken the extra year and they felt they were much better able to tolerate the academic shock and hassles of the plebe year compared to those who came into the Academy right out of high school. Those from NAPS were also happy to have nearly 200 friends from their prep school class when they arrived at the Academy.

The parents who were interviewed were unanimous in their praise of the program and felt that the extra maturity gained by their sons and daughters made their Academy experience much more worthwhile. A father from Maine, who admitted being skeptical about the program initially, was asked what he would say about the program if a good friend called and asked his advice. He said:

"If they make the offer, jump on it. I absolutely, strongly recommend it. It is a great transition and it makes them a year older when they go. Instead of the double shock of being away from home and encountering the pressures of the Academy, they just have the Academy to stress them. But I would also tell a friend that he is inviting disaster if the kid really doesn't want it."

One final point about the admissions process was made by a Tennessee father who also is a Blue and Gold Officer. He said:

"Warn parents that the Naval Academy is usually the slowest of the service academies to send out their appointments. I have lost some of my candidates because of this. They had applied at other academies and when they were notified of an appointment to one of them, they accepted immediately and then became ineligible for the Naval Academy appointment which came later. Advise parents to have the kids wait until the deadline for accepting the appointment for a second-choice academy-- usually the deadline is around the first of May. That way they can have the backup and perhaps still get into the Naval Academy if that is their first choice.

On I-Day a long line results while nearly 1200 are checking in.

Courtesy USNA Photographic Branch.

PLEBE SUMMER

Around the first of July the new appointees have to report to the Naval Academy for induction. The day they report, called I-Day, is a traumatic experience, both for the inductees and their parents if they accompany them.

It is traumatic for the inductees because, in the words of a New Jersey mother: "They go there being told how wonderful they are; they have been at the top of their class; they had all the people at home telling them how proud they were of them; they get a wonderful send off; then within a span of two hours and a quick welcome aboard, they become dirt. They are treated like second-class citizens; their squad leader starts pushing them around; they put on a uniform that doesn't fit; they get all those shots and then their head is practically shaved..."

And if the parents go along for that day, they spend their time trying to catch glimpses of the son or daughter, until, late in the afternoon after the swearing in ceremony, the new plebes get to spend a few minutes with their parents before they disappear into Bancroft Hall and embark upon six and one-half weeks of rigorous training called Plebe Summer.

Should the parents accompany their sons and daughters on I-Day?

Most parents who have done that also recommend it for others, saying that it is a momentous occasion in the family's life and it is something that will mean a lot in

215

Parents get to watch the swearing-in ceremony if they are there on I-Day...

Courtesy 1/C Jimmy Parker.

future years. Advocates also felt that it is a way to tell sons and daughters that they have the complete support of the family.

Some of the other parents felt that it was not that important to go on I-Day. A few thought that it would be a nice thing to do if the family could afford the trip or if they were close enough so travel was no problem.

More negative was a California mother who has had two sons at the Academy and who has been co-president of a parents' club. She said: "My sons and others we have spoken with don't think parents should be there on I-Day. They felt that it was harder on the inductees. Also, the kids from this area all leave the day before in a group and they start making friends right away--and those friendships will help keep them going after the swearing in."

Another California parent said: "I have had two sons go there and in both cases we felt that it would be less stressful on them if they didn't have to think about us. Also, we felt that we could better use that travel money for a visit later in the year. Parents should also realize that Thornton Studios in Annapolis video tape the I-Day proceedings and that they can see their son or daughter at least three times on tape--if arrangements are made ahead of time."

There was absolutely no disagreement on what parents should do right after I-Day. Their admonitions can be summarized with three words: *support your mid*!

First and most important are the letters that you should write. Most parents said they tried to write something every day even if they had to strain to think of things to write about. Said a mother from Michigan: "Write even if it is only one page saying we had hamburgers for supper and the dog has been sleeping all day."

216

...but the goodbyes are hard.   *Courtesy USNA Photographic Branch.*

And said a mother from Minnesota: "The important thing is to be regular with your writing. If you only write twice a week, that is okay as long as you keep it up because that kid will get used to expecting two letters a week. Just keep the routine going. And the letters don't have to be great and grand. Just tell what is happening at home. That is enough."

Many parents, especially the fathers who had also gone to the Naval Academy, stressed the importance of humor for the survival of the midshipmen. They say it is the humorous things that really keep the midshipmen's burdens from being oppressive.

Humor is also something that can be sent in from the outside by the parents. Several told of the hours they spent in stores shopping for funny cards that they could send. Said a mother from Virginia: "I shopped continuously and was able to send a different funny card for six weeks--all during Plebe Summer. He just loved them."

And said a mother from Maine: "I wrote a letter every day that whole first year and he said it really meant a lot to look in that mail box and know that something would be there. I clipped a lot of stuff out of the paper and I sent the Charlie Brown cartoon every day just so he would have a little laugh."

Some parents also mentioned some unique kinds of correspondence. Said a South Carolina mother: "Just before our daughter left that summer, I collected several books of quotations and started pulling out those that would be inspirational. Then I bought a six-month supply of postcards and copied a different quotation on each card. I sent one of those out each day and she really appreciated them. She shared them with her roommates and eventually I sent some to her roommates as well."

The most unique form of correspondence was described by a Florida mother: "Our daughter knew it was going to be very difficult and before she left she sat down and wrote 49 letters to herself. It was a big stack and she told me to mail one each day so she would get one during each day of Plebe Summer. I finally read one of them and it was very detached as though she was writing to another person. It said things like don't take it personally when they are screaming and yelling at you--it is something they have to do. Also that you have to keep your sense of humor and think how ridiculous they look screaming at you for things that don't matter. And this was all her idea. We had nothing to do with it."

Parents reading the above comments may wonder: What about e.mail?

Here is the story on e.mail. The mids all expect to get an average of 40 e.mail communications every day. Many are "in-house" memos from professors, announcements of Academy activities, etc. But many of them are from friends in the Brigade--friends made during Plebe Summer but who are now dispersed throughout the huge Bancroft Hall. And, yes, there are also many e.mail letters from parents, brothers and sisters, and high school friends who are in other colleges. So e.mail is an important part of the mids' life, and, in terms of advice for parents, the author makes a strong recommendation that you join the cyberspace revolution and stay in constant contact by e.mail.

However, after recently speaking with about 200 mids--mostly plebes in the late part of their year--their overwhelming advice was to tell parents not to forget about regular mail! They were adamant about this advice. They feel strongly that e.mail is sort of a "quick and dirty" way to communicate, while regular mail takes more time and effort. The plebes emphasized that the extra time and effort means a lot to them-- that it is a way parents can demonstrate that they really care. Also, it gets them through the depressing days when they go to their mailbox and find it empty. (Most extolled the great value of just receiving junk mail because it showed that they were important to somebody--and that kept them from having to face an empty mailbox.)

Regarding e.mail, a couple from California with a son at the Academy offered an idea that seems to have a lot of merit. They said: "We communicate often by e.mail, but we make it a point to print out all letters--to him and from him. We then put all the letters in a notebook and we are very happy that we did this. Now we have a priceless record of those years, and, reading what he was experiencing during that difficult plebe year will mean a lot to him someday."

Besides sending letters, almost every parent, and especially the midshipmen, strongly recommended the sending of care packages. Said a mother from Connecticut: "I sent a package every week with things like homemade cookies and brownies--also granola bars, nuts, trail mix and Kool-aid. We also sent cocoa mix, and various dried soups which they can make in their room because the water is so hot. They really need this extra nourishment during Plebe Summer."

Other parents recommended a variety of other things for the care packages. Cough drops were recommended because the plebes have to yell a lot and are often hoarse. Powdered drinks were recommended because the plebes are always dehydrated because of the high heat and strenuous exercise. Vitamins were recommended because of the inconsistent eating patterns that result from harassment during meals.

Several parents cautioned against making a fuss about a plebe's birthday during

Plebe Summer. The rule for the plebes is never to draw attention to themselves so they do not want to give their detailers any excuse for picking them out of the crowd for special recognition.

How should the care packages be sent, by parcel post or UPS? Over the years there has been a running debate on this point and because of changing policies, it is not possible for the author to make a recommendation that will hold up for any length of time. About all that can be said at this point is that parents and mids are about equally divided on the merits of the two parcel services and that parents should quiz their plebe at the first opportunity and follow his or her recommendation.

One of the most frustrating things for parents is the difficulty they have communicating with the plebe. At the Naval Academy parent telephone calls to the plebes are discouraged--except for emergencies, of course, and it is the rare parent who is going to see much written correspondence from their plebe. The reason for the latter problem is that the plebes simply do not have enough time to do everything they are supposed to do--and during what little spare time they might find, they are better off spending it getting a few moments of rest. So what happens is that parents end up doing all, or practically all, of the letter writing and the plebes end up communicating with their parents by telephone.

So be prepared, say the parents who have been through it. Get your mid a telephone credit card (some carriers issue cards that are only good for calling home), or get an 800-number the mid can use. The important thing is to make it as easy as possible for them after they have stood in line to use a pay phone.

And be ready for some hefty telephone bills, especially if the plebes are given a general purpose credit card and allowed to call their friends. (Several parents recommended that they be allowed to do this, saying that they, themselves, are getting off cheaply not having to pay tuition and that such calls are great for boosting morale.) Monthly phone bills of one-hundred to two-hundred fifty dollars are not uncommon say the parents.

For the parents who live closely enough to drive to Annapolis on a weekend, it is possible to visit with your mid for about an hour on Sunday mornings. At the chapel, between the Catholic and Protestant services (10-11 AM) the chaplains have a social hour that plebes may attend.

The parents who spoke about such visits expressed mixed feelings about them. Some felt that it was a wonderful opportunity to buck up the morale of the homesick mid. Others felt that such visits make it harder on the mid and that they negate one of the purposes of Plebe Summer, which is to cut the ties to mom and dad and shift the mids' dependence to their own support group--their peers.

Then there was the "Hey, Ralph!" story.

A father from New Jersey told about he and his wife's frustrations when their daughter went to the Academy. Not only were they lonely, but they wanted to support her. Yet, even though they lived relatively close, they knew they could not go there and visit her. But, then they came up with a bright idea. They checked with their daughter during a phone call. "Do you have anybody in your company named Ralph?" they asked. She said, no. Shortly afterward they went to the Academy and observed the formations. Then, when they saw their daughter, the father yelled, "Way to go,

Ralph! Hang in there, Ralph!" Said the father when he related this story: "This was great. She didn't dare show any expression--she had to look straight ahead. But you could see it in her eyes. She knew we were there and even though it was just a little thing, it meant a lot to her to know that we cared."

This story is related, not to encourage parents to do the "Hey, Ralph" number, but to illustrate the type of creativity that parents use while trying to support their mid. The message that you want to communicate is, "We love you, kid, and we are 150 percent supportive of what you are trying to do." So, go to work out there in Alabama and Iowa and Oklahoma and Oregon and put on your own creativity hat. Show your mid that you, too, can be creative.

Now for the other side of the story. Numerous parents, especially those involved in leadership roles in parents' clubs, as well as Academy officials, have told stories of parents who created problems for their mids--some of them severe. As an example of the latter, during a recent visit to the Academy, the author was told by a senior official of two plebes who were interviewed as a part of the dropout process. (Before plebes can leave, they must go through a series of interviews.) The official, with deep emotion showing on his face, explained that the two plebes had been told by their parents that they were being disowned for leaving the Academy. Luckily, one was going to live with a sister or brother, but the other young person left with no place to go.

The above cases are extreme, but not uncommon. Parents can become extremely emotional about the Academy, but the actions manifested from the emotions can go both ways. Equally as difficult, say those who work with the mids, are parents who cannot cut the parental cord with their mids. The author heard stories of mids, while struggling to keep their heads above water in Plebe Summer, receiving calls from mothers crying and telling their mids how desperately lonely it is at home without them. Everyone associated with those mids has told of the demoralization that occurs after such phone calls.

The irony of the latter problem is that it is often caused by otherwise excellent parents. Said a parents' club president: "The parents who cause those kinds of problems are wonderful people. They have been very involved in their kids' lives. They helped at the school and with extracurricular activities. They really care. But they can't cut loose. They still want to feel needed. But, they have to realize that they are going to have to suffer heartaches and hurt feelings--even anger. But that is the only way their mids are going to develop the independent traits they can be proud of on graduation day."

Part of the problem is with the Academy itself. The Superintendent greets parents who go to I-Day and they are told, "If you have any problems, you be sure and call me--I'm here to help you and serve you." Typically, parents also get a letter from the mids' company officers giving them their phone number and telling them to call if they think there is a problem. Well, some parents take them literally, and they call. Then the problems start when the information goes downhill through the chain of command--company officer to the firstie who is company commander, then down to the

The advice from mids and their parents is emphatic: do what you have to do to attend Plebe
Parents' Weekend! *Courtesy USNA Photographic Branch*

upperclassman who is directly above the plebe. Of course, the last thing the plebe
wants is to draw attention, and guess what dear mother or dear father has done to the
plebe? The plebe is now in more trouble than before!

There is also another aspect to this problem. The plebes cannot complain to their
upperclass supervisors. Nor do they dare complain to their roommates in the privacy
of their room. In short, nobody wants to hear griping and moaning; it is too
demoralizing. So, to whom can the plebe vent his or her feelings and frustrations.
Well, dear old mom and dad have probably held the crying towel for years, so I guess
they will have to put up with a little more. That is what some conclude. However,
what do plebes do if they think mom or dad is going to call their company officer? Do
they vent their frustrations knowing that? Of course not. They have enough trouble
without bringing more down upon their head. So they bottle it up--which is okay, to
some degree, because they are at the Academy to learn lessons of leadership, one of
which is the loneliness of command. But, many young people have been closely
nurtured at home and need a crying towel from time to time while they are maturing
and learning to become independent. Such young people need parents who will
continue to listen to their problems, but who will keep the communication within the

family. An alternative for parents who cannot do that is limited or lost communications with their plebe.

PLEBE PARENTS' WEEKEND

About five and one-half weeks after Plebe Summer begins, the Academy sets aside one weekend for the visitation of parents. It is called Plebe Parents' Weekend. And of the advice given during all the interviews with parents, by far the strongest recommendations were aimed at convincing plebe parents that they should not miss this weekend. Here are some samples:

A father from Minnesota: "We were strongly encouraged to go but I thought it was rather silly to spend that much money. But, by the time the weekend was over,

During Plebe Parents' Weekend you will be proud of your mid, but you will also see dramatic changes. *Courtesy 1/C Jimmy Parker.*

222

I realized it was definitely NOT silly. If there is any way in the world parents can go, I think they should. It is extremely important at this stage that they [the mids] know you are proud of them."

A father from Maine: "It is absolutely a must. I would come from Alaska if I had to. As a parent you owe it to yourself and you owe it to the plebe. It is a real boost for them. They realize that they are not there alone [when the parents show up] and they need your support."

A father from New York and a Class of '52 graduate: "You just don't want to miss seeing that kid at that time. The transformation they have made in five weeks in something to behold--you have to see it to believe it. They take that scruffy little kid on the fourth of July and by the middle of August the transformation is impossible to comprehend. You look at her and wonder if it is your kid. They mature so much in that time. They are very confident. I pride myself in being a good sailor, but when we went down I pulled out my old sailing card from my days and said, 'How about going sailing?' We took one of the knockabouts and she very quickly took charge and told me what to do and what I was doing right and wrong. I was speechless the whole time. I couldn't believe that this had happened in just a little over a month. She had learned not only to sail but to sail well."

A mother from Illinois: "If they can manage it financially, I think it is a must. One just can't describe the feeling of pride you feel when you see your mid march out on that parade field. Do it for your mid's sake. They are looking forward to it so much. There were some plebes there whose parents were unable to come and those poor kids just isolate themselves and try to avoid any contact to avoid the hurt. We invited a young lady from Oregon and she didn't want to go and didn't want substitute parents. [Other parents said that you should almost force "strays" to go out--that even though they object, deep down they do want to get away.]"

A mother from Arkansas: "There are some things you cannot put a value on and that weekend is one of them. It really has nothing to do with money. It has to do with loving your child and saying I am here for you. It has to do with saying I am so proud of you I am about to bust my buttons. It has to do with getting up there and seeing what your son or daughter is doing--up there with the cream of the crop in this country. You'll come back so patriotic!"

A father from Ohio: "Come hell or high water, you get there! Borrow the money if you have to. Somebody has to be there when that kid comes out. That is the loneliest time in the world when the kid comes out of there. He is exploding to say, 'Look what I've done; I've accomplished something.' That youngster needs somebody to say, 'Here's a hug.' That means more than anything in the world. When that formation is over and they come out looking among two thousand parents who are waiting, he might understand it if his parents are not there, but he is hurt. He needs encouragement from those that he loves."

A father from Connecticut: "Even if it is a sacrifice, you should go. They are not through Plebe Summer yet and they have a hard road ahead. They need that support. Also, the bond you build up that weekend will last the next fifty years because it is such an emotional experience. They work so hard for the week or two before that weekend to get themselves in shape for the parents. It is a milestone and if you absolutely cannot make it, arrange for a surrogate. Just don't leave the kid hanging there for the whole weekend. That would be a most horrible thing."

Are you convinced? If so, there is more that you should know.

For example, you must make your room reservations early, not only because of all the parents who will be in Annapolis that weekend, but also because there is . You are advised to get the latest list of available motels[1] and make your reservations just as soon as your son or daughter has accepted an appointment. And do not forget, if grandfather and grandmother or other relatives will be going, they will also need rooms.

It is also recommended that parents stay as close to Annapolis as possible so little time is wasted in traffic. And do not accept offers to stay with friends in the Washington, D. C. suburbs even though freeway connections make the distance look minuscule.

Most mids will be dying to get to a room where they can get out of their uniform and "crash" for a few hours. That is one reason for staying close to Annapolis. Another reason is that you will, in the words of one unhappy parent: "Spend a helluva lot of time on the beltway that you could be spending with your kid."

Those who manage to get motel reservations within walking distance of the Academy do not have to rent a car if they fly into Baltimore-Washington International--the airport of choice. There is a limousine that departs hourly that delivers passengers to the Annapolis motels.

Also, you are strongly advised to take the opportunity to eat an evening meal in King Hall where all the mids eat. However, if you desire to do this, notify your mid so he or she can make reservations. Because there are so many parents, some have to dine there on Friday while others have to dine on Saturday. Some of the parents felt that, given a choice, Friday is better and that you should ask your mid to get reservations for that night.

Many parents also want to do some sightseeing in Washington, D.C. while they are in the area. If that applies to you, it is recommended that you go early and get all the sightseeing out of your system before you greet your mid--or stay afterward and plan on sightseeing later.

That weekend will be the mids' first chance to get out of Bancroft Hall since I-Day. Mostly they will want lots of junk food, a long cold shower, a few hours of sleep, a chance to watch anything on television and, most of all, the opportunity to unload and talk about everything that has been happening to them. It would definitely be an exceptional mid who would want to do much sightseeing. (Also they are restricted to a certain number of miles from the Academy on that weekend.)

---

[1] Check your parents' club--they may have an up-to-date list with prices and recommendations. Also, you can call the Annapolis Chamber of Commerce, phone number: 410-268-7676 or RoomFinders (rooms in private homes, 3-night minimums), phone number: 410-263-3262 or Annapolis Accommodations (hotels, motels, bed and breakfasts) phone number, out-of-state: 800-715-1000, in-state: 410-280-0900.

Wear comfortable walking shoes, dress casually and take lots of changes because of the high heat and humidity, say parents. Also, read everything the Academy sends and duplicate all maps and schedules in case the family wants to split up. In addition, always have a meeting place agreed upon if someone in your party gets lost in the crowd--a not uncommon experience.

Be ready to see some dramatic changes in your son or daughter say the parents. Here are some of their comments.

A father from Oregon: "Be prepared for an emotionally mummified kid. They all look the same. They are almost catatonic. She sat at attention in the chair when we got into the motel. It took her awhile to unwind. Later she relaxed and took us sailing and she was more normal."

A mother from Pennsylvania: "When you see him, he is no longer your little boy-- they have matured a lot. We teased him about one thing. He was always walking ahead of us and looking at his watch worrying about being on time--that was a big change."

A father from Florida: "We picked him up at Wendy's and while he was in the back seat on our way to Burger King [where he wanted to go] he went to sleep while we were talking to him."

A single mother from Arkansas: "I thought he looked great--he was really handsome even though he had lost about 30 pounds. He was really proud of making it through Plebe Summer and to see him there getting along okay made everything right. But all he wanted at first was to go to the room and crash; then he wanted pizza; then he slept some more. I just sat and watched him sleep. Later we walked around the school; then we sat by the water and talked for a long time."

A father from New York: "They need sleep desperately and the best thing is to let them sleep for a few hours right after you meet them. Then you can visit. But many parents are in for a shock when they see their kid. Ours lost twenty pounds and looked like a skeleton. But don't worry; they put it back on after the school year starts."

Another father from New York: "We took her directly to the motel and had planned on going to the pool, then to dinner. But she sat on the bed and talked for three solid hours. I regret now not having a tape recorder because she told of experiences that she will never tell in that way again. I recommend that parents take one for that first long conversation. To see her so charged up was the high point of the visit."

A father from Minnesota: "They want to talk, to tell you everything and the worst thing parents can do is yawn when the kid is excited and telling all those things. Don't be judgmental and say that it is immature or silly. Just sit and listen."

A mother from Arkansas: "Expect a new son or daughter because they are different. They are more respectful of their parents and of each other, and all the parents we spoke with commented on how much the kids had matured. One woman said they had taught her son more in five weeks than she and her husband had in eighteen years. Unlike most, however, our son did not look haggard and tired. But I can't forget that look on his face in that crowd of a thousand mids. He had a stern look but a big grin was about to bust out and you could tell his eyes were on nobody but us. He hugged us and talked--we had never been greeted like that before--that is why it

Many parents recommend that girlfiends and boyfriends should visit later for a football game or dance.   *Courtesy 1/C Jimmy Parker.*

stands out in my mind so much."

A father from Connecticut: "One of the nice things you can expect is that all of a sudden you feel closer than at any other time in eighteen years. He talked to us more than he ever did when sitting at the dining room table. One day we talked for two and a half hours and I can't remember ever having more than a fifteen-minute talk with him in his life. He talked about everything--even about torpedoes and things like that because he knew that I had been in the Navy thirty years ago. You can see that they appreciate their parents--they see that we are real people. Before he just took us for granted--like we were just there--like we were nonentities."

One controversial issue among parents is whether or not girlfriends and boyfriends should go along on Parents' Weekend. Here are some sample comments:

A mother from Georgia: "The girlfriend went with us and it was a bad experience. We strongly recommend that you leave the girlfriend home--although it might work out with the right kind of girl. Our son was going with an immature girl. And there he was, emotionally drained from six weeks of constant trauma and he had to divide his time between us. It was not a relaxing weekend and it should have been. Let the girl go later for a weekend dance or a football game. Of course, now they have broken up."

A mother from California and co-president of a parents' club: "Girlfriends cause more trouble than anything. We suggest that you leave them home. This is where you lose kids--she puts in a plea and hurts his morale--and he has to divide his time. The girlfriends can go at other times of the year. We strongly recommend that you leave the girlfriend or boyfriend at home. We flat out tell the parents to be strong about this."

A mother from Minnesota: "We thought the girlfriend did him a lot of good--that it helped his morale a lot. We look at her as a good friend of the family and we didn't feel torn. We knew the girl pretty well. Our family has always been very open with comments and feelings and we just talked about everything all the time as though she was a daughter and we didn't feel that she was an imposition. But he is looking around now and we noticed that this summer things were kind of cool."

A mother from Connecticut: "I put my foot down and said that was our weekend. It is unfortunate that the Academy has a dance that weekend. They make it an option that might not come up otherwise. Of course, if it becomes a major issue, I think parents should acquiesce. The mid doesn't need any more stress and it is probably better to bring her along if that is what the mid wants."

A mother from Virginia: "I am biased because I was the girlfriend when my husband was a plebe at the Academy. Obviously it worked out okay. I still treasure the picture his parents took of the two of us on the capitol steps."

A mother from New Jersey: "We took the girlfriend along and we don't think it is a good idea. It is such an emotional experience for the parents and the girl, and the mid is very torn about spending his time. Trying to satisfy both parents and girlfriend makes it hard on the mid and it makes his life more complicated. If we were doing it again, we wouldn't bring her. We would tell her to go down later to one of the dances."

A single mother from Kansas: "I'm glad his girlfriend didn't go. When we began loading up the limo to leave, there was this girlfriend who was just hysterical, screaming and wailing to this mid. How awful for that boy to have to go back after that kind of experience."

A mother from Illinois and co-president of a parents' club: "Our daughter's boyfriend went along and we now advise parents not to let this happen. The young man wanted her to spend her free time with him rather than us. That created problems between the two of them as well as with us. Fortunately that relationship was over by Thanksgiving."

A mother from Arkansas: "The problem with most girlfriends is that they are rather immature and self-centered. They want the boyfriend to think about them; they want to be taken care of. The problem is that the plebe needs to be nurtured--he doesn't need to be the nurturer. The plebe needs to let it all hang out. He doesn't need to be the strong one that weekend. He needs to say that he hates the damn place if he wants to. If the girlfriend is along, he has to be the strong one. Of course this has to be judged on a situation-to-situation basis, but in general I think it is a bad idea. I think it is a good compromise for the girl to go to a dance later.

A mother from New Jersey who has been active in a parents' club for several years: "About 75 percent say it was a negative experience because it is very rare that the girlfriend is really serious--it appears to be serious and it becomes more intense because of the intense experience down there. But she remains a stranger and can't talk about certain matters with the mid and the mid won't talk to the parents because of the girlfriend--he is not going to open up, yet that is one of his real needs. I recommend that the girlfriend go down for the Plebe Mixer in October unless it is an unusual situation and the girl fits in with everybody. If everybody feels comfortable and it is a very close, mature, genuine affection-love relationship, then it will probably work. But that is a lot to expect from a 17-year old girl."

One of the hardest things during Parents' Weekend is saying goodbye, especially after the mids tell their parents what they can expect when they return to Bancroft Hall Sunday night. The mids call it Black Sunday because the first classmen are just waiting for them. As the mids gather to say goodbye, the first classmen are hanging out the windows with Christmas music playing loudly on their stereos, saying that you are not going to be seeing mommy and daddy until Christmas. And when the plebes return to their rooms, they are subjected to all kinds of harassment just to get them back into the groove of Plebe Summer. As an example, one mid told how his room had been trashed and how, with the lights out, he and his roommates had to put it back in order.

So, make your goodbyes short, said many parents. And try to be good actors and actresses. Do not let your emotions run over because the mids have some very difficult hours ahead of them. They do not need the haunting images of mom and dad or girlfriends crying, say the parents. What they need is to be left with strong, positive feelings of support, and a conviction that the parents will continue to support them in the future. After all, they have only gone through about five and one-half weeks of the plebe indoctrination system. They still have one very long, difficult plebe year ahead of them.

Said a parents' club president from Massachusetts: "Also be sensitive to the mids' time restrains. Remember, 900 mids are trying to get back to Bancroft Hall for the same curfew. And, if they are late, they can't say to their company officer, 'I'm sorry, my mother just wanted to go into one more shop.' You have to respect their time schedule. Allow adequate time to get back to the yard and plan for traffic jams! If your mid is at Gate One five minutes before the curfew, he is going to have trouble getting to Bancroft Hall on time."

One final bit of advice regarding Parents' Weekend comes from an Arkansas mother. She said: "Don't forget about the siblings. It is so easy to get caught up in talking about the midshipman all the time, especially when everybody in the town is calling and asking about him. It is real easy for the brothers and sisters at home to feel that they have become second-class citizens. Try to give them attention, too, and

228

involve them in the planning for parents' weekend if they are going. They have to feel that they are important, too."

HANDLING THE DOWNER PHONE CALLS

It is very easy for plebes to get depressed from time to time, and some parents would say that cycles of depression are normal behavior.

There are many possible causes for the depressions. The stresses of plebe indoctrination are especially hard on young men and women who have experienced nothing but laudatory comments for all their previous achievements.

Another major cause is the academic shock that most plebes experience during the first semester of the school year.

Typically, the plebe is very bright and was able to get excellent grades in high school just by sitting in classes and listening. Most have never been held accountable for assignments and therefore they do not know how to study. They try, of course. But they are loaded down with far more academic work than they can accomplish with their inefficient, wheel-spinning-type study habits. Also they are pressured by upperclassmen to learn a lot of extraneous information called "rates." Assignments pile up and many are left undone. Then the plebe gets behind and the situation deteriorates. Plebes who carried a near 4.0 grade point average in high school find themselves with an unsatisfactory 1.72 at midterm and, perhaps before an academic board that decides whether to keep them or send them home.

Another type of depression results when mids discover that they are really not at the Academy for the right reasons.

Often the problem is the parents themselves. Sometimes mids "get through the cracks" of the screening system designed to keep out those who are being pushed by parents. But in other cases the parental pressure is more subtle and inadvertent on the part of the parents.

While interviewing parents, the author found three different parents who admitted, after their sons dropped out or were expelled, that they, themselves, were the real cause. The typical comment was: "He was really there for us. He knew we were so proud of him that he just kept plugging away until the system got to be too much for him." Those parents strongly advised others to look at themselves closely when the mid gets depressed, and then really try to find out who it is who wants the mid to stay there.

Physical problems can also cause depression. Two parents from Oregon, both medical doctors, advised parents of females to expect a call telling them that she has not had her menstrual period for a month or two. They said that condition, called amenorrhea, is not uncommon for females under stress and that the problem will typically solve itself later.

Now it is time for the parents to speak for themselves. Almost every parent who was interviewed said that new parents need more help with downer telephone calls than anything else. The following comments present a broad sampling of that advice.

A father from Georgia: "In our parents' club we always ask parents from each class to talk to the new parents and the subject always gets around to the downer phone calls. The thing we always stress is this. Those young men and women are a bit selfish and their world has turned upside down. They will make calls home and it will put great demands upon your time and emotions. They will call one Sunday and be at the bottom of the pit. The next Sunday they call and they are up and okay, yet the parents will worry all week. The new parent must realize that their [the mid's] whole temperament can change in 30 seconds--that's just part of it. If possible, parents should share those experiences and laugh about them. We had one mother call us--she was upset because her son had chosen to go there and then he calls up and complains all the time. We explained that he needs someone to dump on--that he is being yelled at by everybody and can't do anything right because that is the system. We explained that there is no way to change any of that so the mid needs someone to talk to."

A father from Oregon: "When they call and start hinting around about quitting, it is common for parents to start worrying. They have to realize that such thoughts are normal--there's hardly anyone who doesn't think about quitting any college. But what is important is for the mid to know he has your support if he does quit--that it is not a social stigma. The Naval Academy is not for everybody. Of course, it is important not to quit on a whim."

A mother from California with one Academy graduate and another there now: "They need encouragement to stick it out when they call and are down. You've got to say, 'You've made it this far--there's only a couple of weeks to this or that--there's only a couple of weeks to the Army-Navy game or a couple of weeks till Christmas. It is normal that they want to quit."

A father from Pennsylvania: "We would get one phone call and he would be up; then the next one would be such a downer that the two of us would mope around all week and wonder what we were going to do. Finally we got used to the ups and downs, and generally we would get more upper calls than downer ones. I think parents have to be positive to downer calls. I also think it is helpful to call somebody else who has had this experience. One thing we learned is that parents should really listen. Lots of times after the call the kid won't even remember that he was down because he unloaded on you. Also parents should realize that the kid can't complain to other plebes--they have their own troubles. So who else does the kid have to complain to?"

A father and Blue and Gold Officer from Tennessee who was in the Class of '47 and whose father was in the Class of '21: "Our son had heard about all the plebe problems since he was a little boy but he was very determined to go. But right after he got there he started screaming to come home. I was adamant. I said, 'You are going to give it a year. You have taken somebody else's place who could have gone and a lot of people have gone out on a limb for you and it isn't like you went in there blindfolded.' Well, you know what? By November he couldn't say anything bad about the place. Parents have to realize that it is common for plebes to think they want to quit. Why even Admiral Zumwalt (former Chief of Naval Operations) admitted that he wanted to quit during Plebe Summer."

The wife of the above Blue and Gold Officer went on to add, "You know, when our son was making those calls, if it had been up to me, I would have told him to come on home. I'm very glad now that my husband held firm--it would have been a terrible

230

mistake to have let him come home. He is a pilot now and is very happy."

A mother from Florida: "Deep down you may feel that it is all coming to an end [the daughter went before several academic boards] but when you speak to them, you make every thing positive. You emphasize positive thinking again and again. I remember finding this wonderful article on personal fortitude by a Vietnam POW and I sent that to her. You can't let your barriers down when they call--they don't call for you to tell them negative things. She knew I was feeling it but I couldn't tell her how much. When you hang up, then you cry. You have to be a good actress. The happiest day of my life was when I saw her graduate and I said, 'Thank you, God!'"

A mother from New Jersey who has one son who is a graduate, one son who was dropped for academic deficiencies and one son at a prep school: "You have to prepare yourself to have silent telephone calls. You have to talk to the silent line because if he said something, he might cry. So you just keep talking. What do you say? You run the gamut, depending upon what kind of gut feeling you get. 'Listen I know it's horrible and obviously you are in no mood to talk. I know how difficult it is but it can't always be horrible like you feel now. Probably you are exhausted. Probably you haven't eaten enough.' Then you make a joke if you can. Mids are always open and looking for something to laugh about. Tell them anything to cheer them up. The silent telephone calls are difficult, not only because you are having trouble thinking of things to say but because you are also ready to cry yourself. The moment you hang up and you start to cry, the kid grins and feels much better. He walks away with a big smile and you stand there shedding tears. I know that because you get that confirmation later on when he says, 'I felt so much better after talking,' and I say, 'Umm hum, I know.' Other mids have confirmed it, too. You think the poor kid is being persecuted by the most horrible creatures that walk on earth and that he is the only one who is getting that kind of treatment. You say, 'Oh, my goodness, how is he going to survive?' You have to realize that others are going through the same thing."

There was a suicide at the Naval Academy just a few weeks before some of the parents were interviewed. From what the parents said, it was a plebe who was either told not to come home if he quit, or who was afraid he would hurt his parents if he did quit. This tragedy influenced the parents' thinking and several wanted to caution parents to listen carefully to their depressed mids. Here are some of their comments.

A father from New Jersey: "We both told our son, 'Hey, you're going to a school and you don't know what it is like even though you have been there and talked to mids. But if you have any personal problems, pick up the phone and call home and you tell us what is going on, and above all else, take each day as it comes. The best thing you can do is talk to us and let us know what you are feeling. It is going to be awfully lonely down there and there will be moments when you are depressed. Pick up the phone and call us.' It's not that hard for them to get to a phone--they just have to do a little exploring and use their creativity."

A father from New York who was in the Class of '52: "You have to encourage them but you should also know your child well enough to listen. You have to ask them [when they start talking about quitting] what plans they have and what alternatives they are thinking about. But you have to be very careful to make sure what a parent considers encouragement is not strong encouragement. You owe it to them to continue to encourage them, but if they make up their mind to leave, you also owe it to them to encourage them at that. Just make sure that they are doing it for a good reason."

A single mother from Arkansas: "I never felt he would do something drastic, but I did know that he felt awfully low because of his grades. What I said, and he said it helped, was, 'You have chaplains there just to talk with,' and that is what he did. Later, he said that it helped a lot. He got to know some who had been in combat. He was surprised by that. He didn't know that Marine Corps chaplains were right in the trenches with the men. I have advised a lot of parents about these calls and I recommend that they go over the reasons why the mid wanted to go in the first place just to be sure that their goals are the same. Also, I advise them to find a graduate and ask that graduate to write a positive letter to the mid. The graduates will be sympathetic. And they can say things like, 'I wouldn't take anything in the world for the confidence I gained from going through what you are suffering now.' Some old timers like my uncle can write and tell how they were actually beaten. That made my son appreciate it more."

A mother from Connecticut: "After that suicide we have become a little more cautious about telling other parents to encourage them to stay--it is easy for parents to get too hard about it. We still suggest that they tell the mid to hang in there and that the parent should be upbeat even though they don't feel like it. But after a lot of thinking about it, we believe now that the best advice is to tell the parent not to worry much about just one downer phone call. But if a parent gets two or three bad calls in a row, that may be an indication that the kid really needs to come home. Normally a bad call is followed by one that is upbeat. Two in a row might be a reason to become concerned. Three in a row may be something to worry about and probably should be followed by some positive action."

A father from Texas, a graduate in the Class of '58: "I found that there were some down days and perhaps a couple of downer calls that caused me some worry. But then I would get a call two days later and he would say that he had it all together now and that things were going well. When should a parent be worried? You need to know the son or daughter. You need to know what their stress points are versus what you think they might be. I do think that when the second and third phone calls are downers, that is the time to be concerned. My best advice would be to tape all the phone calls, particularly with a son who is having some difficulty." [2]

The next question is: What should a parent do if they believe their mid is becoming severely depressed?

---

[2]A father from Florida who has a son in the Air Force Academy started taping all his son's calls when, after a phone conversation when mother, daughter and little brother passed the phone around, they struggled to recreate the whole conversation. Now, the father says that the tapes are priceless mementos of those years and even the son loves to listen to them. Radio Shack sells an inexpensive device that links telephone and recorder.

The first question to ask the mid is: Have you talked with anyone there at the Academy about your problem? If the mid answers in the affirmative, there is less reason to worry. At least the mid is not bottling up his problems, which is a harbinger of potential trouble.

If the mid has not spoken to anyone about his problem, then two courses of action have been recommended. One is to get on the phone with the Company Officer and discuss your concerns. Many of them are sensitive to the kinds of problems the mids encounter because they are graduates themselves. However, they may not have as much empathy as the parent would expect, partly because of the "so what else is new?" syndrome--after all, most mids are depressed at one time or another. But also the officer you speak with will generally not be old enough to fully appreciate how parents think and worry.

The other course of action is to phone one of the chaplains. And you do not have to know their number. Just call the Academy switchboard (410-293-1000) and tell the operator that you need to speak to a chaplain. They rotate duty on off-hours and carry beepers, so within a short time you can always get in contact with one.

There are two advantages to speaking with a chaplain. First, problems such as you will be presenting are routine for them and they have lots of experience handling them. Also, they can check into the mental health of a mid without the mid ever knowing that the parents have inquired.

The second advantage is that all communications are privileged--the chaplains do not have to tell anybody about matters that you wish to keep confidential.

Also chaplains routinely field a lot of wild pitches. As an example, one parent told of a brief phone call with her son when he suddenly exclaimed, "Oh, my God!", and broke the connection. And that was the last she heard. He did not call back. She worried for three days, then called one of the chaplains. He was very understanding and reported back shortly that there was nothing to worry about. Her son had looked down the hall and seen that Admiral Rickover was coming to inspect their rooms. And then he forgot to call back!

But what if there is an apparent real emergency that has to be handled immediately and it is after hours? The advice from the Academy is to tell the switchboard operator that you have a possible emergency and that you must speak to the Officer of the Watch.

There is also the possibility that a mid will get injured or become ill and be placed in a hospital. If this happens, parents are sometimes frustrated when trying to get information. If this should happen to your mid, call the Company Officer first and get the name of the mid's attending physician and the number where he or she can be reached. If the Company Officer does not have that information, have the switchboard operator connect you with the Branch Medical Clinic in Bancroft Hall and they should be able to tell you what you need to know. If the preceding steps fail, then speak with one of the chaplains who will be certain to help you.

OTHER ADVICE

Many parents warmly praised the Naval Academy Plebe Sponsor Program. This

If possible, try to visit when there is a home football game. Many parents from the region organize "tail-gaters" and will gladly welcome visitors from afar. Said one New Jersey parent: "When a mid or parent says, 'Oh, I'm from Florida,' we just say, 'That's just South New Jersey; have a drink and a hot dog!'" *Courtesy 1/C Jimmy Parker.*

is a program where families from the Annapolis area "adopt" one or more plebes and bring them to their homes on weekends when the plebes are free. The idea is to give the plebes a "home away from home"--a place where they can relax and get away from all the pressure. Often the sponsor relationship continues after the plebe year and in some cases the mid-sponsor relationship becomes a lifelong friendship. (A parent in Ohio told of their son's sponsor who traveled to Ohio for his wedding!)

What parents should realize about the sponsor program is that it is too valuable not to be used by a plebe. In some cases the first visit does not go well and the plebe decides just to stay in Bancroft Hall. Encourage your plebe not to do that. Encourage your plebe to contact the Plebe Sponsor Program Coordinator and ask for another sponsor. An alternative, which many plebes stumble into, is to tag along with a roommate who has a compatible sponsor. Just remember, your plebe needs to get away once in awhile and a good sponsor can make life at the Academy much more bearable.

Midshipman support is a very important role for parents. But that support should also be broadened, where possible, to mids other than the son or daughter. Several parents mentioned the son or daughter's roommates and how much they appreciate a funny card now and then or a little note wishing them well on a chemistry test.

Also, if you live reasonably close to the Academy, you might want to invite one of your son or daughter's friends who can't get home for Thanksgiving to your own home. Parents who have done that highly recommend it to others.

Also, do not forget your son or daughter's friends when you visit the Academy. They like to get away and greatly appreciate a chance to be with another family. They also appreciate the more elemental things, such as what was described by a Texas father who had a son and daughter there:

"I was back for a visit and I was taken to my son's room where I greeted him with a big hug. His roommate, about six-five and a basketball player looked down at me like I was a midget and asked, sheepishly, 'Can I have a hug, too, sir.' All he wanted was a touch of family. About the same thing happened one time when I greeted my daughter with a hug. The girl with her handed her books to my daughter and, for reasons I can't go into now, the hug I gave her might have been a turning point for that kid. So my advice is just don't hug your kid; hug them all!"

A mother from Virginia had two other suggestions. When visiting the Academy on a weekend, she suggested that a picnic at Hospital Point is great for the mid and his or her friends because they can go there in their exercise clothes and thus can relax more. Her second tip was to call the mid's company in Bancroft Hall occasionally, not to speak to the mid, but to leave little messages like: Good luck with your chemistry test tomorrow.

A FINAL BIT OF ADVICE FROM THE AUTHOR

This whole book is loaded with advice but practically all of it has come from those who are directly associated with the admissions process or the Academy itself-- and parents, of course. Now it is time for the author to add a bit of his own advice to parents. No, he has not had a son or daughter attend the Academy. But he has been a high school teacher and educational consultant for many years and the advice that he wishes to pass on is well within his professional competence and his knowledge based upon the research done for this book. So here is the advice.

During Plebe Parents' Weekend, while your son or daughter is much more likely to be receptive to your advice, he or she should be given a short lecture which could go something like this:

"We are leaving tomorrow and you are about to encounter what many midshipmen feel is the most dangerous threat to your survival here. You are about to start your academic studies and you should realize, that even though you are bright, you made good scores on your SAT and you made excellent grades in high school, that you are almost surely going to suffer academic shock right after you start your classes.

"I have some advice when this happens. My advice is to forget about that stubborn pride of yours--the pride that we all admire because it has gotten you through most of Plebe Summer. It is extremely important, when you first start to see yourself falling behind in any course, to forget your pride and *immediately* seek extra instruction (EI) from the professor. I know this is something you will be reluctant to do because your pride wants you to do everything on your own. But that is when your pride is leading you down the wrong path. Throw away that pride and knock on your professor's door during the hours that he or she has set aside for EI.

"Just think of your impending academic struggle as an arm-wrestling exercise. When you first get into an academic class (your opponent), you probably have enough strength to keep your arm upright in the match--at least for a few days. But your opponent is stronger than you think--and you are weaker than you think. So once your opponent gets your arm moving downward, you are going to be defeated very shortly afterward. In other words, when you get behind, particularly in your chemistry and calculus classes, it is like the arm going down in the arm-wrestling match. It will happen quickly and then you will be hard pressed to ever catch up.

"Do not let that happen to you. Be extremely vigilant when you start your academic classes. Just as soon as you even smell a hint of trouble, *get help*! To procrastinate--to let your pride tell you that you should be toughing it out on your own--is a serious potential pitfall. Do not let that happen to you."

End of lecture, and, also, the end of the chapter. And if you, the parents, are lucky enough to have an enthusiastic, strongly-motivated candidate get into the Naval Academy, CONGRATULATIONS AND GOOD LUCK!

WLS

ACKNOWLEDGEMENTS FIRST EDITION

While at the Pentagon, and later while on assignment in Italy, Lt. Raymond P. Kempisty was tremendously helpful with this project. He helped get it started and during the research phase he gave much helpful advice. Later he spent many night hours reviewing two different manuscripts and his many comments and suggestions based upon his own days as a midshipman were very helpful.

Admiral Don Boecker and his wife Gay were also helpful with advice during the planning phase for this book.

Most important of all was the complete support and cooperation I received from all of the officials at the Naval Academy.

Commander Stephen Becker in the Public Affairs Office was my official liaison and he made sure that this project had the green light from the beginning to the end.

My day-by-day contact, and the man who probably spent at least a hundred hours either tagging along with me, arranging interviews, answering questions, reviewing manuscript or resolving problems--always with enthusiasm--was Mr. Jim Kiser, the PAO Media Director. After spending over a year pestering Jim to find "just one more source," I wondered when he would run out of patience. That never happened. Fifteen months after he started helping with the project he was coordinating manuscript reviews and still arranging interviews with as much enthusiasm as on the first day. For all of that, Jim, thank you.

Publications Director Susan Worsham screened hundreds of photos in order to find the types that we requested. Carol Feldman helped us find a cover photo. Photography Director Dave Eckard announced at the beginning of the project that he was ready to take any photo we needed and he proved to be as good as his word. Thanks, Susan, Carol and Dave.

Thanks also to Ralph Henry, Desiree Johnson and Martha Thorn of the PAO office for helping with a variety of chores during our visits.

Captain Harry A. Seymour Jr., the head of the Candidate Guidance Office was also a major source of help. He personally spent over three hours in interviews. In addition, he and his entire staff made themselves available on the telephone whenever they were needed, and they reviewed and critiqued the manuscript. For all of that, many thanks Captain Seymour.

Thanks are also due Lt. Commander Linda B. Scott and Lt. Dan McElroy from that office for all their advice and information.

Out west Mr. Tom Teshara runs a branch of the Candidate Guidance Office. He, too, was very helpful in providing information, materials and assistance in locating key parents and congressional staffers who could be interviewed.

Captain Bill Flight, Director of the Naval Academy Foundation is gratefully acknowledged for giving much helpful information and for reviewing the manuscript.

The Commandant, Captain Howard Habermeyer Jr. officially and enthusiastically opened the doors in his division for whatever information we needed. His cooperation is gratefully acknowledged.

237

Most helpful in that division, with interviews, follow-up calls and manuscript review were Lt. Colonel Richard Kunkel Jr., the Director of the Plebe Summer Program and Lt. Marjorie Rawhauser, the Brigade Honor Officer.

In the Academic Division Vice Dean Richard Mathieu gave a long interview to discuss academic matters, then made the entire staff available whenever they were needed for information. His cooperation was most helpful.

Several professors were consulted and some were kind enough to review and make helpful corrections in the manuscript. They are (in no order of importance): Karel Montor, Ed Peery, Heinz Lenz, Jim Gehrdes, Lt. Nancy Hoffman, Mike Chamberlain, Lt. Commander Dave Smith, Fred Fetrow, Mary Howland, Michael Parker, Carol Burke, Mark Myerson, Charles Rowell, Lt. Commander Mike Lemieux and Boyd Waite.

Lt. Commander Mike Lemieux's father, Nick Lemieux, an award-winning high school chemistry teacher in Colorado, helped with advice and by reviewing part of the manuscript.

Captain Paul Evans, the coordinator of the Plebe Sponsor Program gave a helpful interview as did Lt. Commander James Morgan, one of the brigade chaplains.

Many midshipmen were interviewed during two different visits to the Academy and their advice forms the real core of this book. Unfortunately some of their names are missing from the following list because of a computer disk crash late one afternoon. Many thanks to the following mids and my apologies to those who cannot be listed: Kevin McGoff, Wyman Howard, William Burkhart, Rich Hager, Jeff Smith, John Dachos, Lewis Glenn, Steve Ohmstede, Scott Valentine, Herman Cestero, Jeff Cogan, Mark Bauermeister, Scott Pappano, Jack Likens, Ephraim Garrett, Luther Archer, Tom Warner, Steve Alexander, Randy Wootton, Richard Edwards, Douglas Thiry, Anthony Calandra, Craig Prosser, Kent Churchill, Nora Ernst, David Bradley, Gerald Graham, Dave Hitt, Tim Trampenau, Kirby Scott, John Sewell, Dan Tejada, Glenn Weinstein, Sandra Hill, Steve Vanni, Stephanie Karasick, James Manchester, Jim Stewart, Dwight Neely, Jerome Wallace, Katrine Jacobson, Barbara Rapson, Kara Flatley, John Nobers, Darren Duke, Mike Eagan, Steve Velotas, Tom Chandler, Ron Mobayed, Rodney Ward, Troy Byers, Suzie Kline, David Shewfelt, Miguel Peko, Margaret Gibson, Ross Chears, Kale Moberg, Tim Tousignant, Marty Shue, Andrew Kirkland, Richard Neitzey, Robert Barr, Kristen Roper, Brian Kelly, Thomas Booth, Kevin Harres and David Hauth.

For over a week Ensign Dave Biddinger, Class of '87, served as my escort and also helped arrange interviews with some of the above midshipmen who were in his old company. Later, Dave read parts of the manuscript while participating in the very demanding nuclear training program. Thank you, Dave, for all your help and advice.

Special thanks is also due First Classman Jim Clautice the Brigade Honor Chairman for a professional briefing on the Honor Concept.

Also special thanks to Ensign Jim Stewart, Ensign Susan Williams and Lt. Junior Grade Stephanie Kish for in-depth interviews and for reviews of the manuscript.

Numerous congressional staffers interrupted their busy schedules to allow themselves to be interviewed and to contact panelists who had served on their committees. With deep appreciation I thank the following: Patty Shay, Ruth Ann

Norris, Celie Nelson, Dolores Dunn, Pam Barbey, Jeff Subco, Betty Burger, Carolyn Kegley, Clayton Hodgson, Shelly Wilkins, Ginger Yates, Susan Gurekovich, Helen Scheurer, Helen Hiestand, Randy Forster, Jenny Irwin, John Seager, Alisa Sokolis, Grace Garrelli, Carol Leffler, Valorie Watkins, Melodi Moor, Karen Mollenauer, Sally Testa, Donna Faunce, Karen Parsley, Jeanne Zappone, Susan Wilson, Anne Mackey and Tom Andreason. Thanks also to Helen Hiestand for reviewing parts of the manuscript.

The following panelists were interviewed and I wish to thank them for sharing their philosophies and opinions: Dennis Hawker, Jeri Smith-Fornara, David Motta, Dr. Robert Elliott, Arnet Ward, Mary Jo White, Captain Richard Hartmann, John Brandon, Donna Staver, Kelly Tobin, Paul Breon, Lt. Colonel Vic Straub, Al Hoberman, Dave Lesko, Steve Getzow, Paul Shalita, Pauline Riel, Dr. Hiram Carr, General Robert Teater, Colonel Bill Trice, Donna Buol, General James Abraham, Teresa Bloomingdale, Captain Bob Kaufman, June Milson, Ray Walton, Mary Lou Berry, Commander Maury Cartier, Bob Venefra, John Augenstein and Betty Runion. I also want to thank one of the panelists, General Abraham, for reviewing and commenting on parts of the manuscript.

Numerous Blue and Gold Area Coordinators and Officers gave interviews and helped locate parents who would be helpful with advice. Thanks to the following: Captain John Natter, Captain Earl Stephen Jr., Captain Lionel Banda, Lt. Commander Marvin Williams, Commander Thomas Murray, Captain Hugh Albers, Captain Charles Evans Jr., Captain James Clark, Rear Admiral Will Yamanouchi, Captain John Lester, Commander Richard Bell, Captain William Barr, Commander Theodore Curtis, Commander John Lepore, Captain Joseph Walsh Jr., Rear Admiral J. Rodneyu Grubb, Captain James Donovan, Mr. Kenneth Moyer, Captain Charles Shallcross, Commander Salvatore J. Indiviglia, Captain Douglas Storey, Captain Richard Hartmann, Captain David Weidenkopf, Captain John Augenstein, Commander Dave Fluaitt, Lt. Commander Albert Burton, Captain William McCann, Rear Admiral Frank Anderson, Captain William Meek Jr., Commander Ernest Flynn, Commander Ira Hanna, Captain H.J. Petersen, and Commander Maurice Cartier.

I also want to express my deep appreciation to the many parents who were willing to share their advice and experiences with others. I gratefully acknowledge: Robert and Karen Behning, John and Susan Kendrick, Ken and Mary Ann Frack, William and Anita Pappano, Wally and Lorraine Stopkey, Jay and Ann Holland, Drs. Eric and Hanne Jacobson, Kirby and Pat Scott, Dr. and Mrs. Newell Bowman, Commander and Mrs. Thomas Murray, Dan and Nancy Bryan, Jim and Sandy Waters, Connie Olson, Bob and Cindy Wainscott, Al and Marian Burr, Ray and Patricia Vandenberg, Mark and Mary Boyd, John and Penny Dennis, Thomas and Nancy Moody, Fred and Ellie Kramps, Roger and Helke Phelps, Ken and Claire Rathjen, Tony and Barbara Monaghan, Ivan and Eleanor Samuels, David and Grace Henderson, Bill and Pat Gill, Roger and Sue Gregory, Lester and Alice Vincent, Dennis and Helen Bruce, Mike and Barbara Velotas, Bud and Jean Eason, William and Franziska Chandler, Robert and Margaret Rupp, Richard and Margaret Kline, Loren and Deborah Dawley, Darrell and Diane Duke, Bill and Cathy Eagen, Edward and Annette Lowe, Alfonza and Betty Butts, Dick and Sally Uhde, David and Barbara MacRitchie, Bill and Judy Plohetski,

Joan Bietz, Mary Ellen Thien, Jim and Salley Downs, Dave and Carol Tousignant, J.C. and Carol Tipton, Roger and Betty Augenstein, Dennis and Sarah Renshaw, Clyde James, John and Peggy Gibson, Thomas and Mary Booth, Arnold and Karen Moberg, Bob and Shirley Kelly, Joseph and Patricia Kalas and Bill and Joyce Clautice.

ACKNOWLEDGEMENTS SECOND EDITION

Since 1989, when the first edition of this book was published, I have made several visits to the Naval Academy, some brief, and some for extended periods. During every visit I received outstanding cooperation and assistance from numerous individuals, however, I did not faithfully record the names of all who helped me. For example, at one luncheon in King Hall, some of the mids who had used the first edition suggested that I include a chapter in the survival section on the "sleep problem." I agreed to do that (see Chapter 22) but, unfortunately, cannot record the names of the mids who made the recommendation. With apologies to those not included, I share the names of those who found a place in my research notes:

Martha Thorn and Karen Myers in the Public Affairs Office head the list of those who have been helpful. They coordinated my visits, arranged appointments, and rounded up mids who took time from their busy schedules to drop into whatever room I happened to be using for interviews. I would also like to thank Diane Olmstead, Director of Naval Academy Publications in the PAO, for responding so warmly and generously to my many requests for special photographs.

The Admissions Office has strongly supported my efforts over the years. Recently, Captain Tom Butler, Director of Admissions, invited me to attend a one-day session in his department and made all of his personnel available to me. In addition, he let me observe and photograph the Admissions Board in action, and arranged for me to attend an evening session with visiting educators in order to get their perspective on the Academy. I am deeply grateful to Captain Butler and to the following persons in the Admissions Office who, during one or more visits and telephone follow-up sessions, have been most helpful: Nick Pantelides, Capt. Garry Holtzman (chief medical officer), Cmdr. Patrick Rearden, Lt. Cmdr. Jim Jarvis, Don Nelson, Frank Gren, Delma Miller, Lt. Paul Tortora, Lt. Mary Kay Williams, Lt. Jared Keyes and Lt. Mike Barber.

The chairmen, or former chairmen, of the English, chemistry and math departments (Michael Parker, Mark Elert and Jim D'Archangelo) gave long interviews and much valuable insight into the problems plebes have with their academic programs. In addition, Michael Halbig, Associate Dean of the Faculty added much insight on the overall academic program.

Also, Doug Afdahl and Louis Giannotti spent almost two hours briefing me on all phases of the Academy computer system.

The good folks who inhabit the Naval Academy Alumni House have always been very helpful, and this was especially true during recent visits. Special thanks to the head of the program, now retired, Captain Bill Busik. And extra special thanks to Captain Harry "Chip" Seymour, who has fielded numerous challenges for me, and Babs Miller, the dynamo lady who coordinates the Naval Academy Parents' Clubs.

It is always a pleasure to meet with the officers who run the professional programs at the Academy. On recent visits the following gave me long, informative interviews: Cmdr. Michael Herb, Maj. Christopher Breslin, Lt. Cmdr. Michael Carlin,

241

Lt. Col. Duane Hegna and Cmdr. Charlie Jones.

Now for the mids--without the generosity of their time, this book would not exist. Many thanks to the following (and to those whose names did not get recorded): Leon Ingleright, Chris Georgi, Gina Martyn, Brian Reardon, Bill Conner, Sean Rough, Clay Doherty, Brian Kalamajka, Laura Herath, Kevin Johnson, Cory Christensen, Matt Murphy, Robert Flickinger, Midshipman Rudd, Randy Stoker, Robert Daniels, Richard Klauer, Kelly Hanrahan, Jeff Rogers, Christopher Barnard, David Collins, Ty Biggs, Bard Hubard, Melissa Hiler, Deke Egger, Chris Wunsch, Christopher George, Gabriel Kelly, Stephen Clark, Becky Mills, Gary Buxton, Stephen Earl, Andy Peng, Jessica Groff, Autumn Kosinski, Frank Gould, Adam Crecion, Robert Najoris, Jeb Kucik, Michael Neill, Bernic Javier, Ben Stickney, Jody McGovney, Daniel Wiegrefe, Vijay George, Brett Holdiman, Nathan Conner, Jason Mendenhall, Timothy Moore, Micah Zimmerman, Glenn Larson, Katharine Nease, Brian Earp, Aaron Massey, Brien Croteau, Andrew Grubler, Chad Redmer, Jeremy Pelstring, Robert Diamond, Time James, David Ostwind, Jesse Rehus, Adam Johnston, Sebastian Pacheco, Josephine Nguyen, Joe Troyan, Susan Smith, Kevin Simmons, Joe Slaughter, Gregory Clancy and Amy Voy Doll.

Over the years I have heard from a number of Blue and Gold Officers, and recently, for this edition, I specifically interviewed (or reinterviewed) some whom their colleagues describe as the most outstanding. For their support and assistance I would especially like to thank Captain Wendell Suydam, Captain M.R. Byington, Jr., Tom Teshara, Captain Myron Fleming, Captain Richard Hartmann, Captain John Lester, Commander John Lopez, Al Burr, Captain Joe Sciabarra and Captain Joe Walsh.

I also heard from many parents over the years who were grateful for the parent advice in the first edition. Most said the information was just right, but, for this edition, I also interviewed a few more parent club presidents and former officers just to update my perspective. For their kind help I would like to thank: Mike and Diane Madore, Carla and Tom Fortmann, Hugh and Marian Mauldin, Mr. Joe Anderson and Mr. and Mrs. Bob Frauenzimmer.

For the many hours spent transcribing my interview tapes--some of which were garbled and filled with static--I would like to thank Mrs. Doris Bills for her fine work.

Also, I would be remiss not to thank Shelly Ann and Gayle Marie at Schabot and Deagle, both of whom have remained their cheerful selves while fending off irate purchasers who were not able to buy this book during the time it was out of print.

Another cheerful person who should be acknowledged is Tamara Toberer whose artistic abilities were used for the design of the cover and the book pages.

Finally, I want to think my wife, Patricia, for her wonderful support, and my oldest son, William M., who continues to be a great friend and most helpful critic.

INDEX

AVAILABLE FROM BEACON BOOKS

THE NAVAL ACADEMY CANDIDATE BOOK $16.95

THE WEST POINT CANDIDATE BOOK $15.95

THE AIR FORCE ACADEMY CANDIDATE BOOK $16.95

SET Price--All Three Candidate Books $45.95

4th Class shipping and handling. $2.50

Priority shipping and handling $4.50

For each additional book shipped, either 4th class
or priority, add $1.00 shipping and handling.

To order, send check to:
Beacon Books
1020 Main Street
Buhl, Idaho 83316

For faster service using Visa or Mastercard, call:
1-800-794-1724
or purchase online from
Amazon.com

Note: We discount 20% to Parents Clubs
on orders of 10 or more books.